THE STORY OF THE
YORKSHIRE DALES

To Bet and Eileen.

Enjoy the read,

Jean and Andy
+ family.

East Stonesdale and Keld, Swaledale, with High Seat and High Pike on the skyline.

THE STORY OF THE
YORKSHIRE DALES

W.R. MITCHELL

PHILLIMORE

1999

Published by
PHILLIMORE & CO. LTD.
Shopwyke Manor Barn, Chichester, West Sussex

ISBN 1 86077 088 6

Printed and bound in Great Britain by
BUTLER AND TANNER LTD.
London and Frome

CONTENTS

List of Illustrations vii

Preface ix

Introduction xiii

1   Landscapes 1

2   Man in the Landscape 11

3   Transport 29

4   National Park 35

The Yorkshire Dales:

5   Malham and Malham Moor 41

6   Three Peaks 51

7   North Ribblesdale 63

8   Sedbergh, Dent and Garsdale 75

9   Swaledale and Arkengarthdale 85

10   Wensleydale 95

11   Wharfedale 109

12   Nidderdale 123

13   The Dales Today 131

Bibliography 137

Index 139

TO JACK MYERS

LIST OF ILLUSTRATIONS

Frontispiece: East Stonesdale and Keld, Swaledale

1.	Langcliffe, North Ribblesdale	2
2.	White Scar Caverns, Ingleton	3
3.	The Carlow Stone, Semerwater, Raydale	6
4.	Upper Hodder valley	9
5.	Stone circle near Yockenthwaite, Langstrothdale	13
6-7.	Fountains Abbey near Ripon	17-18
8.	The big wheel, Killhope, Weardale	19
9.	Friars Head, Winterburn	21
10.	Lady Anne Clifford	21
11.	Lodging place used by lead-miners, Killhope	23
12.	Chapel at Widdal Foot	26
13.	River Ure, Wensleydale	30
14.	Fell pony	31
15.	Stable yard at Malham Tarn House	33
16.	Charles Stanley Sharland	34
17.	Swaledale above Gunnerside	35
18.	A Swaledale sheep	40
19.	Clapper bridge, Malham Cove	41
20-21.	Walter Morrison at Malham Tarn House	44
22.	Fountains Hall	45
23.	Malham Cove	47
24.	Gordale Scar	48
25.	Domed chapel of Giggleswick School	50
26.	Ingleborough	55
27.	Penyghent, North Ribblesdale	58
28.	Reginald Farrer	59
29.	A Farrer watercolour	60
30.	Thornton Force, Ingleton Glens	62
31.	Driving sheep at Old Ing, North Ribblesdale	65
32-33.	Ribblehead viaduct	67
34.	John Delaney	69
35.	Edward Elgar and the Wilkinsons, Hellifield	71
36.	Settle Market Place	73
37.	Giggleswick Post Office	74
38.	Sedbergh and Winder	75
39.	The 'down' platform at Dent	80
40.	Upper Swaledale	85
41.	Old Gang, part of the Swaledale orefield	87
42.	Lead-miners at Nenthead	88
43.	Thomas Armstrong	89
44.	Mr. Harker, Muker, 1900	90
45.	Low Row Common, Swaledale	92
46.	John Wesley	95
47.	Market day at Hawes	98
48.	Fred Taylor with dairy utensils	99
49.	Semerwater in Raydale	101

50.   The Low Falls at Aysgarth 104
51.   Middleham in Wensleydale 107
52.   Jervaulx Abbey 108
53-54. Hubberholme Church in Langstrothdale 111
55.   Langstrothdale in 1900 113
56.   Grassington 115
57.   Barden Tower in the 1970s 118
58.   Bolton Hall in Wharfedale 119
59.   The Cavendish Pavilion at Bolton Abbey 121
60.   Almshouses, Beamsley, Wharfedale 122
61.   Scar House, Nidderdale 124
62.   *Yorke Arms*, Ramsgill 126
63.   Gouthwaite Hall, Nidderdale 127
64.   Pateley Bridge 128
65.   Bewerley Hall, Nidderdale 129
66.   James Herriot 132
67.   A Dales farm 133
68.   'Sweeping up' hay 134
69.   Newhouses, in Langstrothdale 135

LIST OF MAPS

Glaciation around Ingleborough 5
The Yorkshire Dales 38
Malham and Malham Moor 42
Around Ingleborough 52
North Ribblesdale 64
Dentdale and Cowgill 78
Garsdale and Grisedale 83
Swaledale and Arkengarthdale 86
Wensleydale 96
Wharfedale 110

LIST OF COLOUR ILLUSTRATIONS

Between pages 80 and 81.

I   Addleborough from Howgate, Askrigg, Wensleydale.
II   Hawes and Abbotside Common, from Wether Fell, Wensleydale.
III   Semerwater dale from Blean Lane, Wensleydale.
IV   Askrigg and Ellerkin Scar, Wensleydale.
V   The *Moorcock Inn*, at the head of Wensleydale.
VI   Weets Cross above Malhamdale.
VII   The inflow stream at Malham Tarn.
VIII   Bolton Priory in Wharfedale.
IX   Fountains Abbey near Ripon, North Ribblesdale.
X   The Strid, Wharfedale.
XI   Kilnsey Crag, Upper Wharfedale.
XII   Muker in Upper Swaledale.
XIII   The Cross Keys and Cautley Crag, between Sedbergh and Kirkby Stephen.
XIV   Former railway workers' cottages, Garsdale.
XV   The Folly at Settle.
XVI   The lead mining museum at Earby.
XVII   One of the Buttertubs, between Wensleydale and Swaledale.
XVIII   Giggleswick Scar, North Craven.

PREFACE

This book has been over fifty years in the making. An avid note-taker since I became a journalist at Skipton, 'Gateway to the Yorkshire Dales', I kept a record of what turned out to be a rural revolution, little realising when the task began that I would be observing the passing of a centuries-old way of life, one which was born in isolation and demanding self-reliance, frugality and hard physical toil. For centuries the dalesfolk had coped with thin soils, with fickle weather and unbearably long winters. Theirs was a relatively quiet world, with dark nights except when there was a moon, which an old man at Austwick called 't'village lantern'.

The first big changes, between the wars, came with improved transport and the availability of urban goods and services. During the Second World War, young dalesfolk had their first glimpse of the big world while, at home, older folk watched the meadows being turned 'brown side up' by tractor-drawn ploughs for arable cropping, a novelty in this pastoral region. Mechanisation on the land subsequently reduced the need for a large labour force. Life was transformed by electrification. Now, on dark nights, you could see where the farms lay by the pinpricks of light. Rupert Hart-Davis, the London publisher, who had a holiday cottage on Kisdon Hill overlooking Keld in Swaledale, recalled that the only electric light to be seen from that cottage in the late 1940s was in the far-off telephone kiosk.

In 50 years many people have shared with me their knowledge of the Dales way of life. The work of geographers and archaeologists has explained the natural forces which have been at work over millions of years and painstakingly assembled details of human activity over a mere 12,000! Harry Gill, of Gargrave, who taught me history at school, infused me with a love of the Dales past. His special interest was in traces of a Roman villa at Kirk Sink, Gargrave. Tot Lord, of Settle, an amateur archaeologist of renown, showed me round his museum of cave finds. As I reverently handled a reverse-barbed harpoon made of antler, or patted the skull of a great cave bear, Tot would speak of the folk who ventured into the Dales when the area still had the Pleistocene chill upon it.

Arthur Raistrick, Dales historian, stimulated my interest in the remote past by talking about Lea Green, with its Romano-British settlement of oblong hut shapes and a dewpond which, he said, could have been the reason Jack and Jill went *up* the hill to get a pail of water. I watched him supervise a dig at a half-forgotten colliery above Wharfedale, and at his home at Linton-in-Craven he showed me photographs and artefacts relating to his special interest, which was lead mining.

With such acquaintances, wherever I walked in the Yorkshire Dales I was conscious that somone had been there before me. A low-slung winter sun accentuated traces of the remote past in bumps and indentations on the landscape. My morning walk was in part on a stretch of road which originally was a lynchet or terrace on which ox-drawn ploughs prepared the ground for a cereal crop. A glimpse of a cross base by Mastiles Lane brought to mind thoughts of monastic traffic between Fountains Abbey and Malham Moor, or even further afield, for it was part of a route linking the abbey with the Lake District in the days before the Dales landscape had acquired its pattern of drystone walls. While resting on a lead miner's trod above Swaledale I might picture a small group of men, stopping briefly to smoke their clay pipes during the long slog from their cottage homes in the valley to work in cramped mines on the fells.

Drystone walls, field barns and hay meadows are special features of the landscape of the northern dales—a landscape which the Yorkshire Dales National Park regards as 'one of the most distinctive and appealing in Western Europe'. My good fortune has been to chat with people with first-hand knowledge of the workaday life and to record their observations. So I have chatted with wallers and, during spells in haytime, to fellow workers forking hay into barns. Through my work as a journalist, I was always more interested in people than in places. To list all those who have helped would be to invite writer's cramp. Several people who were born and bred in the Dales deserve a mention because they cheerfully tolerated my questions and in their replies filled in many fine details.

Kit Calvert of Hawes, dalesman extraordinary, talked about his Dales upbringing in a house littered with papers and old books. He told me about cheese-making amid the clanging of milk kits at the old Creamery, which he had helped to save in the 1930s when closure seemed inevitable. Kit took pleasure in reciting for me part of his translation of the gospels into the Wensleydale dialect. Matthew Cherry, of Swaledale, was my guide through the Swaledale orefield. Clara Sedgwick, one of the last authentic speakers of the old Dentdale dialect, yarned at length about domestic matters and, though born in the simple days before the First World War, was unconcerned when I held the microphone of my tape-recorder close to her lips. William Alderson, of Keld, in Swaledale, better known as 'Gurt Bill up t'Steps', happily recalled childhood memories of life on the land. He had foddered young cattle at the outbarns on his way to school. At home, he had found a seat beside a fire formed of peats he had helped to cut and transport. The coal his family used had been brought by the cartload from a drift mine on Tan Hill, a few miles away.

These genuine people, all of whom are now dead, were proud of their Dales background and happy to have details of it recorded. Of the present chroniclers of Dales life and industry, Marie Hartley and Joan Ingilby, the authors of many authentic books about the region, are still researching and writing and justifiably proud that the gift of their collection of Dales bygones has blossomed, at Hawes, into an outstanding museum. Marie and Joan were awarded MBEs in 1997. Edith Carr, an indomitable daleswoman with vivid memories of an upbringing in Malhamdale and farm life at Capon Hall, on Malham Moor, has been another fount of information.

During the compilation of this book, Robert White, archaeologist with the Yorkshire Dales National Park, and Dr. J.O. Myers, have read various sections and made helpful comments. Writing this book has led me to a rediscovery of the Yorkshire Dales, a fresh assessment of things taken for granted and a quest for facts and figures to fill in many a gap. Since I first wrote about the Dales, there have been revisions of geological nomenclature. The familiar Yoredale Series is now 'Wensleydale Group', and that grand and romantic name, Great Scar Limestone, has become obsolete among academics. In my schooldays, the Pennines were 'the backbone of England'; I must learn to think of them now more as an elevated plateau. Drumlins are not just heaps of glacial mush; many of them have rock cores which have become overlain with boulder clay. It made a big difference.

When, 50 years ago, fresh from two years of naval service as a conscript, I visited Harry J. Scott at Clapham, in response to his invitation to talk about the future, I could not have foreseen that I would complete half a century with *The Dalesman*, Scott's world-famous little magazine which he founded in 1939 and which at its peak had a circulation of 74,000 copies a month. As magazines go, this was special, with each reader encouraged to think of him or herself, Quaker-style, as a member of a large Dales family. J.B. Priestley contributed a message to the very first issue of what was originally called *The Yorkshire Dalesman*. I never visit Hubberholme, where his ashes were laid, without thinking of his joy at revisiting this normally quiet spot at the head of Wharfedale which, to Priestley, and many another, has been the nearest approach to heaven on earth.

ACKNOWLEDGEMENTS

I would like to thank the following for allowing me to use their illustrations: Jim Nelson, 15; Dr. J.A. Farrer, 28; British Rail, 32-33; J.F.C. MacMillan-Collins, 35; Fred Taylor, 48; the Yorke family, 65; Trevor Croucher, I-IV; A. David Leather for drawing the diagram on page 5; J.J. Thomlinson for the map on page 38; and Christine Denmead for drawing the maps that appear throughout the book. All other pictures are from the author's own collection.

What a vast procession of friendly ghosts must haunt the village on quiet nights ... Tall, fair men of the Bronze Age; smaller, darker men of the Celtic Brigantes ... Angles, Danes, Norsemen; farmers, shepherds, monks and miners.

Arthur Raistrick, *Malham and Malham Moor* (1976)

INTRODUCTION

The Yorkshire Dales occupy the central part of the Pennines between Stainmore and the Aire Gap. Within this region, 680 square miles are given special protection as the Yorkshire Dales National Park, which is largely the area covered by this book. The term Park is a misnomer, suggesting a tract of well-manicured land which has been nationalised, whereas in fact some 96 per cent of the Dales Park is privately owned. It takes in the slaty Howgill Fells of the north-west, which the boundary revisions of 1974 transferred from Yorkshire to Cumbria, but unaccountably leaves out the valley of the upper Nidd, which I have included. A large and increasing portion of the Dales is owned by the National Trust, which when I first explored the area had but one property, and that was Stainforth's packhorse bridge, in North Ribblesdale.

Colin Speakman, founder of the Yorkshire Dales Society, has written of National Parks that they are 'landscapes of excellence, whose special qualities have been recognised by the nation'. The Dales Park was designated in 1954 in recognition of its scenery, notably the largest outcrop of limestone in Britain, which lies in the north-west. There was always an awareness of the need to preserve the farmed landscape, such as Swaledale and Arkengarthdale, with its stonescape of walls and barns. But the Dales National Park has a diversity of wildlife habitats, including grouse moors which are a haven for upland waders– for golden plover, dunlin, redshank, tewit [lapwing] and curlew. Also taken into account today is the rich cultural heritage and peacefulness, though–in common with many other rural areas–it is much less peaceful than it was, and suffers from the strident sounds of quarry lorries and low-flying aircraft.

The concept of National Parks was based on the wartime ponderings of John Dower, a town planner of indifferent health who was living a quiet life at Kirkby Malham when he compiled the report which became the basis of the 1949 Access to the Countryside Act, which brought the Parks into being.

Each dale was given its final shape by glacial action but each has developed its own special character. Swaledale is narrow and steep-sided, with a web-like pattern of drystone walls and dozens of field barns. Wensleydale, broad and relatively shallow, is open ended, with some splendid tabular hills. Wharfedale, beginning austerely, with a stubble of indigenous woodland on its steep sides, narrows at the Strid, where dense woodland has some affinities with a rain-forest; it then opens out into the classic, park-like landscape around Bolton Priory. Little Malhamdale has a superb backdrop in a limestone cove. North Ribblesdale's limestone is being nibbled away by quarry interests but, though generally thought of as industrialised, has many pleasant and quiet parts. The valley of the Rawthey is offset by the rounded Howgill group of fells which someone compared with a herd of elephants which had lain down to rest.

The dale-country is drained by rivers whose names have the melodic charm of a litany–Swale, Ure, Wharfe, Nidd and Aire (flowing eastwards to the North Sea), plus Ribble and Rawthey (which take a westward course to the Irish Sea). Walkers on the 250-

mile long Pennine Way, which extends from Derbyshire into Scotland, see the dales in context—as glaciated valleys in upland settings. The well-known valleys occupy about a third of the Yorkshire Dales National Park. Much more extensive is the high ground in between. Twenty fells overtop the 2,000 ft. contour line, the highest being Whernside, at 2,419 ft., which lies within the National Park but in other respects is shared by North Yorkshire and Cumbria.

For every major dale, there are several tributary dales and numerous gills (water-carved gorges). Wherever you go you will hear the sound of tumbling water, which is at its most spectacular at Hardraw Scar, in Upper Wensleydale, where a beck pours over a cliff and falls almost 100 ft. without touching any protruding rock until it seethes on rocks beside a crystal plunge-pool. On Ingleborough, Fell Beck leaps 340 ft. from a lip of lime-stone into the main chamber of Gaping Gill. In Littondale, and some other limestone dales, the river runs underground unless there is heavy rain. Some waterfalls, like Cotter Falls, in upper Wensleydale, are tucked out of sight but worth seeking out, this one having a frame of greenery in summer.

Watercourses indicated by blue lines on an Ordnance Survey map resemble the pattern of veins on the back of a leaf. From Cam Houses, formerly a small farming community and now a single occupied farm at 1,450 ft., there is a clear-weather view of two adjacent gills, one producing the main feeder stream of the Wharfe, which flows to the North Sea, and the other being Cam Beck, a principal tributary of the Ribble, the course of which is westwards, to the Irish Sea. These springs are only a few hundred yards apart. The Ribble builds up its strength in the Three Peaks country and flows along fault-lines. Those who introduced fluoroscein, a green dye, into Alum Pot were astonished to detect it at a tarn on the opposite side of the Ribble; there had been an intervening layer of impervious material. Westwards, too, flows the Lune, receiving transfusions of water from a trio of fast-flowing rivers—Rawthey, Clough and Dee—which were in Yorkshire until local government reorganisation in 1974. Two becks which blend their waters half a mile south of Malham become the Aire, which swings east, through the Aire Gap, to have its waters polluted by industry.

Almost three-quarters of the visitors to the Dales Park who were quizzed for a survey of 1994 gave the landscape/scenery as the main feature of interest. The fells look austere but no true wilderness is to be found here. Indeed, overstocking with sheep during and since the Second World War has resulted in a debasement of the upland habitat and the disappearance of vast tracts of heather. Within living memory there was a purple glow on a hill like Ingleborough in late summer as the ling blossomed. A scheme for 'gripping' (mechanically draining) the uplands also resulted in the loss of many of the boggy areas which were prime sources of food for moor birds.

It is the walker who sees the Dales at their best, but car-borne visitors are aware of their vastness when they follow a road connecting the head of one dale with its neigh-bour, such as the highway, in a literal sense, over Fleet Moss, between Langstrothdale and Wensleydale, or Buttertubs Pass, named after limestone shafts, which provides a high-level connection between Wensleydale and Swaledale. A dalehead farmer might say, 'There's a terrible lot of unseen grund up theer!' Arthur Raistrick wrote, 'Dalesfolk live in the valleys—but look to the hills.' The Dales landscape has been manipulated by over fifty generations of farmers and workmen: the high hills have been honeycombed with shafts and levels by lead-miners, scarred by quarrymen and kept bare by the incessant nibbling of a third of a million sheep.

Those making their first visit to the Dales tend to be fascinated by a feature which the native takes for granted—the pattern of drystone walls, thousands of miles of them, mostly built during the Enclosure period of the 18th and early 19th centuries when the commonland was taken in hand by progressive farmers. In a relatively short time, the landscape of the Dales obtained a gridiron pattern of walls and innumerable field barns where wintering cattle were fed with hay taken from the land immediately around them. Lee Gate, a large farm above Malhamdale, has no less than 17½ miles of drystone walls. In 1931 A.J. Brown wrote exuberantly of the Craven walls, 'amazing, straggling, limestone walls, that go swarming from the deep valley to the top of the fells: to the top of the world–and beyond'.

A Pennine wall is really two walls in one, bound together by long stones known as 'throughs', any space at the centre being packed with small stones, and finished off by a row of copings which also helps to protect it from bad weather. A wall built by a craftsman lasts a century and more. These mortarless walls reflect the underlying geology, because no one carried stone further than he must. At a fault-line, such as the head of Buckhaw Brow, near Settle, differences in walling material are clear to see. East of the Brow, which means east of the fault, the wall is composed of grey limestone, and west of the road it bears the darker tones of gritstone. There is a mottled effect where both types of stone intermingle at around the fault.

Change is a natural process which affects both the landscape and the community. A strong Norse flavour, associated with settlers of the ninth and tenth centuries, is evident in the place-names of the upper dales, the word 'dale' being derived from the Norse *dalr*, and 'fell', for hill, coming from the Norse term *fjell*; And yet the dalesfolk should not be thought of as latter-day Vikings; the blood of Angle, Dane and Viking was intermixed, and industries like lead mining and textiles drew in labour from other parts of the country. A Dales farm which began life as a *saeter* (summer grazing area) of the Norsefolk, and in the Middle Ages was a vaccary (a ranch for cattle) may now have outbuildings like aircraft hangers for in-wintering cattle or accommodating sheep at lambing time. There may be a small park for visitors' caravans, a bed and breakfast sign on the gate, and a string of ponies bearing trekkers along the green lanes on a day's holiday jaunt.

The population of the Yorkshire Dales National Park is about 60,000 and almost a third of those in employment have jobs connected with the land. There is a subtle cultural divide between valleys, and even villages, mostly in the speech and intonations of the local people. An example is provided by Hawes, which is hemmed in by the Pennines. Hawes tends to look to the east and the native speech is more closely related to the eastern region than to the west, even to a place as close as Dent. For example, the Dent word for being chilled is 'carled', whereas in Hawes it is 'cawld'. A resident of Hawes might detect subtle differences in the dialect of old Hawes (Norse) and that of Askrigg, a few miles away (Danish).

As Richard Muir has pointed out, because the dale-country is largely made and maintained by man, the Pennine landscape is vulnerable to changes in human society. 'It can live no longer than those who care for it.' Within living memory, a farmer with a dozen cows, rather more sheep and limited inland, and with fell-going rights for his stock, had an income which was small but, by living frugally, was sufficient for a large family. Dales life has long been economically fragile and hill-farming is now under threat. The income of many a farmer today is no more than between £5,000 and £7,000 annually.

The native-born population is relatively small and much of the old dialect is no longer heard. Margaret Batty, in her booklet *A Bonny Hubbleshoo* (1970), recorded some dialect words still in use, discovering something far more expressive than Queen's English. There were over 20 words relating to the weather, including 'tewtlin' (a few snowflakes) and 'dusslin' (driving snow), 'snaw broth' (when the snow is melting) and 'brimmin' (when steam rises from the hills after a thaw). The Dales-born had some fine names and expressions when talking about nature, such as 'moorpoot' (a young grouse) and 'mowdy-warp' (a mole), 'dowdy-cow' (a ladybird) and 'tenglether' (dragonfly).

Gone, too, is most of the robust nonconformity which began with the Quakers, continued with the Congregationists and reached its most popular and dynamic stage with Methodism. Today, chapel congregations are much reduced. Where there are exceptions, an old-time liveliness endures. Years ago, there was pride in belonging to specific areas, which was reflected in the work of local poets. Tom Twisleton, of Winskill, near Settle, wrote movingly about his native Craven landscape:

> On some heigh hill now tak yer stand
> An' view the plats o' dark green land
> Which down the valley lie;
> Then to the north just turn yersel,
> Whar Pennyghent and Fountains Fell
> Cock up their crests on high.

The old way of life has not so much died as adapted itself to changed circumstances. Tourism is an economic lifeline–and a threat to the environment. The Yorkshire Dales, which had a trickle of visitors during the Romantic Age, now experiences a mighty flood of people, most of them touring by car. A National Park visitor survey in 1994 recorded 8.3 million visitor days, 93 per cent of the visitors arriving by private car and six per cent by public transport.

The remaining Dales farmers still face up stoically to conditions on the high Pennines–to thin soils, to notoriously fickle weather and to a long northern winter. There are not many of them left: Daleheads are ranched; milk production has virtually ceased in the high dale-country, even in as fertile a valley as Littondale, where the last milk producer put away his dairy equipment in 1997. An income from sheep is augmented by alternative ventures, such as providing bed and breakfast facilities to tourists or keeping exotic creatures like red deer, ostriches, even water buffalo.

There is hope. It is evidenced at dalehead hamlets like Halton Gill, where the old chapel and 17th-century barns have been tastefully converted into dwellings; at least they survive as buildings. The farming landscape of walls and field barns is being conserved in several dales through National Park grants and the efforts of the National Trust. Off-comers have, in the main, been absorbed into local society and some of them are keen to make a contribution to Dales life, through such as music-making and local studies. The life of Dales communities in the immediate past now charms us by its quaintness and simplicity.

1

LANDSCAPES

THE YORKSHIRE DALES are a series of glaciated valleys carved into the upland area of the Pennines between the Stainmore and Aire Gaps. They form a landscape of rocks of the Carboniferous period, with major faults abruptly separating them from the slaty Howgill Fells of the north-west and from the gritstone of Bowland and the South Pennines, to the west and south. The three main rock types are Great Scar Limestone, Yoredale Series and millstone grit, which are marine sediments laid down from about 345 until some 280 million years ago. The mass was uplifted into an elevated platform which has suffered considerable erosion.

The dale-country forms a block which, buoyed by the underlying Wensleydale granite, tilts slightly to the east and vanishes beneath the Plain of York. The district of the west and south-west is conspicuously limestone country as far as the Craven Fault Zone, where the cavernous limestone ends abruptly. To the east, the limestone dips under the Yoredale Series of rocks, with Wensleydale offering the most prominent exposures, while millstone grit, younger still, is the main visible rock to the east. The tilting effect is evident in the river system. The Ribble and Dee, flow swiftly westwards and enter the Irish Sea. The Swale, Ure, Wharfe and Nidd flow much more gently eastwards, entering Ouse and Humber to flow into the North Sea.

Carboniferous strata overlie the slaty rocks of the Silurian and Ordovician periods, which originated as muds and sands deposited by river action into the ocean deeps between 395 and 500 million years ago. They have been brought to the surface under the impact of two continents squeezing together. Originally the Silurian and Ordovician rocks, tightly folded and uplifted, created mountains which were considerably higher than any to be found in the country today. The Howgill Fells, large, rounded and wall-less, are composed of rocks of these periods. Seen in a triangular area in the north-west, the Howgills crest at the Calf, 2,200 ft. They lie partly within the Yorkshire Dales National Park but are more akin to the Lake District. Travellers using the M6 through the Lune Gorge see these fluted fells at their best. Fine exposures of the Silurian rocks occur in the road cuttings.

Cautley Crag, an exception to the typical aspect of smooth slopes and steep, V-shaped valleys carved by lively becks, is the most prominent feature of glacial erosion in the Howgill group. At Cautley water tumbles down a steep slope in a series of waterfalls collectively known as Cautley Spout. The fell called Winder is an impressive backdrop to Sedbergh, the little town at the southern apex of the Howgill group. This and its neighbours were described by the Lakeland poet William Wordsworth (1770-1850) as Sedbergh's 'naked heights'. The Craven historian Thomas Dunham Whitaker referred to them in 1823 as 'the piked points of Howgill'.

THE BASEMENT ROCKS

Ordovician deposits, much contorted, are visible in the Glens of Ingleton, a famous scenic walk representing a sortie in the 'basement' of the district, below the level of the Great Scar limestone, where the rocks are between 440 and 500 million years old. At Thornton Force, above the almost vertical Ingleton green slates of the Upper Ordovician age, is a conglomerate containing boulders and pebbles of Ingleton slate, representing an ancient beach deposit when the Carboniferous sea invaded the land. Silurian rocks appear conspicuously at Combs Quarry, near Helwith Bridge. Above the terrace of Foredale Cottages on Moughton Fell, the upjutting slates support the horizontal limestone in a classic unconformity.

LIMESTONE DEPOSITS

Great Scar Limestone, some 600 ft. thick, was laid down in a tropical sea over 300 million years ago. It so dominates the landscape in the Craven district of the south-west that the name Craven possibly means 'land of crags'. For millions of years the limestone which now brightens the Dales landscape lay buried under later depositions. Movements of the earth caused folding and fracturing. After yet more millions of years, the limestone was exposed by the removal of the rock which had overlaid it and was then subjected to weathering, especially to solution and the freeze-thaw process of winter. Generally, this limestone is fine-grained and very pure. It consists of the shell fragments, corals and skeletons of animals and limey mud. Some layers of limestone are particularly rich in fossils of shell-bound creatures. In others, such evidence of life in the remote past is sparse. Mostly cream or pale grey, the limestone weathers almost to pure white. In bright light, the effect of its exposure is softened by the light green of turf and the darker green of yew and juniper, the last-named forming a conspicuous mat in the unexpected setting of limestone outcrops on Moughton.

1 *Limestone country. Above Langcliffe, North Ribblesdale.*

2 *Mr. Long at the original entrance to White Scar Caverns at Ingleton.*

Limestone has been much eroded by glacial meltwater, as at Malham Cove. Here a former waterfall cut back from the Mid Craven fault scarp, though the cutting-back process may owe much more to the presence of the active cave at its foot. Water action is still evident at Gordale Scar, where the limestone walls overhang grandly. Elsewhere, Trow Gill, at the approaches of Gaping Gill, is typical of the narrow limestone gorges which are now dry, the water having found courses at lower levels. Alcoves along major bedding planes were once taken as evidence of a collapsed cave, which was not the case. Another spectacular limestone gorge which no longer has a regular flow of water is Conistone Dib, in Upper Wharfedale.

In limestone country, beauty is more than skin deep. Once exposed to the air and rain, and thus to a weak solution of acid, a slow process of erosion occurs which, at the fault lines, has led to the creation of extensive systems of potholes (vertical shafts) and caves, the water coursing underground to debouch as a beck above the impervious slate of the Silurian system. Ingleborough and its neighbours are honeycombed with natural shafts and galleries, the cave systems which are no longer active being adorned by a variety of calcite formations, as a visitor may see at the show caves—Stump Cross (on Greenhow Hill), White Scar (Ingleton), and Ingleborough Cave (near Clapham).

The last named, one of the oldest show caves in the country, decked by imposing stalactites, stalagmites, pillars and 'curtains' of glistening calcite, was discovered in 1837, when James Farrer, who presided over the Ingleborough Estate, instructed his workmen to demolish a series of natural barriers at the end of the Old Cave and opened up a system which had been the main resurgence for Clapham Beck. This had subsequently found a lower course, emerging at Beck Head.

The earliest book devoted mainly to the caves is *Tour to the Caves, in the Environs of Ingleborough and Settle, in the West-Riding of Yorkshire*, by John Hutton, published in 1781, this edition including a dialect glossary. Two versions of the book appear as appendices to West's pioneering *Guide to the Lakes*. John Hutton (1740?-1806) was ordained in 1763 and from 1764 until his death in 1806 he was vicar of Burton-in-Kendal in Westmorland. He had many stimulating ideas about cave formation which did not stand up to later study, but geology was then in its infancy and belief in the literal truth of the Book of Genesis was a great hindrance. In Hutton's day open shafts giving tantalising glimpses into the under-world were considered by some to be vents through which water poured at the time of the Flood. They remained conveniently open against a time when the Almighty might decide to teach humanity another lesson.

Hutton's references to caves are charming, an example being this paragraph from 1761 which includes references to systems which have not been positively identified, the names having doubtless been supplanted by others:

> There are a great many more holes, or caverns, well worth the notice of a traveller: some dry, some having a continual run of water; such as Blackside Cove, Sir William's Cove, Atkinson's Chamber, &c, all whose curiosities are more than I can describe. There is likewise, partly south-east, a small rivulet, which falls into a place considerably deep, called Long-Kin; there is likewise another swallow, or hole, called Johnson's Jacket-hole [probably Jockey Hole], a place resembling a funnel in shape, but vastly deep; a stone being thrown into it, makes a rumbling noise, and may be heard a considerable time.

A cave system which sent shivers of terror down the spines of early tourists is that in and around Weathercote Cave, in Chapel-le-Dale, which is no longer open to the public. South of the *Hill Inn*, streams cut through the Great Scar limestone and, other than in exceptionally wet weather, the drainage is underground, the surface bed, with its smoothly eroded rock being dry. Weathercote Cave, a large gash rather than a true cave, is one of the 'windows' into this system. The features of Weathercote can be observed in daylight, the approach to the main chamber being down a rock slope, which in the old days had a good flight of steps, and along a passage under a rock arch to where a 77 ft. waterfall is seen, appearing from behind a perched boulder known (since the days of John Hutton) as Mahomet's Coffin, he having compared its appearance with the feature in Medina. At midsummer, when sunlight slants down, a bright rainbow appears in the spray far from the surface.

YOREDALE SERIES

Rising above the limestone in a series of gigantic steps are the Yoredale Series, now more commonly referred to as the Wensleydale Group, a repeating sequence of deposits. Here is somewhat impure limestone, shales within which are seams of coal, and millstone grit, so called because when used in grindstones it did not overheat the grain. The name Yoredale was given by the geologist John Phillips, a contemporary of Adam Sedgwick, the distinguished native of Dent who became Woodwardian Professor of Geology at Cambridge. Phillips's geological excursions took him to many parts of the Dales in the summer of 1832 and spring of 1833. He studied a characteristic section in Upper Wensleydale, formerly known as Yoredale.

The beds are conspicuous on Ingleborough, where about 1,000 ft. form a major part of the hill. In Wensleydale, and at the head of Wharfedale, the limestone beds tend to stand stepped and proud along the dale sides, best viewed in profile, as when using one of the moorland roads from Swaledale into Wensleydale and pausing as a vista of Wensleydale appears. The prominent steps led to the formation of waterfalls, notably Hardraw in Upper Wensleydale, where weather-resistant beds of limestone have held together a scar from which a 100 ft. waterfall leaps into a narrow gorge.

MILLSTONE GRIT

Above the Yoredales is a wide covering of millstone grit, a rock formed of material which accumulated in the equatorial swamps of a huge delta. The Three Peaks of Whernside, Ingleborough and Penyghent are among many which have a capping of gritstone and are tabular in form. In the east, as at Brimham Rocks above Nidderdale, the eroded gritstone has taken on fantastic shapes.

ICE AND WATER

The Dales landscape was shaped and polished by the Quaternary Ice Age. Over a spell of some two million years, glacial ice advanced from the north and retreated in three successive periods which have been named Anglian, Wolstonian and Devensian. The first was the most severe and during this period the troughs of what are now known as the Dales were gouged out. The two other glaciations did not overwhelm the main summits, such as the Three Peaks, which remained exposed as 'nunataks'. The last glaciation wiped out most of the deposits of the others and thus the greatest impact was created by the Devensian, which was at its peak some 20,000 years ago. It was then that the top beds of the Great Scar Limestone were scoured, exposing the so-called limestone pavements, the surface being modified by post-glacial solution, producing tabular clints and fissures, known as grykes, which are of varying depth and thickness.

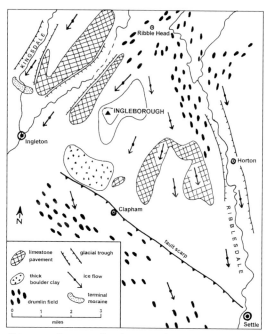

Diagram showing the glaciation around Ingleborough.

The pavements girdling Ingleborough formed around 12,000 years ago. Moving ice scraped the landscape down to bare rock. Winskill Stones, above Langcliffe, is a tract of pavement purchased with a Lottery grant in 1997. It might otherwise have been quarried for use in ornamental rockeries. Other areas in which pavements are exceptional and have been given special protection from theft and damage are to be seen near Kettlewell and also between Cray and Hubberholme, in Wharfedale. An especially dark, fine-grained type of limestone exposed in gills at the head of Dentdale is notable for its conspicuous white fossils. For many years, it was quarried, polished and sold as Dent marble.

In limestone country, a beck has a predilection for going underground, as in part of Littondale, where a whole river, the Skirfare, normally flows out of sight. A similar situation is found on the upper Dee and in Chapel-le-Dale. Some areas are pockmarked with neat funnel-shaped hollows known as shakeholes. Such a depression developed where the boulder clay overlying a fissure in the limestone was thin. An especially large shakehole is seen by walkers on the Ingleborough path which begins east of the *Hill Inn.*

Ice deposited boulder clay to an elevation of some 1,500 ft. As the grip of ice was relaxed, glacial drift, composed of small stones and clay, formed the low, rounded hills we know as drumlins. Many drumlins have solid rock cores. An extensive drumlin field came into being at the head of Ribblesdale, and on the map the effect has been compared with 'baskets of eggs'. The hillocks are aligned north-west-south-east, indicating the direction in which the ice flowed. Another drumlin field is seen by travellers on the A65 just south of Hellifield. Where a moraine blocked a valley, such as at Gunnerside in Swaledale, the consequence was a lake. As the ice melted, what is now the dale-country assumed a lakeland appearance. Where a powerful beck bearing rocks and other debris entered a major valley, a delta was created, providing a stretch of high ground above the boggy valley–and an ideal situation for a settlement, such as at Buckden in Wharfedale. Powerful streams of abrasive meltwater eroded much of the limestone.

3 *An erratic boulder known as the Carlow Stone, Semerwater, in Raydale, off Wensleydale.*

The Norber boulders, on the hill of that name near Austwick, are an outstanding example of 'erratics'–chunks of Silurian slate which were plucked by glacial ice from the head of Crummackdale about 11,000 years and borne to their present position on the limestone of the valley side, about half-a-mile from their source. With the melting of the ice, the boulders came to rest on the limestone itself which, being soluble, was later eroded, except for the areas sheltered from the weather by the stones themselves. Stones on Norber rest on pedestals which are from 12 to 15 inches high.

DENT AND CRAVEN FAULTS

Of the geological fractures which occurred at the close of the Carboniferous period, the Craven and Dent Faults have had the greatest visual impact. Evidence of the Craven Fault is readily seen from Giggleswick to Grassington in Wharfedale, and is also evident above Pateley Bridge in Nidderdale. The Dent Fault divides the Carboniferous stratum of the Dales and the much earlier, mainly Silurian, landforms of the Howgill Fells. It was Adam Sedgwick who first drew attention to the Dent Fault. In 1838 he noted that it

> passed along the south flank of Casterton Low Fell up Barbondale then across the valley of Dent, through the upper part of the valley of Sedbergh, and along the flank of Bowfell and Wildboar Fell; and that along the whole of this line there are enormous and complex dislocations.

Towards the end of the Carboniferous Age, from about 275 million years ago, the ores of lead and other minerals were intruded. The origin is still debated, but opinion has been moving away from the idea of a link with granite or other deep igneous sources. The more favoured idea is that highly saline trapped water in the thick crust sediments of the Bowland area to the south and the Stainmore area to the north have been squeezed out by pressure and migrated into the rocks of the Askrigg Block. The two main orefields are those centred on Swaledale, taking in Arkengarthdale and the north side of Wensleydale, and the field which incorporates Greenhow Hill and Grassington Moor. The veins are quite narrow, being usually measured in inches, sometimes in feet. They consist of lead ore, also fluorspar and barytes. Friarfold, at the head of the Swaledale field, was rich but complex, extending from about Keld to east of Arkengarthdale. When mining took place the metallic ore might be no more than five per cent of the filling and the mine proprietors were rich indeed if the yield was 10 per cent.

BLUE FLAGSTONE

The tough old rocks which form a platform for the Carboniferous deposits have had and continue to have a commercial use, being quarried and broken down for use as 'metal' in roadwork. An early reference to flag production appears in a statement outlining a case in support of a canal for Settle in 1774. The writer mentions 'many inexhaustible quarries of blue-flags, grit-flags, excellent blue-slate and grit-slate in the neighbourhood of Settle, which will undoubtedly pass along this canal'. The watercourse was never made. The laminated nature of the flagstone was mentioned by John Hutton, the clergyman author of *Tour to the Caves*, published a few years after the canal scheme was broached.

Hutton noticed at what he called Coombs Quarry that 'the stones are of a blue kind, like slate, from one to three inches thick'. Quarries at Ingleton and Helwith Bridge yielded 'slate' for a variety of uses, that at Ingleton specialising in roofing material; a directory of 1822 noted that two slate dealers were in business. Roofing slate of a kind was associated with Helwith Bridge and known as 'Swarth Moor Jacks'. The flagstone was hammer-trimmed. The Horton Flags, in North Ribblesdale, were used since time immemorial but their main commercial exploitation lasted for a period of rather more than 200 years, ending as recently as the 1920s. It was then that the last of the quarries to be worked on traditional lines acquired a crusher and the Silurian heritage was henceforth reduced to fine chippings for spreading on the roads.

In the heyday of the flag industry, half a dozen small quarries were in operation and flagstone prepared for domestic and farm purposes, the former including flagged floors, benks (shelves in dairies) and cisterns for soft water, the rainwater being collected from the roof of the house and made available for washing purposes in an area of hard (limestone) water. Field troughs were also made, cisterns and troughs having their sections bolted together using metalwork provided by a blacksmith. At Horton-in-Ribblesdale churchyard flags form the roofs of lych-gates, paths, the bases of foot-scrapers and many of the grave-stones, though, being laminated, edges exposed to the weather led to flaking. On the farm, flagstones were used as boskins (divisions between stalls in a byre or shippon) and even as field boundaries, a good example being seen on the side of Moughton Fell between Austwick and Helwith Bridge. The largest of six quarries, at Helwith Bridge, was that on the riverside below the Ribble bridge. Little of the building remains but the water-filled quarry is now used as a fishery.

USES FOR LIMESTONE

Limestone is represented in many Dales buildings, though as a building stone it is difficult to carve. In drystone walling limestone is the most difficult of mediums to use. Economically, the Dales limestones have been most important as lime to be spread on acidic land or where the high Pennine rainfall has leached the lime from shallow soils. Ironically, this has frequently occurred in limestone areas. The many field kilns, which from a distance look like short towers and at closer range are identifiable from the capacious mouth, date from about 1760, a time when much common land was being enclosed and new ideas developed in agriculture. The burn was initiated with the use of brushwood, and lime to be burnt was fed into the top, with local coal used as fuel. The proportions were usually one part of coal to four of limestone and the process of charging a kiln with these two commodities might last for several days. The last 'burns' were in about 1860.

As transport improved and the demand for lime increased, kilns of a continuous burning type, designed in 1856 (patented 1858) by a German, Friedrich Hoffman, were made available in a rectangular form, and in 1872 one was constructed at the Ingleton Patent Limeworks at Mealbank, Ingleton. Credit for the introduction of Hoffman's design to the locality is shared by John Clark and Michael Wilson. In 1873, lime from the Hoffman, 'on account of its superior bleaching qualities', was being sent by rail to Gateshead, a distance of 120 miles. Large quantities of burnt lime were also being sent to Bradford and other Yorkshire towns. A writer in the *Lancaster Guardian* of 1873 noted that 'the demand for it at Halifax is so great the price is only a secondary affair'. Eventually, a Hoffman kiln three times the size was built at Langcliffe, in North Ribblesdale. The Ingleton kiln is little more than a heap of stones, but the main kiln at Langcliffe survives virtually intact and will probably be preserved.

COAL MINING

Coal seams in the Yoredale beds have been mined at high altitude at Cowgill Head above Garsdale, at Tan Hill, above Swaledale, where mining took place in bell pits or drifts, and on the vast plateau of Fountains Fell, the highspot of Malham Moor. The coal, though brittle, was acceptable until the coming of the railway permitted the distribution of much better deep-mined coal from South Yorkshire. The coal industry extended over at least seven centuries. The canons of Bolton Priory burned coal mined on the Wharfedale moors. Lady Anne Clifford, whose vast estates extended from Skipton to Brougham in Westmorland, enjoyed the heat of a fire of Tan Hill coal at her castle in Appleby.

During the later part of the 19th century, coal from Tan Hill was being delivered to the smelt mills of Swaledale and Arkengarthdale as well as being collected by private customers. Turner Fell Pit, some six miles from Hawes, in Wensleydale, was worked by the Metcalfe family and supplied coal to the greater part of the dale. It was a day hole, with a coal seam some two feet thick. Mining ceased just before the First World War.

In its heyday, the Fountains Fell colliery, a collective name for numerous bell-pits needed for seams which were invariably too shallow to be followed, produced up to 1,000 tons of coal a year, which was transported off the fell by packhorses using the bold diagonal of the Coal Road, now a rough and much eroded track, which was constructed about 1810 to provide ease of movement to the Silverdale road between Halton Gill and Stainforth. At about the same time, a squat building was constructed on the fell as a coke oven. It is still virtually complete today. The Dales coal industry came to an end some fifty years ago, when Tan Hill coal was being sold as cheaply as fippence (five old pence) a corb (about two cwt).

Ingleton New Colliery, which tapped the coal measures, began with borings to a depth of 300 ft. during 1913 and was employing about five hundred men between 1917 and 1920, but lived fitfully for less than 25 years. In one memorable week over 2,000 tons of coal had been lifted. The engineers were thwarted by the Craven and Hollin Tree Faults, the last-named extending from the scattered workings around Ingleton to Burton-in-Lonsdale. The Craven Fault cut off the deep coal seams to the east.

DALES VEGETATION

When conditions ameliorated after the last ice advance, the first humans to venture into the Dales found a well-wooded landscape, with trees thriving to an elevation of some 1,500 ft. Today, tree cover of any significance is found only on rocky dale sides, where ash trees have survived. The Howgills, smooth hills composed of slates and grits, are covered almost exclusively with grass, though with less trampling by cattle and a much reduced use of braken as bedding for young cattle in winter, bracken is spreading fairly rapidly.

On high ground, where peat and heather occur, the cloudberry fruits in mid-July and the berry turns yellow when ripe. It is usually consumed by the grouse and is rarely found by human visitors. On the ill-drained gritstone moors, which were once wooded, the landscape is open. Dry ground sustains ling, the commonest species of heather, with its associated bilberry and crowberry. Controlled burning of strips of heather in March, if there is an especially dry spell, destroys the rank vegetation and encourages the formation of new shoots, which are basic food for sheep and grouse. The burning is done in strips, so that heather of various ages remains. The thicker growth provides shelter and nesting places for the grouse.

The wettest areas on the moors are known as 'mosses', and here the distinctive plants are cotton-grass, which is actually a sedge, sphagnum moss, cross-leaved heath and sundew. The cotton-grass, in its early stages of growth, provides a nourishing bite for the sheep and

4   *Conical heaps of peat, drying in the sunshine and wind, upper Hodder valley.*

is known to Dales farmers as 'mosscrop'. The moors being relatively ill-drained, peat is in places over 10 ft. deep. Dales peat, composed largely of cotton-grass, was cut for fuel. Much erosion has been caused by peat-cutting and also wind-blow where the peat has dried out. Years ago, the moorland vegetation and the peat held the water like a sponge, releasing it gradually. Now there is a rapid run-off after storms. Over-grazing during and since the Second World War has led to the loss of considerable areas of heather and the degeneration of hill land into expanses of mat-grass (*Nardus*) which is unpalatable to sheep and, being tussocky, is not liked by those who walk upon it.

It is in the free-draining, sweet limestone areas that plant life is both varied and profuse. Geoffrey Grigson, a modern botanist, in a pen portrait of Ingleborough, found a 'wild garden of streams and natural sculpture and flowers'. Here grow, among a mosaic of diminutive form and pastel shades, the mountain pansy, the yellow type being common in the Craven district. Rock rose and thyme impart a fragrance to the summer landscape. The bird's-eye, or mealy primrose, was joyfully greeted by botanist Reginald Farrer, who noted its umbel of up to a dozen lilac-pink flowers, each with a yellow 'eye' on a slender stem.

The limestone areas have been a classic ground for botanists since John Ray of Cambridge explored and described its plant life around 1677. For example, he saw the alpine bistort 'in a mountainous pasture about a mile and a half from Wharfe'. (It still grows there.) The community of plants to be found in the grikes of the limestone pavements is akin to old woodland vegetation and survives here because between the clints, or blocks, conditions are shady and moist. Two outstanding nature reserves are Colt Park, North Ribblesdale, where ash grows from a limestone pavement, and just round the corner of Ingleborough at Southerscales in Chapel-le-Dale, where a more open pavement area is maintained as a reserve by the Yorkshire Wildlife Trust.

In spring, the marsh marigold, also known as kingcup, adds a patch of yellow to moist places, and also to be seen are globe flowers, the strong stems of which support globes which have a sulphur-yellow hue. Dorothy Wordsworth, who was no stranger to the Dales, wrote of the globe flower as 'a beautiful yellow, palish yellow, flower that looked thick, round, and double, and smelt very sweet'. A riverside stroll where there is woodland reveals carpets of ramsons, known to most people as wild garlic. Road verges hold the frothy white of meadowsweet. Here, too, is sweet cicely, with its aniseed tang, cow parsley and the purple-blue flowers of meadow cranesbill.

CLIMATE

The Dales climate is fickle, being frequently cool and cloudy as weather systems from the west meet the north-south barrier of the Pennines. The winter is long, often hard, the snow-season being mainly towards the end of January into February. May and October are usually sunny, if cool. Indeed, there have been several springtimes of drought, when Dales becks have dried up and vegetation on the fell was crunchy underfoot. Precipitation is recorded on over half the days of the year, with a rainfall of around 70 in. at the daleheads. July and August have their bright spells but usually develop into a stormy time of the year. Around Christmas there might be a mild spell, leading to chill easterlies and frost in January. There are climatic differences between the high and middle reaches of a dale, and between a dale and the high fells.

LANDSCAPE MODIFICATION

The story of man in the Yorkshire Dales will be told in the next chapter but our section on Landforms cannot end without a mention of humankind, who soon began to modify the landscape to suit himself. Stones indicate the presence and shape of Iron-Age settlements and field systems. The oldest remaining walls, of medieval times, are low and rough, doing little more than provide a demarcation or use up a surfeit of stone which littered the landscape to increase the area on which the livestock might graze. At the monastic sheep farm of Middle House, between Malham and Arncliffe—a farm associated with Fountains Abbey—the attendant crofts were bounded by walls made of blocks of weather-worn lime-stone, forming an erratic pattern.

A medieval traveller in the Dales used tracks through an open landscape. He or she would observe people at work on common land divided into strips. William Camden (1551-1623) wrote of 'mountains waste, solitary, unpleasant and unsightly'. John Houseman, writing about a descriptive tour in 1800, referred to 'those numerous and extensive bleak moors which present themselves on all hands to the eye of the traveller'. When the need arose to define boundaries, it was difficult to find sufficient features for reference, as between Swaledale and Wensleydale in 1679:

> ... to Stony gill head, from thence towards the west (as Heaven water falls) to the great stone in or near the Tarne, from then to Ogaram Currock or Ogarum Syde, from thence to Cogill head Beakon ... from thence further towards the west by a little rukle of stones that is on the west side of Lovelysyde to Bull Voggin the cliff head.

The intake (pronounced 'intak') signifies where land was taken in from the moor at a time of population growth. Some intakes date from the 13th century, but most are historically recent. The golden age of Dales walling was the period from about 1750 to 1840, the heyday of the Enclosure Awards, which transformed what had been a tousled, open region into a landscape with a park-like neatness. Richard Muir has described the Enclosure period as 'a massive and ruthless campaign of privatisation'. The walls of the Parliamentary Enclosures were the ultimate expression of a process of land reclamation which began thousands of years ago with the clearance work of early settlers.

2

MAN IN THE LANDSCAPE

MAN WAS A LATE ARRIVAL in the region which is now known as the Yorkshire Dales. Animal life thrived during a warm interglacial period about 120,000 years ago, judging from remains found in 'bone caves' on the limestone scars near Settle. The fauna included straight-tusked elephant and narrow-nosed rhinoceros, long since extinct, as well as hippopotamus and spotted hyena, now restricted to the tropics. The bones of such large beasts were probably deposited piecemeal when the caves were hyena dens.

The discovery and exploration of Victoria Cave yielded information about Early Man of some 10,000 years ago. He would not be predominantly a cave-dweller. A reverse-barbed harpoon found in Victoria Cave in the early 1870s and cherished by Tot Lord at his unique Pig Yard Club museum of cave finds, is an indication that the first people to reach the area hunted or fished in glacial lakes. A so-called 'prehistoric' boat found when Giggleswick Tarn was drained about 1840 was later judged to be medieval. The boat, with an appealing setting, occupies a case at Leeds Museum.

Victoria Cave, and others in the limestone scars of North Craven where the remains of early animal and human life were preserved, provide a key to life in the Dales in those times. The rediscovery of this cavern, as recounted in 1896 by George H. Brown, minister of Zion chapel at Settle, took place in May 1837. Michael Horner and two other young men from Langcliffe were walking on the hills when they encountered John Jennings of Settle, the proud owner of two terriers. Jennings suggested they might visit the Fox Holes. One of the dogs was put in the lower hole and eventually emerged from the upper hole. A week later, when the young men were back at Fox Holes, a stone was dragged away, enabling Michael Horner to enter. He told Joseph Jackson (1816-1886), a local plumber who employed him, and they excavated the cave in secret, building up an impressive collection of human and animal objects.

Jackson has been described by a modern archaeologist, Thomas C. Lord, as 'the first cave archaeologist in the Yorkshire Dales'. The year 1838, which is more commonly used for its discovery, was adopted by the archaeologist Boyd Dawkins in the 1870s, the reference being to the year of the Queen's coronation. Charles Roach Smith, who described Jackson's cave finds in 1840, referred to 'the Caves near Settle'. It is presumed that Jackson subsequently named the cave, and as it was 1837, the year of the Queen's accession, it was called Victoria Cave in her honour.

Later excavators enlarged the hole to its present size as they dug through layers associated with Romano-British times and through an upper cave earth in which were the bones of bear, lynx, fox, badger, horse and red deer. A layer of laminated clays, assumed to have been deposited during the Ice Age, divided these from the bones of ancient beasts and provided a useful point of reference. No trace was found below the clay of a human presence. Birkbeck of Anley found a human tooth, then confessed it was his.

THE FIRST HUMANS

Mesolithic people (8,000-3,700 B.C.) visited the Dales to hunt during the short, hot summers. Strings of glacial lakes occupied the major valleys. Upland locations, such as Malham Tarn and Semerwater, have yielded microliths, made of flint, which were used as barbs on shafts. Archaeologists associated with the University of Bradford, on a research project in the 240-square-kilometre area between Settle, Grassington, Kettlewell and Horton-in-Ribblesdale, have reported that among over 3,000 artefacts discovered during three years of a five year research programme were arrowheads, barbs and even a stone-age hearth. Mesolithic 'pygmy' flints were recovered from Lea Green and High Close, north-west of Grassington in Wharfedale.

Hunters and their families would follow the reindeer herds and other animals to their upland grazings on the mossy tundra which lay beyond the tree-line. Moss sustained the deer. The deer in turn were a rich source of protein for prehistoric man. They also provided him with hides to be cured and used for clothing, footwear or the construction of simple shelters. Pieces of antler had a variety of uses and a complete antler was a versatile instrument. It was the opinion of Major E.R. Collins of Pateley Bridge, based on discoveries in the early 1920s, that chert, the hardest rock locally available, as well as imported flint, were used for implements and weapons. The Major had found what he took to be an ancient implement made of chert when he explored Goyden Pot, in Nidderdale. Chert was certainly used but some of Major Collins's finds are now considerable to be natural.

When, in the same period, the level of Gouthwaite Reservoir fell nearly 20 ft., exposing the hillwash lying beneath the soil on the sides of the valley, he found artefacts which suggested that in early times hunters had camped beside what was then a glacial lake. The skeletons of several adult reindeer found in Stump Cross Cave, on Greenhow, may have been those of animals which were washed into an open system by sudden natural disaster, to be sealed off by clay and peat until in more recent times the remains were found by prospecting lead-miners.

With climatic warming, the dale-country was overspread by pine, elm, oak and lime. Alder and willow established themselves in the wetter places. At its maximum, natural woodland in the Dales must have covered about 90 per cent of the land surface. Neolithic man, arriving in Britain from the east some 5,000 years ago, introduced improved hunting and herding skills, as well as rudimentary farming, cultivating wheat and barley. Few Neolithic remains have been found. Neolithic man did possess a formidable implement in the polished Cumbrian Axe, made from a volcanic tuff of Lake District origin.

Evidence of the Neolithic presence has been found at the Fox Holes, just off the dry valley above Ingleborough Cave. When excavated in 1914 it was judged to be a Neolithic camp and interment site, there being pottery, flints and burial remains. Neolithic man also found convivial circumstances beside Semerwater, in Raydale. It is from this period that the first known Dales pottery is dated. Burial sites include a chambered cairn, such as the so-called 'Giant's Grave', at the head of Penyghent Gill, a site which yielded skeletons when it was excavated in 1805. Dry caves may have been used in Neolithic and Bronze-Age times as burial places, judging by the recovery of bones, some of them charred. Also found were leaf-shaped arrowheads and fragments of what is now known as Peterborough Ware, a thick dark type of pottery.

BRONZE AND IRON

At the close of the Neolithic period a measure of social organisation is hinted at by circular, earth-banked and ditched enclosures named 'henges', examples of which have been found near Aysgarth and at Yarnbury, above Grassington. Were these tribal focal points, associated with religious and/or trading purposes? Rather less than 4,000 years ago Bronze-Age folk laid out stone circles, though doubt has been cast on the origin of two Dales examples: at Bordley, on the edge of Malham Moor, opinion swings between chambered tomb and stone circle; the extremely fine circle at Yockenthwaite, in Langstrothdale, may be what remains of a tomb or an enclosure for stock. A crouched position was favoured for the dead, who were often buried below mounds of stone or earth.

Two cave divers in the limestone country abutting the Howgills, in that part of the Dales National Park east of Sedbergh, followed a water-filled passage to where they were able to climb a boulder slope into a cave which contained the remains of people deduced by radio-carbon-dating of bones taken on the first visit to be of the Bronze Age. Also found, crisp and clear, was a prehistoric footprint, the first to be observed in an English cave setting. The bones in the cave were left intact but a skull which had slipped into the boulder slope was removed for detailed study and proved to be that of a woman of about 48 years of age who lived 3,500 years ago. A specialist at Manchester University rebuilt the skull and then moulded a face from clay. The appearance of this prehistoric woman may not have been unlike that of a middle-aged woman today.

Barrows and burial cairns are numerous in the Dales. Bronze-Age people possibly had a lake-dwelling at Semerwater, which may explain an old folk tale of a city which was flooded because of its inhospitality to a visiting beggar. Semerwater is notorious for its flash-floods. From this area was recovered a bone spearhead of about 1000 B.C. Modern researchers, using aerial photographs, have plotted over 700 hut circles, single or in groups, some of the Bronze Age but mostly of the Iron Age, in the limestone areas of Craven.

5   *Stone circle near Yockenthwaite, Langstrothdale.*

The Iron Age (third century B.C.) formed the last stage of prehistoric settlement, the new society gradually evolving into a political grouping known as the Brigantes. They were nature worshippers and named some of the rivers—Dee, Swale, Cover and Ure. Among the hills, Penyghent and Addleborough have Celtic names. The Iron-Age folk lived in circular huts, kept goats and sheep, and used iron for axes and the tips of ploughs, clearing away much of the remaining woodland cover. Still visible on many limestone plateaux, especially in the Grassington and Malham areas, are outlines of their field systems, where oats and other crops were cultivated, to be ground in querns for bread-making.

THE ROMAN PRESENCE

When the Romans moved north they encountered the Brigantes, who were ruled by a queen, Cartimandua. She readily adopted Roman ways, to the disgust of her consort, Venutius. He was incensed when, in A.D. 52, Cartimandua handed over to the Romans a kinsman, Caractacus, who had sought refuge among the Brigantes. Cartimandua divorced Venutius and married a Roman. One of the Brigantean strongpoints was a hill-fort on the summit of Ingleborough, at 2,350 ft. The area was ringed by a wall 3,000 ft. long, traces of which remain, along with evidence of some twenty hut circles. As a defensive position it would be good in the short-term. Most likely it was a retreat in time of danger rather than a round-the-year habitation.

Roman policy was to contain the native folk in blocks, using forts linked by good roads. The remains of villas have been found at Kirk Sink, near Gargrave, and at Middleham, in Wensleydale. An intriguing survival from the first century is a Roman marching camp, possibly from the days of Cerialis who, appointed Governor of Britain in A.D. 71, set about subjugating the Brigantes. The remains of such a camp, which pre-dated the forts, lie beside an ancient track, Mastiles Lane, linking Kilnsey with Malham Moor. The camp was a temporary structure, used by troops spending a night in potentially hostile country.

The Roman road system extended north and south on either side of the Pennines with an important crossover point between Low Burrow in Lunesdale and Bainbridge in Wensleydale, where from about A.D. 80 a fort was garrisoned by a cohort of 500 infantry. Bainbridge stood at a meeting place of roads, notably Cam High Road which headed westwards over Wether Fell at an elevation of 1,900 ft. and continued over Cam End to Chapel-le-Dale and Lunesdale.

DARK AGES

For five-and-a-half centuries between the departure of the Roman forces and the Norman Conquest is a period once known to historians as the Dark Ages. There are few written records but much evidence of folk activity through an incursion of Angles, Danes and Norse settlers. The Anglians, a people of North Germanic stock who first appeared along the east coast as raiders, had by the middle of the seventh century become Northumbrians, a people living north of the Humber. They were urged to go west, and in the Dales their tenacious farming methods, assisted by heavy axes and ox-drawn ploughs, opened up the cultivable areas.

Banks were made to indicate important boundaries, examples being a series around Grinton, in Swaledale, and Tor Dyke, between Wharfedale and Coverdale. The last named represented the north-east boundary of Craven, a district recorded in Domesday Book as Cravescire. It later assumed an ecclesiastical importance as the Archdeanery of Craven. Christianity, a minor religion in Roman times, was re-established, as indicated by fragments of stone crosses found in the eastern part of Wensleydale. Early villages with a central green include Linton and Burnsall in Wharfedale, Arncliffe in Littondale, and Reeth in Swaledale.

Farming was a blend of arable and pastoral. A group of villagers shared strips of land which were run on a basis of triple rotation. Village names frequently ending in -*tun* (a township, as at Airton), -*ham* (a settlement, such as Clapham) and -*ley* (a cleared area, as in Wensley) give a good idea of the area of colonisation, which was mainly in the middle or lower stretches of the dales.

Place-names associated with early settlement, such as Anglian and Danish, indicate a general location and not necessarily the present settlement, which has normally evolved, shifted, expanded or shrunk over time. Villages with a linear formation, which were possibly planned settlements of the 12th century, include three Wensleydale examples–Aysgarth, Castle Bolton and West Witton. Such settlements are identifiable through names ending in -*by* (a homestead), as in part of Kirkby Malham and Carperby. As both Angles and Danes were competent arable farmers, their cultures would quickly merge.

Skipton, the 'gateway to the Dales', has an Anglo-Danish origin, 'sheep town', with Sheep Street as one of its main thoroughfares. Fragments of Anglo-Danish crosses at Burnsall church in Wharfedale testify to an allegiance to the Christian faith. The appearance of lynchets or cultivation terraces on steep hillsides, to augment the arable land in the main dale, came with a rising population, the ploughing being carried out using oxen and plain wooden ploughs with iron tips. Though the lord of the manor owned unenclosed areas of the uplands, local people had rights to dig peat or turf or to graze stock. Austwick has a survival of this custom in its stinted pastures.

NORDIC SETTLERS

The Norse folk who arrived via Ireland in the 10th and 11th centuries made the upper dale country their own. They were several generations removed from those intrepid folk who had left Scandinavia on a migratory route which lay across the top of Scotland and down the Irish Sea from the Hebrides to Ireland and the Isle of Man. The migration into the dales, more properly referred to as an Irish-Norse migration, appears to have been via what is now the Cumbrian coast, through Garsdale and upper Wensleydale. Little tangible evidence remains of their settlement, though three hogsback grave covers favoured by Vikings with means are to be seen, alongside fragments of a stone cross, at Burnsall in Wharfedale.

A Viking farmstead excavated at Ribblehead consisted of a building taken to be the house, a flagged path leading to a kitchen which was kept separate from the living space to lessen the fire risk, and a third building taken to be a workshop. Such buildings would have had heather thatch or turf roofs. A Norseman, like the archetypal dalesman of recent times, would be no lover of crowds. Present dales farmsteads, spaced out along dalesides, where there is a copious water supply in the form of a spring or beck, are invariably on sites of Irish-Norse settlement when a name terminates in -*thwaite*, -*gill*, -*garth* or -*rigg*, among other topographical references.

Norse names became a major part of the language of topography. An exhaustive list would include *crag, clint, scar, beck, moss* and *tarn*. A Norse settlement was a *thwaite* or clearing, as in Thwaite, upper Swaledale, or *holme*, an element in the name Hubberholme, by the Wharfe. The suffix -*sett* is derived from *saetr*, originally a summer grazing area, in hill country apart from the winter home. Well-known examples in Wensleydale are Appersett, Burtersett and Countersett. The place-name Keld, in upper Swaledale, is derived from a Norse word for spring. Norse folk were at home in farmsteads scattered across Malham Moor judging by hard Norse names like Thoragill and Stangill. Arthur Raistrick believed that Middle House may be Norse, the old name, Midlow House, being related to Mootlow, the hill where the Norse councils were held. He pointed out that Midlow Hill is almost central to the Norse farms.

NORMAN RULE

The return to administrative tidiness came with the Normans and their Domesday Survey of A.D. 1086. After the Conquest huge tracts of land were granted by William I to his followers, the Norman lords, who had made themselves secure quarters behind the walls of their castles at Richmond, Middleham and Skipton. When Norman scribes were active, the Yorkshire Dales were still recovering from a depopulation which followed the 'harrying' instituted by a vengeful Conqueror in 1069-70. The Domesday record stopped at the forest edge, which in Wharfedale was at Starbotton and in Swaledale at Reeth. Some development updale would be for the accommodation of foresters.

Much of the northern dale country was granted to Count Alan of Brittany, whose Honour of Richmond became one of the largest feudal holdings in the county. Roger de Poitou's territory incorporated Craven, a district which included the choicest limestone country, parts of Bowland and the upper valley of the Wharfe. As feudal estates flourished, the names of Percy, Neville, Clifford and Scrope (pronounced Scroop) began to dominate the Dales story.

The aforementioned forest, at the daleheads, was a term derived from *foris*, undeveloped land suitable for hunting. It was not necessarily well wooded. Creatures of the chase, notably deer and wild boar, were protected by strict laws. Waterhouses near Malham Tarn housed the forester of Gnoup or Darnbrook, which included Fountains Fell. Bainbridge, the old Roman centre, was developed greatly in the twelfth century to care for my lord's interests in the Forest of Wensleydale, where the settlements, originally lodges, included Stalling Busk, Mossdale and Snaizeholme. Place-names like Laund and Drebley mark the early points of habitation in the Forest of Barden, which was part of Skipton.

Langstrothdale Chase, Bishopdale and Arkengarthdale were further large tracts where hunting was regulated (and poaching decisively opposed) at special courts with their bevies of officials. Ranulph, lord of Middleham early in the 13th century, asserted that 'Beyntbridge belonged to his ancestors by service of keeping the forest, so that they might have abiding there 12 foresters, and that every forester should have there one dwelling house and 9 acres of land'. Earl Conan of Richmond in 1171 granted Jervaulx Abbey free pasturage in the New Forest of Arkengarthdale. The Earl insisted that the monks should have no hounds or mastiffs. A commoner was not to keep any large dog unless it had three claws cut from each forefoot so it would not be able to hunt.

The mere presence of red deer could put neighbouring landowners at odds with each other, for such animals represented not only sport but an acceptable source of protein in the long, lean winter. The Cliffords of Skipton were at odds with their neighbours, especially the Yorkes, over hunting the red deer. Between 1606 and 1633, Sir John Yorke of Appletreewick did not discourage those who sought deer on Clifford land, as in Littondale where, on a summer day in 1607, a marauding band carrying crossbows and guns and with greyhounds, pursued a herd of 30 deer they found near Halton Gill on to Penyghent, thence to Malham Moor, where two hinds were accounted for. Two others fell from a crag and were killed. Tempers ran high and, at Appletreewick Fair in 1621, faithful supporters of the two families came to blows. By this time, however, hardly any free deer remained in the district. The last of the stock of what had been wild red deer survived in parks, such as that at Bolton Abbey, until modern times. The Chatsworth estate at Bolton Abbey in Wharfedale endures as an area of recreation, both for the owning family and for the tourist, having passed through the hands of Cliffords and Cavendishes, each proud of its status and heritage. It is possible that some of the ancient hollow stumps of oak trees had begun their long lives before the Norman Conquest.

GIFTS TO THE MONKS

The rich and powerful, having achieved affluence and power in this world, and anxious to secure favourable conditions in the next, made gifts of money and parcels of land to the monasteries in exchange for burial within the grounds and prayers for the well-being of their souls. In course of time monastic interests held most of the land now included in the Yorkshire Dales National Park. The chief religious houses were Easby Abbey near Richmond in Swaledale, Jervaulx Abbey in Wensleydale, Coverham Abbey in Coverdale, and Bolton Priory in Wharfedale, founded by Augustinian canons. Abbeys which had territorial claims but were not situated in the immediate area included Fountains near Ripon, Furness, at the edge of modern Barrow, and Salley, now called Sawley. Granges were established on the outlying land. Five monasteries, namely Fountains, Byland, Sawley, Furness and Jervaulx, had territorial interests in High Craven. Marrick Priory, in Swaledale, and Ellerton Priory were associated with Benedictine nuns.

In the Dales the great abbeys had a mainly pastoral economy, whereas in other areas arable farming was practised. Mineral resources were exploited. Sheep produced wool which was then highly regarded throughout Europe. In the exploitation of natural resources, such as lead, iron and coal, monastic interests laid the foundations of much of the later wealth of the Dales. Granges, or cotes, were a form of decentralisation, each grange being a combination of chapel and farm, the staff including a monk and lay brothers who did the day-to-day jobs. Visiting officials from the monastery ensured a grange was running according to rule and also made the necessary arrangements to victual the place and collect its products, such as fleeces, cheeses, corn, hides and stock on the hoof.

Trade routes were opened up. Wool from Kilnsey went by packhorse or ox-hauled wain to Fountains Abbey. The fleeces clipped from the backs of sheep around Ingleborough were despatched from the grange at Newby, between Clapham and Ingleton, to Furness Abbey, a range of buildings which stood in red sandstone majesty near the northern shore of Morecambe Bay. The Priory at Bridlington and Rievaulx Abbey, land-owners in upper Swaledale, developed their pastoral farming, enclosing land as meadows and ranching cattle.

Fountains Abbey (1132-1539) was founded by rebellious 'black' monks from York who were accepted into the Cistercian order, becoming 'white' monks and making the customary vows concerning poverty, chastity and obedience. Fountains stands in the secluded valley of the Skell near Ripon. The strict monastic routine was governed by the ringing of the big bell. Silence was maintained at meal-times. Being enjoined to renounce wealth and luxury, the Cistercians originally accepted gifts of uncultivated land where they might construct austere buildings and live frugally, the manual work

6 *Fountains Abbey, in the valley of the Skell, near Ripon.*

7   *The Cellarium at Fountains Abbey, near Ripon.*

being done by lay brothers. By the year 1150 Fountains had seven daughter abbeys, one of which was situated in Norway. The crowning glory of Fountains was to be Abbot Huby's Tower (*c.*1520), which rises in gleaming magnesium limestone to a height of 170 ft.

The Cistercians were particularly skilful at sheep farming. Granges and outlying farms were connected with the parent abbey by a web of routes, some of which, like Mastiles Lane, between Malham Moor and Kilnsey, were marked by stone crosses. The monastic route was intended not simply to connect with the properties of a big Dales estate; it continued into the Lake District, where the most outlying estate took in part of Borrowdale. There were legal disputes about grazing rights with a powerful neighbour, Furness Abbey. To Fountains Abbey came the representatives of Italian merchants from the affluent city states of Florence and Venice. Deals negotiated at Fountains Abbey led to wool clipped from the backs of sheep at the grange of Kilnsey in Wharfedale, which specialised in farming sheep, being transported by wagon or pack-horse to the Abbey, and thence to the medieval city of York, where the wool was loaded on to sea-going ships.

The development of sheep-farming on a grand scale transformed the appearance of large areas of the Dales. The animals effectively prevented the natural regeneration of timber. Land denuded of trees had its minerals leeched from it by the northern weather. Cattle and horses were more important than sheep in some places. One Ralph Buck, aged 80, of Darnbrook on Malham Moor, was summoned by Thomas Proctor, who had land at Fornagill on Fountains Fell, during a tithe dispute in 1598, and stated that he had seen cattle and horses brought to the area from Fountains Abbey. Ralph also witnessed 'heardes[men] milk the Abbeis Kyne in the same ground lying their swords and bucklers besides them whilst they were milking'.

Mining for lead was important in Dales life in the 12th century, when mines were operating above Grinton in Swaledale and in the New Forest, Arkengarthdale. Count Alan of Brittany, Lord of the Honour of Richmond, bestowed on Jervaulx Abbey the right to mine lead and iron, for their own use, in the Forest of Wensleydale. Much timber was needed for smelting lead and to produce charcoal for iron working. Abbeys squabbled among themselves over mining rights. When, in 1365, Thomas Musgrave, the sheriff of York, bought lead for Windsor Castle, part of it was transported from Coldstones on Greenhow and borne to Boroughbridge in 'two waggons each with ten oxen'. The mountains crossed by the carters were stated to be 'high and rocky' and the roads 'muddy'. The lead was shipped from Boroughbridge to York, thence to London. Other supply routes for Swaledale lead were via Stockton.

Scottish raids in the 14th century led some Dales families to fortify their houses. For others, the embellishment of a house was surely a status symbol. Nappa in Wensleydale and Barden Tower in Wharfedale are examples of imposing early stone buildings in the dale country. The Black Death's fearful death toll led to a serious labour shortage. Fountains had to pay servants to do the manual work and was empowered to sell the ruined granges as self-supporting farms. The population at Fountains Abbey, which peaked at over 500, not all of them monks, declined steadily so that by 1500 there were about thirty monks and relatively few servants. Fountains ceased to exist in its original sense on 26 November 1539, when Abbot Bradley and the monks, assembling in the chapter house, surrendered 'the whole of our said monastery, its site, precincts and church' to the King. He received some 60,000 acres together with a vast number of cattle and sheep. The monks were pensioned off.

The Dissolution of the Monasteries was bitterly opposed by many dalesfolk, who supported the Pilgrimage of Grace, a rebellion which reflected Catholic/Protestant antagonisms. The rebellion was soon put down and the ringleaders were hanged. Some land was bought by a few entrepreneurs, many with connections at Court, and sold in smaller parcels. Subsequently, there arose in the Dales a class of yeoman farmers, not unlike the 'statesmen' of the Lake District, a few of whom were to prosper. The majority became tenant farmers, some of whom had the qualities of the proud, self-reliant yeoman type. Dissolution also liberalised trade and industry.

A QUEST FOR LEAD

Lead was mined in Roman times, judging by the discovery of 'pigs' of lead of this period. The next evidence for mining comes from post-Conquest times when, needing vast quantities of lead for roofing castle and monastery, Count Alan of Richmond mined in Swaledale and Arkengarthdale. The monks owned lead mines: Jervaulx, in Wensleydale, was given the right to dig lead and iron ores locally; Byland Abbey benefited from iron ore and lead taken from Nidderdale; Fountains mined lead on the east side of Greenhow.

8 *The big wheel at Killhope, Weardale, where lead mining processes are demonstrated.*

Mineral rights were normally retained by the lord of the manor and mining remained a part-time activity until the 17th and early 18th centuries, the miners working under a 'bargain' system. Those miners skilled in sinking shafts or driving levels, who were not able to mine as such, would be paid wages, but it was not until the late 18th and 19th centuries that this applied to miners in general. Lord Wharton had mining interests in Swaledale and Arkengarthdale. The Conyers operated in Swaledale and in Wensleydale, where the Metcalfes were developing mines. In Wharfedale, the agents of the Earls of Cumberland realised the potential of the Yarnbury and Grassington Moor orefield, the workforce including miners brought from Derbyshire. At Linton, a smelt mill was one of the best examples of its kind, about fifty of which were to be found in the Dales.

GOLDEN FLEECES

The wool trade switched from the exportation of wool to become a domestic industry, one aspect of which was the knitting of stockings. As the 16th century waned, Richmond had become a major Yorkshire market for knitting. Kendal, whose motto was 'wool is my bread', sent wool into the north-west dale country to be knitted into socks, gloves and mittens for wide sale. Wool was borne to the West Riding, via Settle, where a crossing point of the Ribble is still known as Kendalman's, harking back to the old packhorse days. The Border troubles lessened with the Act of Union, which united Scotland and England in 1603. Cattle-droving from Scotland to the English graziers, thence to market, greatly increased.

THE YEOMEN

A Craven example of the 17th-century rise of the yeomanry is the Dawson family. In the 16th century Christopher was a tenant of the Cliffords at Halton Gill and Foxup at the head of Littondale. His grandson, also named Christopher, had the old Hall built at Halton Gill. His son, Josias, in turn acquired Langcliffe Hall, in North Ribblesdale. And his son, yet another Christopher, married Margaret Craven of Appletreewick and moved to nearby Hartlington.

An outstanding example of an Elizabethan house is Friars Head at Winterburn, in the Craven lowlands, which graces a tract of gentle countryside between Eshton and Winterburn. This large house was built by the Proctor family, probably Sir Stephen Proctor who, according to West's *History of Furness*, managed the Furness Abbey estates in Craven before the Dissolution. Friars Head has four lofty gable bays, with mullioned and transomed windows. In the gables these are surmounted by three light ogee-shaped windows. The property has affinities with Fountains Hall, near Ripon, Proctor having bought land formerly owned by Fountains Abbey. Thousands of visitors to Bolton Abbey in Wharfedale see another wondrous dwelling, the Old Rectory, latterly the home of the estate agent. Burnsall School in Wharfedale, founded and endowed by Sir William Craven in 1602, also testifies to the unpretentious but attractive use of local materials.

Many families were involved in what the historian Hoskins was to call the 'great rebuild', expressing their new-found wealth and confidence in the future by constructing new homes of stone—dwellings which used local materials and therefore had a textural link with their environment. The great period of farmhouse building began in about 1600, though not for another 70 years was it fully under way, long tenancies at low rent enabling farmers to invest in status housing. Constructed of local stone, with sandstone for quoins and dressings, the new homes conformed to the notion of 'fitness for purpose' and were based on a long, rectangular plan, several bays wide but only one room deep. A typical

9   *Friars Head at Winterburn.*

house had a central porch and a passage from front to back, dividing the ground floor into two, and an inglenook with a wall cupboard near the fire so that salt and spices could be kept dry. Another conspicuous feature was the mullioned window, complete with dripstone. Pride in ownership was proclaimed by an stone above the main door inscribed with the initials of those concerned in the building and the year in which it took place.

CLIFFORD PROPERTIES

Lady Anne Clifford, the last of her illustrious family to bear the Clifford name, became almost a queen in the Dales when, after the Civil War, she returned north to take over her family estates, which she had not seen for half a century. She set in train a reassertion of her rights and a restoration of her properties, taking no account of new ideas but simply preserving for a few more years the feudal way of life. This was carried on to the extent of her being borne with all the pomp of a monarch from one place to another. Using a horse litter or a coach, she traversed 'mountainous and almost impassible ways' between her native Craven and Westmorland, where lay her favourite castle, Brougham, and near where she bid a last farewell to her much-loved mother, erecting a pillar emblazoned with family heraldry to mark the spot. Lady Anne, intelligent and characterful, earned the admiration of Cromwell himself; hearing that she was engaged in rebuilding the castles which should have been slighted and left in a ruinous state, he allowed the work to proceed unhindered.

10   *Lady Anne Clifford.*

THE DROVERS

As the urban population of England grew, cattle-breeding increased in the Scottish High-lands and on the islands. The cattle, which appeased the craving for fresh beef by the residents of the new towns, were driven to trysts near the Border, and from here along well-established drove roads to fairs held in the Dales. John Birtwhistle of Skipton traded directly with Scottish breeders in about 1745, despite an upsurge of Jacobite fervour, and is reputed to have had up to 15,000 cattle on the move at one time and to be organising fairs on the Great Close, Malham Moor. The cattle were subsequently traded at fairs such as those at Middleham Moor and Askrigg, the first-named being on such a scale that it issued its own £5 notes, illustrated with pictures of local beauty spots. Droves of cattle from Askrigg were driven along the course of the old Roman road through Bainbridge and over Cam Fell to Gearstones, near Ribblehead, where a sale of Scotch cattle was a regular occurrence.

The Dales landscape would soon be transformed by walls built without mortar. The old walls were near the villages and around the dispersed farms. At the monastic sheep farm of Middle House, between Malham and Arncliffe, the attendant crofts were walled using blocks of limestone, forming an erratic pattern. Arthur Raistrick described this area as 'a small oasis of curly walled enclosures'. A maze of such walls also occurs at Gunnerside in Swaledale, enclosing small fields with irregular shapes. A 'mere' wall was one which defined a boundary, such as in the Manor of Ingleton and Bentham (*c.*1592), where a local document noted that 'the water runneth to a place called Toddabb and then by ffrearwood South east to a place called mearewall ascending directly up the meargill unto the sd bounder called Cawdeell knott aforeside ...'.

ENCLOSED BY WALLS

The first enclosures came about by local agreement, which was the case at Grassington (*c.*1605), when the open west field was split into a number of long, walled enclosures. The main beneficiaries of these changes were people with means and influence. Small peasant holdings were eliminated. For a scheme of enclosure to succeed, the support of only a third of the total interest was needed for a petition to Parliament which, if successful, led to the publication of an Enclosure Act. Commissioners, usually three in number, assessed the various rights and gaits on an unenclosed pasture before dividing it into allotments in the proportion of the old rights. Provision was made for roads, quarries, lime kilns and tradi-tional areas of recreation. In Kingsdale, near Ingleton, in around 1820, enclosure and reclamation of some land included straightening the beck, which gives the valley an unu-sually neat appearance.

In the reallocation of land, the new owners had to attend to the walling, any costs being charged upon the land. They worked to a map prepared by the Commissioners, who were inclined to divide up an area using straight lines. When Studfold Moor, near Horton-in-Ribblesdale, was enclosed in 1771, one of the landowners, Dr. Wilson of Beecroft, paid £5 to the Enclosure Commissioners as his share of the cost, the charge being established at the rate of 10s. for each stint which had been in his possession before enclosure took place. Wilson's share of the Moor consisted of two allotments totalling 42 acres. He arranged for the getting and leading of stones needed to make the flanking walls. The work lasted a year and cost him about £25. Having lost their land, the small-time farmer and the cottager either became paid servants of those who acquired it or left the area to find other employment. Ironically, some of the displaced men found work building the walls decreed by the Enclosure Acts.

To some visitors, walls were the proverbial blot on the landscape. The historian Thomas Dunham Whitaker objected to them on aesthetic grounds, stating that

> enclosures, however convenient for occupation or conducive to improvement have spoiled the face of the country as an object. The cornfields were no more. The pastures 'are now strapped over with large bandages of stone, and present nothing to the eye but right lined and angular deformity'.

In the 1770s, William Bray, touring Derbyshire and Yorkshire, crossed over the hill from Wensleydale to Kilnsey. He wrote of the wildness of the scenery and noted that the pastures had been

> lately divided by stone walls of about two yards high, one yard wide at the bottom, lessening to a foot at the top. A man can make about seven yards in length of this in a day, and is paid from 20d. to 2s. The stones brought and laid down for him, cost about 7s. more.

In 1883, the rector of Bolton Abbey, whose joy was a landscape adorned by a thousand shades of green, wrote of 'the cold rectangular boundaries of stone walls'.

In 1805, Charles Fothergill, who was staying with William Fothergill, his uncle, at Carr End near Semerwater, confided in his diary (16 September):

> Immediately after breakfast I set out for Simonstone ... to visit the upper end of the Dale. There is a barn or hovel of stone in almost every field in these parts: they are used for the reception of hay chiefly: the major part of them are built without mortar, something in the manner of the walls, only more regular, and stable, with large corner stones and well slated top ... nearly every field is possessed of a barn which contains the hay of that field together with an apartment at one end for the cattle it is allotted to fodder. By this means the hay is well preserved, the manure kept more from waste and is mellowed, and the cattle feed in shelter from the storm. The more modern barns are built with mortar.

DIGGING 'LEADE OWRE'

For some displaced dalesmen there were jobs in lead-mining. John Leland, visiting Grinton, found himself in 'a little market towne ... The market is of corne and linyn cloth for men of Suadale, the wich be much usid in digging leade owre'. William Camden, a 16th-century antiquarian, wrote, 'The hills afford great store of lead'. The old-time arrangement, whereby a partnership of miner-farmers worked the handiest veins, went early in the 17th century as the industry was transformed. John Sayer developed the Marrick mines in Swaledale and Sir Stephen Procter of Fountains Hall built a smelt mill on Greenhow Hill and began the intensive colonisation of land at between 1,250 ft. and 1,300 ft. above sea level—land which had previously kept little more than sheep. On Grassington Moor, in the 1780s, flues were greatly expanded so

11 *A reconstruction of the lodging place used by lead-miners at Killhope, head of Weardale. Such lodgings were found elsewhere in the Dales where miners stayed near their work from Monday to Friday.*

that lead that had accumulated on the inner sides (as much as six per cent of the total amount smelted) could then be scraped off and sold.

The mining of lead led to considerable changes in the appearance of Swaledale, Arkengarthdale, Wensleydale and Upper Wharfedale. The landscape was despoiled by 'hushing', a process of damming water and then releasing it to pour down a hillside, eroding the soil and exposing mineral veins. The hushes are clear to see in Gunnerside Gill, Swaledale. Turf Moor Hush, near Langthwaite, Arkengarthdale, had an impressive though by no means record length of 1,300 ft., and gouged the ground to a depth of up to 60 ft.

Some miners were also smallholders. In Swaledale, Matthew Cherry, a native who returned to the dale after working elsewhere, and who died in 1996, estimated that during his lifetime over 100 little farms of the smallholder type had been absorbed to form larger units because they were non-viable. The orefield settlements, such as Gunnerside in Swaledale and Grassington in Wharfedale were packed with cottages, many of which were empty after the collapse of mining in the late 19th century until the fashion for holiday and retirement accommodation in the Dales led to their restoration and their value was appreciated. Crumbling remains of old mines cover a considerable area in the Dales, seeming to accentuate an atmosphere of loneliness in those who walk up the gills and across the pockmarked moors. Christopher Dawson wrote of little outlying mines in the limestone hills that had been taken back into the landscape like prehistoric remains of remote antiquity.

TURNPIKE ROADS

Poor roads and basic amenities did not encourage travel for pleasure, but those burning with religious zeal might not notice the discomforts. John Wesley, on a brief visit to the Dales in May and June 1780, preached at Grassington in fine weather, commenting that afterwards it 'rained much'. The second visit took in Wensleydale, which to him was 'lovely' and the most beautiful of the dales. Daniel Defoe, writing in 1724, referred to the dale country as being 'nothing but high mountains which had a terrible aspect ... especially Penigent Hill'. Defoe had a habit of describing places he had not visited and he could have viewed Penyghent from the river bridge at Settle without leaving the main road. Thomas Gray, one of the 'picturesque travellers', returning from the Lakes in the autumn of 1769, lingered in the Dales, where he found Ingleborough 'now completely wrapped in clouds all but its summit, which might have been easily mistaken for a long black cloud too, fraught with an approaching storm'.

Towards the end of the 18th century, new ideas and improved mobility led to the birth of tourism in the English Lake District. War with the French had temporarily ended the Grand Tour of the Continent. Gentlemen (and a few ladies) with taste, leisure and curiosity, became seekers after the 'picturesque', which formalised a new awareness of the natural world. P. Bicknell was to define it testily as the 'art of cooking nature'. What became known as the Romantic Age, from about 1760 to 1840, contrasted with the somewhat stuffy period of Classicism that had preceded it.

Travel was improving with the construction of turnpikes and the first tourists made good use of them. The pioneering if specialist guide book, *A Tour to the Caves*, by the Rev. John Hutton, appeared in 1780. Gratified by the quick sale, the author published a second enlarged edition (1781) in which the description of each cave is 'more exact and particular'. Hutton dedicated his book to Thomas Pearson, Esq., of Burton-in-Kendal, writing

> The amusement you have received in visiting the natural curiosities in the neighbourhood of Ingleton and Settle ... hath induced me to draw up a plain narrative of one of our excursions, in a letter to a friend, by way of an appendix to the *Guide to the Lakes*. This I thought would

not be unacceptable to the southern parties who, for their summer amusement, make the fashionable tour of the lakes. The caves may be visited in their return without inconveniency to most of them ... by taking the Yorkshire road through Settle, Skipton &c.

The Keighley to Kendal turnpike crossed one made to link Lancaster and Richmond, which linked up with the port of Yarm, thus connecting west and east coasts overland. Each of these roads provided ready access from Ingleton to Chapel-le-Dale, where John Hutton described Weathercote Cave as 'the most surprising natural curiosity of the kind in the island of Great Britain'.

William Bray, in 1777, explored the main dales and enthused over waterfalls but, like many another stranger in his day, thought little of hill country. As he crossed from Bishopdale to the upper valley of the Wharfe he found himself on 'a wild and dreary moor ... at the top of which are black and dismal peat-mosses'. He concluded that 'the traveller who sets out on a long journey with the expectation of meeting with the same accommodation on the road that he has in his own house, will soon find himself mistaken'.

Early artists went for those scenes which were picturesque and romantic–for rocks, waterfalls and ruins, preferably overgrown with ivy. J.M.W. Turner toured the Dales on four occasions between 1797 and 1817, putting down his impressions in sketches which would be worked up into watercolours. He toured cheerfully, despite grim weather conditions, cowering under an umbrella which was devised to be converted, if necessary, into a fishing rod.

At the head of Malhamdale, Gordale Scar's vast scale and majesty, and the awesome way in which the limestone cliffs overhung, were captured in a canvas worked up from sketches by James Ward and exhibited in 1815. It supplemented the account left by Thomas Gray, who had visited Gordale Scar in 1769, being both impressed and somewhat scared, for here 'loose stones ... threaten visibly some idle spectator with instant destruction'.

Visitors to the Dales in the second part of the 18th century were aware of the burgeoning of little market towns and improvements in transport, though the droving of cattle was still along traditional routes, avoiding built-up areas and especially toll bars. Thomas Pennant (1772) wrote:

Kilnsey-Scar, ascend and get into a hilly, less pleasing country. Overtake many droves of cattle and horses, which had been at grass the whole summer in the remotest part of Craven, where they were kept for nine shillings to forty per head, according to their size.

At Bolton Abbey, in the heart of Wharfedale, the gatehouse of the priory, saved at the Dissolution of 1539, was now grandly enlarged into Bolton Hall, a residence of the Duke of Devonshire. The Rev. William Carr, Rector of Bolton Abbey from 1789 to 1843, keen to see local beauty spots opened up to discerning members of the public, received permission from the 6th Duke of Devonshire to make paths through Strid Woods. His work was commended by William Wordsworth, who wrote, 'The Rev. Carr has most skilfully opened out its features; and in whatever he has added has done justice to the place by working with an invisible hand of art in the very spirit of nature.'

It was Wordsworth and Walter Scott, on visits to the Dales, who romanticised some local stories. Scott's fancy was taken by Rockeby (Rokeby), on the Greta. Typical of the writing is:

> O'er the high feat of Baron bold,
> When revell'd loud the feudal rout.
> And the arch'd halls return'd their shout ...

Wordsworth, as related, knew Bolton Abbey and converted a strange tale into *The White Doe of Rylstone*. He seems to have got the idea from the writings of Thomas Dunham

Whitaker, historian of Craven, whose source was the utterances of 'the aged people of the neighbourhood'. Wordsworth described the solitary doe which visited Bolton Priory during the servicetime as being white as a lily of June, 'and beauteous as the silver moon'.

When Charles Fothergill toured the Dales, in 1805, he listed fish in the Yore at Middleham, including salmon '... largest size 47lb: instance of 30 taken in a day near Wensley by click hooks as they came to spawn'. Pike of 30lb weight had been taken. This species was common. A trout of 7 or 7½lb had been caught by a trimmer set for pike; '... 'twas fat and healthy'. The river from Middleham to Wensley and the neighbourhood was so full of fish 'as to appear quite alive on a fine summer's evening'.

LIME AND COAL

Arthur Young, touring the north country in 1770, mentioned the high demand for lime to improve the 'black moorland soils'. The demand was met by field kilns in which lime and coal, in alternating layers, were burnt over a period of several days, clouding the Dales with dark smoke. Seams of hard, brittle coal occurred in the upper Yoredale series. Customarily, the coal was recovered by bell-pit sunk to a depth of 30 ft. or more, the seam being worked radially or by drift mine straight into the hillside, depending on the geology. When recovery became difficult, because of foul air and an absence of light, the pit was vacated and another was dug along the seam, creating a line of little spoil heaps.

Coal was transported by pack-pony to where it was required–to the field kilns, smelt mills or farmhouses. An old track, now a highway, connecting the railway stations of Garsdale and Dentdale, is still known as the Coal Road. Anyone who climbs Fountains Fell from Rainscar area uses a track which, cut from the fellside, served coal-pits which were used from 1790 until 1860. Some coal was turned into coke to reduce weight and gases. Possibly the last field kiln employed in lime-burning, using Fountains Fell coal, was at Cowside, on the way from Langcliffe to Malham Tarn. One of the Hunter family, early this century, lit the kiln for 'auld lang syne'.

NONCONFORMITY

George Fox, on his mission through the Dales in 1652, expressed new thoughts about religion which led to Quakerism, the first real break with the practice of the established church. For him, and for many of his supporters, there were trials and tribulations. The persecution of nonconformists lasted until 1689 when an Act of Toleration received Parliamentary approval.

The nonconformists became a dominant force in the ethical and educational life of the Dales. Quakers, and other sects, such as the Baptists and Congregationalists, and especially the numerous Methodists, had their meeting places not only in towns and villages but, for the first groups of Christians, in each other's homes. The early Methodist preachers were not welcomed, being pelted and stoned at Bellerby, in Wensleydale. At Castle Bolton, a Methodist cause was nurtured at the cottage home of John Jackson, whose income came from transporting lead and coal in panniers on the backs of donkeys. The first Methodist society in the dale was formed here in 1765.

12   *The old chapel at Widdale Foot, near Hawes.*

INDUSTRIAL REVOLUTION

The Rev. Charles Kingsley (1819-75) spent short fishing holidays at Malham Tarn House, the 'mountain home' of his friend, the millionaire Walter Morrison, and it is the contrast between 19th-century industrialisation and the unbesmirched limestone country that gives Kingsley's book *The Water-Babies* (1863) its special appeal. Tom, the chimney sweep, escapes from bondage when he gets lost in the chimneys of a house not unlike the mansion beside Malham Tarn. He ventures into a fresh, flowery world and joins the water-babies in a clear, cool stream. The dark marks on the face of Malham Cove are not, as some supposed, streaks of soot left behind when Tom descended into the realm of the water-babies, however. They are damp patches, composed of moss, their blackness deriving in part from airborne pollution.

The images of a beautiful landscape and of a characterful people living their simple, satisfying lives amid great natural wonders, is a modern one, created by writers with urban backgrounds. Robert Southey, in *The Doctor* (1847), invested even death with romance when writing of a yeoman family in Chapel-le-Dale called Dove, who for generations had lived at a house about a bow-shot from the church.

> There they had all been carried to the font; there they had each led his bride to the altar; and there they had, each in his turn, been borne upon the shoulders of their friends and neighbours. Earth to earth they had been consigned for so many generations that half of the soil of the churchyard consisted of their remains.

The Industrial Revolution had its repercussions in the Dales, where many an old corn mill was adapted for processing cotton. Two notable examples of mills which were purpose-built for cotton are Gayle and Yore Mill at Aysgarth, dating from the 1780s. The Hon. John Byng, visiting Aysgarth in 1792, saw an older mill, which was appreciably smaller, and proclaimed that its presence had destroyed every rural thought. Here was 'a great flaring mill, whose back stream has drawn off half the water of the falls above the bridge. With the bell ringing, and the clamour of the mill, all the vale is disturbed.' The old mill had a varied life, including a serious fire. The rebuilding, on a larger scale, was completed in 1853. A hoary story relates how, in the 1860s, some red jersey-like material made from Yore Mill yarn remaining unsold, the merchant who had bought it promptly took advantage of the unification of the Italian states; it is claimed that the material was turned into the red shirts of Garibaldi's revolutionary army. The existing mill of no less than five storeys, now used as a coach and carriage museum, was completed in 1853. A mill at Airton in Malhamdale (now divided into flats) was where the Dewhurst family built up their resources, to be used in the construction of a huge mill with red-brick chimney at Skipton.

AGE OF LEISURE

Lead mining and textiles would fail but tourism, which was being developed in the later part of the 19th century, has, in the later 20th century, become such a feature of the Yorkshire Dales the area is in danger of becoming a theme park. Among the early publications was *A Practical Guide Book to Malham and its Surrounding Scenery* (with illustrations), written by A.M., 'Hon. Fellow of the Society of Science, Letters, and Art (London)', and printed in Blackburn in 1886. The text is mundane and the advertisements give an insight into Victorian tourism. *The Buck* hotel at Malham, 'five miles from Bell Busk station', has a large dining room and private sitting rooms. Parties can be met at Bell Busk or Hellifield railway stations by giving a clear day's notice to Edward Armstrong, the proprietor. *The Lister's Arms* hotel at Malham (proprietor, B. Swinbank) offered 'good beds, stabling, &c'.

At Kirkby Malham, *The Victoria* hotel was similarly well-endowed. 'The Spa Well is 300 yards from the Hotel and Richard Bottomley, proprietor let out post horses and conveyances at reasonable charges.' In 1903, Edmondson and Co. of Skipton published the eighth edition of McFarlane's *Guide to Malham*, and by this time Leonard Lister had set himself up in the village as a landscape and portrait photographer. Clark's *Temperance Hotel* at Malham, 'can dine 50 at one time'. Letters arrived at Malham at 10 a.m. and are despatched at 3 p.m. in winter and 4 p.m. in summer.

Some of the newly-rich of the Industrial Revolution, who built up sporting estates in the Dales, lived congenial lives until the First World War shattered the social system and they were left with their memories of moorland days–plenty of grouse in the air and a large reservoir of inexpensive labour enabling them to enjoy their rural pursuits. Old men recall the days when grouse-shooting involved walking the moors, using specially bred dogs–labradors, retrievers and spaniels–to rouse the birds from the heather just ahead of them. Eventually, grouse were being directed by beaters and flankers to where lines of inconspicuous butts provided cover for men with guns who lay in wait.

THE CONTEMPORARY SCENE

There are now serious threats to the special character of the Yorkshire Dales. In the age of leisure, and at a time when familiar dale-country forms the backdrop to popular television programmes, and thousands seek out Herriot Country or Emmerdale, new development tends to be tourist-orientated, and 'honeypots' like Aysgarth, Hawes, Grassington and Bolton Abbey are congested for most of the year. Efforts to wean visitors from their cars to public transport have not cured the problem. Yet walking from a car park remains a major interest, with certain areas being 'loved to death' and lacerated by booted feet. So many cars visit the Dales in good summer weather, air pollution is becoming a problem. The old peacefulness is regularly shattered by the passage of military aircraft on low-level training flights.

The traditional Dales landscape is suffering. During the Second World War, hill farmers were encouraged to produce more by receiving generous grants for sheep. The hills became overstocked and the vegetational cover suffered. Overstocking has taken place in subsequent years as farmers try to maintain a reasonable income. Heather has vanished from vast tracts of ground. The heather was not only a good 'bite' for sheep and grouse; it provided cover for moorland birds.

The transformation of farming practice has led to the erection of enormous sheds. There is no time nor money to keep all the drystone walls in good repair, except in classic areas, where grants are available. A vast number of field barns are on the point of collapse.

The proportion of native-born within the Dales population as a whole continues to fall and properties which come available are invariably taken up by incomers while young people from old-established families seek cheaper accommodation in town. Yet the planning restrictions which have helped to bring this situation about have ensured that many redundant outbuildings like barns have been splendidly restored as houses.

Visually, the Dales has not fared too badly from decades of exceptional social and economic change.

3

TRANSPORT

PREHISTORIC ROUTES are hard to define but would evolve mainly for trading purposes, such as the distribution of a special volcanic tuff from Great Langdale, used for axe-heads, or of flint from the eastern chalklands. The Aire Gap was a likely trade route with Ireland, with traders keeping to higher ground, or what the historian Arthur Raistrick called 'these "edge" roads', above the swampy valleys. They also offered clear views across any valleyside woods of landmarks which in early times would be used as navigational aids. In the south-west, early folk could travel dryshod on the rim of limestone, in an area now served by the A65.

Firm knowledge about routes through the Dales dates from Roman times, though the most important roads were at the periphery of the area: that in the west connected Manchester with Ribchester, Overborrow, Penrith and Carlisle; the main eastern road extended from York to Corbridge and Hadrian's Wall via Aldborough and Catterick. The only truly Dales route, of some 19 miles, connected Ingleton with Bainbridge (known in Roman times as *Virosidum*) via Cam End, 1,500 ft., and Wether Fell, 2,014 ft. On Warburton's (1720) map of Yorkshire the road is named The Devil's Causeway.

Bainbridge gave the Romans a military presence at a key point in Brigantean territory. Their main aim was to hold the restless tribe in check. The fort, on a drumlin above the Bain river, would be a focal point for several roads, with a possible connection with Catterick. Another routed southwards via Stake Pass and Buckden, in Wharfedale, to the fort at Ilkley, from where a road to Boroughbridge ran northwards via Blubberhouses, its course followed in part today by the modern road between Bolton Bridge and Harrogate.

With the withdrawal of Roman control, there followed a long period when there was no efficient road system. Subsequently, the routes most favoured related to the market towns which were the main centres of commerce. An early market charter was that for Richmond (1144). In contrast, Hawes, at the head of Wensleydale, did not receive a market charter until 1700. During the 400 years or so when monastic establishments had vast holdings in the Yorkshire Dales, and a system of granges, or outlying farms, was in operation, the most frequented long distance routes were those connecting the granges to their parent monasteries. Where one monastery had, as a matter of convenience, to use the facilities of another, an agreement was reached.

Mastiles Lane, between Kilnsey and Malham, was part of a system used by Fountains Abbey. Running against the grain of the landscape between Malhamdale and Wharfedale this route must have been used by Roman troops for the outline of a marching camp is conspicuous. For many years Mastiles was an open track, the drystone walls which now flank it dating from the comparatively recent Enclosure period. Mastiles and other 'green roads' of the Dales had stumpy crosses as an early form of waymarking as well as an

13   River Ure on the Bolton Hall estate, Wensleydale.

assertion of territorial rights. Mastiles Lane had five such crosses, only the bases of which remain. Weets Cross, which has an upland setting between Hanlith and Lee Gate, in Malhamdale, has retained its stone shaft. The derivation of the name Weets is not known, but doubtless the cross stood on the edge of the Malham estates of Fountains Abbey. It marked the meeting point of four townships–Malham, Bordley, Calton and Hanlith.

Early topographers who travelled in the Dales, such as the scholarly John Leland (1540s) and William Camden (1582), put great emphasis on river crossings. Leland, the first great English traveller to provide us with a detailed account of his journeys in this country, at a time when other travellers were preoccupied with descriptions of foreign parts, wrote an account of his travels under the title *Itinerary*, in which there is a reference to a 'tymbar' bridge over the river Ure near Middleham, in Wensleydale, and to 'a great old bridge of stone ... called Kilgram Bridge' spanning the river about a mile below Jervaulx Abbey. 'There is a fair bridge on Swal at Gronton ... the Richemount bridge.' Camden, historian to Queen Elizabeth, lets us know in his *Britannia* that the Wharfe was 'a troublesome River and dangerous even in Summer time also'. A horse was inclined either to slip on the stones or have its legs 'carryeth ... away from under his feete'. Happily for local people, the benevolent Sir William Craven was building a large stone bridge at Burnsall. Celia Fiennes (1690s), a southerner accustomed to using wooden bridges, was enthusiastic in her acquaintance with the Dales about 'those high and large stone bridges I pass'd, which lay across the rivers'.

One of Arthur Raistrick's 'edge' roads made a steep ascent of Cotter End to Cotter Clints, in upper Wensleydale, and then used a limestone terrace in its progress towards Hell Gill and the county boundary. This short cut from Wensleydale into Mallerstang was most suited to packhorses, the beasts of burden which were the main form of transport in the Yorkshire Dales for more than 600 years. On the route to Mallerstang they were rested in a walled enclosure known as the Horse Paddock. Anne Clifford, crossing Cotter End on her way from Skipton to Appleby in 1663, confided in her diary that she 'went over Cotter, which I lately repaired, and I came into the Pendragon's Castle'. The turnpike road avoided this hilly section.

   The many tracks on Tan Hill, between Stainmore and Swaledale, are in part accounted for by the presence of workable seams of coal and deposits of galena associated with the rich Swaledale orefield. Geoffrey Wright, in his survey of roads and trackways of the Yorkshire Dales, records that colliers at Tan Hill were supplying coal to Richmond Castle in 1384, and from the 17th century coal was delivered to Appleby, Brough, Kirkby Stephen, Penrith, Hawes and most of upper Wensleydale and Swaledale. The best coal was for domestic use, the poorer quality having a ready sale to the limeburners who were active from about 1760 until 1850.

   For five centuries packhorse traffic, largely developed in monastic times, sustained trade between Dales communities, though more packponies than horses were in use, there being the choice of Fell or Dales. Many ponies, imported from Germany, were referred to as Jaeger (hunter) ponies. From this period date the attractive single-span stone bridges which enabled the animals to pass dryshod over upland becks or turbulent rivers, two Ribblesdale examples being Thorns Gill, where a small bridge with no parapets crosses a deep ravine, and Stainforth, where a much larger bridge with low parapets was built on a packhorse route by a Quaker landowner in the 17th century. Ivelet Bridge, updale from Gunnerside, is a particularly fine example of a simple but extremely strong structure of the type used in the packhorse days. Arthur Raistrick, writing in *The Dalesman* (1941), said that the leading pony in a pack train had a harness of bells, whose music marked the leader and kept the following ponies together. Each animal was capable of bearing a load of up to 2¼ cwt. (rather more than 100kg). The variety of goods carried was impressive, ranging from salt to lead, from corn to coal. The topographer Harry Speight recorded in 1897 that when the packhorse age came to an end, hundreds of packhorse bells were sold for old metal and the brokers' shops were for a time full of them.

14 *Fell pony in its winter coat.*

One of many examples of a packhorse route is Badger Gate, which crosses the Washburn Valley to Beamsley, and in the late 18th century, when Skipton had a great corn market, was part of a route widely used by badgers [corn dealers] and their trains of packhorses. Arthur Raistrick assessed that in and about the mines on Grassington Moor, and on the 10 miles of roads to Skipton, Gargrave and Pateley Bridge, from 16,000 to 20,000 horse-loads were borne in an average year. Large objects could be moved only in the drier part of the year, as is indicated by the experience of John Robinson, agent for the Coalgrove Head Company on Grassington Moor, who in 1756 asked William Brown, a mining engineer of Newcastle, to design and supply a whim suitable for draining the mine. In January Brown was ready to arrange for the equipment to be installed; Robinson sadly informed him that winter travel was difficult for large objects: 'The roads are so Excessive Rotten that it will be difficult to get Timber and other Materials Led till they be better.' He recommended deferment until spring, 'when one may hope the Weather and Roads will be much better'.

Adam Sedgwick, a native of Dent who became Woodwardian Professor of Geology at Cambridge, harking back to his childhood in about 1790, recalled a time when all external produce was brought into Dent by carriers from Hawes, Kendal and Kirkby Lonsdale. Mrs. Beckett and her daughter Peggy were carriers who travelled to Kendal every Friday for the Saturday market and returned late on Saturday evening with provisions and matching drapery goods. Sedgwick remembered the roads when

> some in Dent were so narrow that there was barely room for one of the little country carts to pass along them ... I remember too when the carts and carriages were of the rudest character; moving on wheels which did not revolve about their axle; but the wheels and their axle were so joined as to revolve together ... Horrible were the creakings and Jykings which set all teeth on edge while the turf-carts or coal-carts were dragged from the mountains to the houses of the Dalesmen in the Hamlets below.

The bell-pits of the local miners were served by a track known as the Coal Road–a route, now macadamed, which connects the stations of Dent and Garsdale across a high fell. Another route, known as the Hearne Coal Road, climbed from Hardraw in Wensleydale by Blea Pot, in upper Wensleydale, and served a line of coal-pits below Pickersett Edge. A branch of this road served the Cotterdale pits, which tapped the same coal seam. Most of the upland roads, with the exception of those serving the mining areas, were abandoned in the 18th century with the development of turnpike roads. Gradients were now suitable for wheeled vehicles.

For many years the duty of repairing the highway in Yorkshire had fallen on the township through which it ran. The Highway Act of 1555 had re-enacted this customary liability and, further, provided that all inhabitants above the position of a hired labourer were to come together with horses and carts and give their labour for six days in the year to repair the roads. Turnpikes, which were introduced between 1750 and 1830, were organised and financed through trusts, the members of which were gentry and business folk who hoped to regain their investment and stimulate local business. In 1927 John J. Brigg observed:

> Much has been written about Turnpikes and a good deal has been said about the greed of the Trusts, but whatever may have been the case with the farmers of the tolls (and even they were controlled by a schedule of tolls), the trustees themselves derived no pecuniary benefit and we may be very thankful that, in times when the central government did nothing, private individuals were willing to find the money for so many of the fine roads we have today.

The Richmond to Lancaster Turnpike Trust of 1751 was, in truth, part of a coast-to-coast system of road transport; a good road connected Richmond with Yarm, a prosperous town by the navigable Tees. The Keighley-Kendal turnpike, of 1753, connected the West Riding textile town with the wool-producing area of the Lake District and adjacent dales. Charges for the use of such roads tended to be exorbitant, and something as modest as a carriage and pair paid 9s. 4d. in toll in passing over the Yorkshire portion of the Keighley-Kendal turnpike. The covered wagons of early times were succeeded by splendid coaches, the most notable of which was the mail coach in its red livery. Lighter vehicles for private use were known as post-chaises. The squeal of the slipper, a wedge-shaped piece of wood reinforced by iron with flanges fractionally wider than a coach wheel, was heard wherever this device was used to retard the coach during a steep descent, to the detriment of the road surface.

Coaches gave people of means high mobility, though progress was measured in a few miles per hour. Horses were changed at prescribed places. One such, on the Keighley-Kendal turnpike, was Switchers, now a solitary roadside farm on the stretch between Coniston Cold and Hellifield. The coaching period resulted at Settle in the development of three coaching inns—*Golden Lion*, *Joiners* and *Spreadeagle*—each having three storeys to provide adequate bedrooms for weary travellers. At nearby Giggleswick *The Hart's Head* provided coaching facilities. Interestingly, both *The Golden Lion* and *The Hart's Head* had a change of situation when the turnpike arrived. The first named, having been by the old route in Cheapside, re-opened in premises just round the corner to attract the new trade. *The Hart's Head* had been at the bottom of Bell Hill, but with the coming of the turnpike spanking new premises were opened up beside the main road, which was re-routed from High Rigg to Buckhaw Brow.

A coaching inn was an extensive group of buildings, providing accommodation and food for travellers, as well as commodious stabling for horses and accommodation for the ostlers who kept the sturdy horses in good condition. The turnpike attained its financial high-water mark in 1835, when the Rimley [Runley] Bridge bar tolls were let for £496. The Leeds and Liverpool Canal, completed in 1816, was close enough to the Dales to enable raw materials to be carted to the Dales mills.

15 *A horse-drawn carriage at the stable yard at Malham Tarn House.*

16   *Charles Stanley Sharland, who surveyed the route to be taken by the Settle-Carlisle Railway.(Photographed in London, October 1869, just before the work began.)*

The coaching period ended abruptly with the coming of the railways, though the Keighley-Kendal Trust was in existence until 1877. In that year, eight toll-houses were sold for £520. On 30 October, Mr. Bradley, the surveyor, was instructed to refuse no reasonable offer for the gates and to see that they were all taken off their hinges at noon on 1 November. By 1847 the railway had been completed from Leeds to Skipton, and the Lancashire & Yorkshire Railway and the Little North Western linked Skipton with Colne and Giggleswick (for Settle) respectively. In the 1870s the Settle-Carlisle Railway, a product of the Midland Railway Company's rivalry with the London & North Western, cut a swathe through North Ribblesdale, storming the high fell country on its way to the Eden valley. On the high-lying stretches, viaducts, tunnels and tracks set on ledges cut from the sides of lonely fells testified to the skill of Victorian engineers.

The Wensleydale Railway, a useful through route, later suffered the fate of many rural lines and was axed, though the stretch between Redmire and Northallerton was kept open to service the Teesside steel industry. When it became redundant and closure seemed imminent, the Ministry of Defence restored this part of the line to transport tanks and other heavy vehicles to the ranges, avoiding the narrow roads of the dale.

Bailey J. Harker, in *Rambles in Upper Wharfedale* (1869), mentioned entraining to Skipton, thence by horse-drawn omnibus operated by Thomas Septimus Airey to Grassington. When Walter Morrison M.P. cut the first sod at the Grassington terminus of the Yorkshire Dales Railway (Skipton to Grassington) on 7 June 1900, the brass band was present, along with many local dignitaries. The relevant part of a busy programme said that 'on arrival at the field, Mr. W.A. Procter will hand Spade to Mr. Morrison, and Mr. Hutchinson and Mr. Ferguson will hand Barrow to Mr. Morrison, and the latter gentleman will cut the sod'.

The story this century has been of an adjustment of the road network to suit increasing numbers of motor vehicles, and especially heavy lorries. Bypasses have appeared around the peripheral towns. Skipton's bypass system was timely in the sense that the High Street, the old bottleneck, could not have coped with the present demand. Improvements to the A59 at Bolton Abbey have provided a new bridge and roundabout, urbanising one of the finest scenic areas of Wharfedale; the wide road continues over Blubberhouses towards Harrogate. Meanwhile, in the high dale country, old tracks between Kingsdale and Deepdale and between Dent station and Garsdale station were macadamed just after the Second World War. Using them is not advised in snowtime.

4

NATIONAL PARK

THE YORKSHIRE DALES National Park, covering an area of 680 square miles, was one of 10 such Parks created during the 1950s under the National Park and Access to the Countryside Act of 1949, and its boundaries take in the best of the landscape while neatly side-stepping all the towns except Sedbergh, which lies in Rawthey valley, between the scenic uplands of Baugh Fell and the Howgills. Here, in fact, the Park takes in an area which was historically Yorkshire but transferred to the new county of Cumbria on changes to local government in 1974.

Moving clockwise, the Park boundary embraces the moorland north of Swaledale, stops short of Richmond and Leyburn, misses not only Pateley Bridge but the upper Nidd too, and crosses the Wharfe near Bolton Abbey. In the west the boundary lies north of Skipton and east of Settle and Ingleton. It is primarily open country, the largest centres being Hawes, in Wensleydale, and Grassington, the 'capital of Upper Wharfedale' and the setting for Colvend, one of two administrative centres of the Park.

17 *Swaledale above Gunnerside*

The Dales Park's aims are to 'conserve and enhance the natural beauty, wildlife and cultural heritage' and 'to promote opportunities for the understanding and enjoyment of the special qualities of the parks by the public'. Over half of the area consists of open moorland and 40 per cent of enclosed farmland, where farmers have been able to erect new buildings, even quite large new buildings, providing they are suited to the purpose intended. A mere 3.6 per cent of the National Park is woodland. The major landowner, with some 4,500 acres, is the National Trust, followed by the Ministry of Defence and the water companies who, on privatisation, also acquired (cheaply) the extensive gathering grounds.

It should be a source of pride in the Dales that John Dower, the architect of National Parks, reflected on the form they might take during a period spent at The Rookery, Kirkby Malham. Writing in *The Yorkshire Dalesman* in 1940, a year after the magazine had been first published, he observed:

> Fate has so willed it that I–a Londoner for almost the whole of my adult life, though by birth and upbringing a Yorkshire Dalesman–should now be living for the first time where I have always wanted to live, in a small Dales village.

John Gordon Dower, born and reared at Ilkley, was the elder son of Robert Shillito Dower, a steel merchant in the firm of Depledge's in Leeds. His father was also a nonconformist lay preacher. John went to Ghyll Royd (prep.) School in Ilkley and then to the Leys School in Cambridge. He was just too young to take part in the First World War. He studied history at St John's College, Cambridge, and moved to London to study and practise architecture, becoming a qualified architect and town planner, assisting in various offices and then, with John Brandon-Jones, working on his own account. In 1929 he married Pauline Trevelyan, one of the celebrated Northumbrian family. Charles Trevelyan, his father-in-law, and Charles's brother, George Macaulay Trevelyan, stimulated John's interest in the campaign for National Parks and for broader protection of the countryside.

A modest, quietly-spoken town planner, whose health had failed, he became friendly with Harry Scott, founder of the magazine, and he contributed to it an article on what he, an invalid, might see of Dales life from his bedroom window. He had first written and spoken about the concept of National Parks as early as the 1920s, when the English countryside was being rediscovered by war-weary people and the out-of-work of the industrial towns. In such a Park the landscape would be protected from abuse and people have reasonable access to it. Youth hostelling had been introduced from Germany to England in the 1930s, and public access to the countryside was a lively topic. In 1932, the Kinder Scout mass trespass re-focused public attention on such matters. Three years later, the voluntary bodies set up a Standing Committee for National Parks to press for their establishment. In 1942 the Scott Report on rural land use foresaw a thriving countryside and restated the case for designating National Parks.

The government commissioned John Dower, civil servant, architect and rambler, to write a report on how the national park idea would work for this country. He was not a stuffy type of bureaucrat, being a good companion on country jaunts and at all times humorous, vigorous, talkative and untidy. John was a passionate countryman, a strong walker and a writer of considerable sensitivity. In the Dales he enjoyed seeing 'the striding patterns of drystone walls' and hearing 'the piping and crying of curlews'. He felt with delight, not anguish, 'a wet west wind in my face when ridge-walking'. Being keen on angling and shooting, he was able to claim with authority that grouse shooting and public access are compatible. John's brother, Arthur, was influential when the young architect became absorbed in thoughts about national parks and related matters. As an active writer and speaker in the cause, John became drafting secretary of the relevant standing committee set up by what is now called the Council for the Protection of Rural England.

In 1938, sensing that war was imminent, John Dower sought a house in the north and found The Rookery, and in the following year he joined the army as a Royal Engineer officer. His wife Pauline and their family, daughter Susan and sons Michael and Robin, settled down to life in Malhamdale. During the first winter of the war, at Shorncliffe Camp near Dover, John contracted tuberculosis and was invalided out of the army. Mercifully, none of the family was aware that a seven-year-long illness would terminate with his death. The tuberculosis waxed and waned in severity.

He wrote articles for what had become *The Dalesman*, including a series of articles about post-war planning in the Dales, his great hope being that the region would be kept attractive for the physical, mental and spiritual refreshment both of resident countryfolk and visitors from the towns. 'It must not be merely a negative job of preservation but a positive job of maintaining and enhancing beauty ... and of making it accessible.' Tuberculosis did not prevent John Dower from becoming a member of the Hobhouse Committee, which in 1947 made formal proposals for the creation of National Parks, building on Dower's report. He died in the same year–just a year before streptomycin, which might have effected a cure, had become available. Thus he did not live to see the passing of the National Parks and Access to the Countryside Act in 1949. In 1972, the Local Government Act and the Sandford Committee reinforced the administration of the Parks, providing a basis for more generous funding by the government.

Dower's great survey of 1945 did not mention a Dales National Park as such. His list of suggestions about areas suitable to become parks included the 'Craven Pennines', some 380 square miles, taking in the upper Wharfe, Aire and Ribble valleys. He visualised as future Parks the 'Swaledale Pennines', with part of Wensleydale, and the Howgill Fells and Upper Lune valley. The North York Moors area, set out as a future Park, was to be designated before that for the Dales. A key part of John Dower's work was writing the White Paper on National Parks in England and Wales, a document published in 1945. Failing health led the family to move home in that year to the house in Northumberland where his wife had been brought up.

John Dower's report was followed in 1947 by Sir Arthur Hobhouse's committee proposing twelve National Parks, each with its own administration. It also recommended the establishment of a National Parks Commission to frame national policy concerning the Parks. Today, the 26-strong committee who administer the Yorkshire Dales consists of a mix of county, district and parish councillors, with members appointed by the government for their specialist knowledge. The annual report for the Yorkshire Dales National Park Authority in the year from April 1996 to March 1997 describes the final year's work of the Committee which, set up in 1974, was superseded by a new National Park Authority in April 1997. The transition was effected by the Environment Act of 1995, at a time when the tempers of some dalesfolk were being tested by what was considered to be rule by outsiders.

The new authority has greater local representation, including more district councillors and, for the first time, members representative of parish councils. There are also increased responsibilities for the economic and social well-being of local communities. In presenting the annual report for 1996-7, Robert Heseltine, Chairman of the Yorkshire Dales National Park Authority, hoped it would 'provide the basis for us all to continue working together to protect this outstanding landscape'.

The Park Authority maintains a network of public rights of way, most of which are well used by visitors, having appeared in various publications describing Dales walks. Of

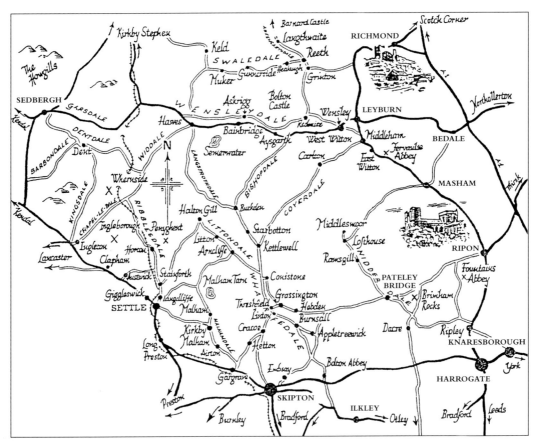

A general map of the Yorkshire Dales.

the long distance paths, the Pennine Way enters the National Park at Malham and leaves it north of Keld, in Swaledale. This route has never attained the highest popularity, if only for the peaty wastes of the South Pennines, and many tackle only the central part, between the geographical gaps of Aire and Tyne. The Dales Way, from Ilkley to Bowness in the Lake District, traverses Wharfedale and Dentdale. Mr. Wainwright's imaginative Coast to Coast Walk traverses Swaledale and is so enjoyable that yet more coast-to-coast routes have been devised by his disciples.

In addition to these footpaths, there are permissive paths, not official rights of way but available through the co-operation of the landowner. Two examples are the western flank of Buckden Pike in Wharfedale, which is across land owned by the National Trust, and the free access to Barden Moor in Wharfedale, courtesy of the local estate. Public rights of way consist of footpaths, bridleways and byways. Footpaths are for foot use only, bridleways may be used on foot, horseback or pedal cycle, and byways are legally open to all traffic, though common sense should decree that where they are unsurfaced they are usually unsuited to the passage of vehicles. The National Park Authority has been looking into the historic rights on the 'green lanes', such as those which were originally monastic ways or droving routes and were flanked by drystone walls during the Enclosure period of the 18th and early 19th centuries.

Grants are available to local farmers who wish to co-operate. Reconciling public demand for access and amenities with a landscape which is being 'loved to death' is an almost impossible mission. In 1994, 8.3 million 'visitor days' were recorded. When all visitors are taken into account, 93 per cent came by private car and only six per cent by public transport, which is no longer adequate for such a large rural area.

Among the schemes is one for Environmentally Sensitive Areas (ESAs), a notion introduced by the Ministry of Agriculture which enables the farmer to enter into a voluntary agreement with the Ministry in return for which he or she receives an annual payment on each hectare of land entered into the scheme. The idea is to sustain a distinctive landscape, in the Dales context this being mainly the preservation of floriferous meadowland, wildlife habitats or historic features.

The National Park contains extensive mineral reserves. Quarrying is a local industry which began in a modest way and now creates enormous scars on the landscape as well as traffic problems, through the despatch of limestone to customers. Swinden, in Wharfedale, which has for long been a considerable eyesore, sends most of its output by rail and there are plans here, as elsewhere, for landscape restoration when the workable deposits are exhausted.

Heather Hancock, who took up her duties as National Park Officer in 1998, was the first woman to hold such an office. When, in 1996, she returned to Littondale–'a return to the real world'–with her husband and son she had already helped the National Park Authority win £4 million of National Lottery money. Around 500 projects designed to bring environmental and community improvements to the Dales were able to go ahead. The more visible challenges she faced were coming from the increasing pressures on the Park from rising numbers of walkers and tourists, and finding the best ways of looking after the landscape for both residents and visitors. At the time of her appointment, there were several urgent problems facing farmers–including a crisis over beef and reorganisation of the Common Agricultural Policy.

Robert Heseltine, Chairman of the Yorkshire Dales National Park Committee, who comes from an old Dales family, writing in December 1997 concluded that the pressures on this National Park are greater than ever before and demand more resources, more effort and even more commitment. New powers given to the Park Authority in the 1995 Act indicates (Section 62) that authorities 'shall seek to foster the economic and social well-being of local communities within the National Park'. If it appears that there is a conflict between purposes, the Authority shall 'attach greater weight to the purposes of conserving and enhancing the natural beauty, wildlife and cultural heritage of the area comprised in the National Park'.

The founder of the National Park movement would have been amazed, as he completed his report in the blissful, stable Malhamdale of the 1940s, had he been able to foresee developments. From two wardens, a large staff has developed and information centres have sprung up, the one at Malham, with adjacent car park, catering for an estimated half a million visitors a year. At another 'honeypot', Aysgarth in Wensleydale, an information centre and large car park are screened by trees and there are short walks, largely through woodland, to the trio of waterfalls which have given this area renown. A collection of Dales bygones by Marie Hartley and Joan Ingilby became the nucleus of the Dales Countryside Museum at Hawes, a costly project which has been redeveloped at a price of £1.7 million.

The Dales National Park has managers concerned with farming and conservation, trees and woodland, public rights of way, development control and planning applications, building conservation, archaeological features, barns and walls and, latterly, development

18   *The famous Swaledale breed of sheep.*

of community services. In what the chairman of the Park Committee calls 'uncertain and volatile times', the authority has brought together all involved with economic and environmental management in the uplands of northern England into an agri-environmental task force. John Dower could not have foreseen the necessity for such a force, but in the circumstances he would doubtless have approved it. No one seems to have found a better name than 'National Park', though it is a misnomer; most of the land is privately owned. There is no automatic right of access to land within the bounds of the Park, where the normal activities of a rural area continue to be enacted.

The emblem of the Yorkshire Dales National Park is the head of a tup, based by an artist on a real live animal, one of the famous Swaledale breed. This emblem was nicknamed Rastus the Ram, which some officials dislike. It does give local bureaucracy a more homely aspect.

5
MALHAM AND MALHAM MOOR

THE CONTRAST BETWEEN MALHAMDALE and the Moor is clearly noticed if the area is approached on foot, as many people do while following the Pennine Way, a 250-mile-long footpath between Edale in Derbyshire and Kirk Yetholm in Scotland. Malham has a special relationship with this long-distance footpath, for in April 1965 the formal opening was held near Street Gate, attended by some 2,000 people, including Tom Stephenson, journalist and rambler, who for 30 years had sought to have this route given official status.

Having spent 50 miles trudging across the peat, ling and *nardus* landscape of the South Pennines, a walker crosses the Aire Gap to enter Malhamdale in a landscape underdrawn by Bowland shales. From a point near Hanlith, the eye takes in a Promised Land. Beyond the low fields, the meandering Aire and the grey roofs of Malham is the majestic Cove, a domed hill called Cawden and the pearl-white crags around Gordale. Then the Pennine Way follows the eastern side of the Tarn in the section between the Cove and the summit of Fountains Fell, so that for some 20 miles the limestone obtrudes like sun-bleached bone, and meadow flowers put on a dazzling show of colour. Then, far north of Malham, the grey-green interlude is over and walkers enter what Christopher Dawson, a member of a landowning family, called 'the desolate highlands of Mallerstang and Stainmore Forest'. The Pennine Wayfarer is left wondering if the Malham interlude was just a dream.

19 *Clapper bridge near Malham Cove.*

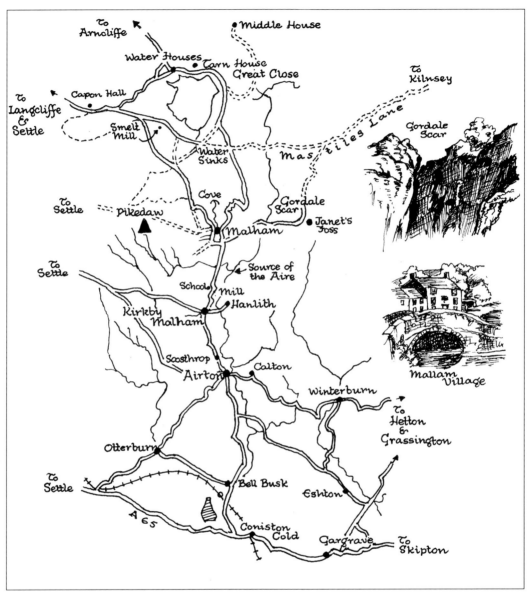

Malham and Malham Moor.

In a region of low horizons, Malhamdale's appeal is based on grand verticals. There is bow-shaped Malham Cove, a feature of the Mid-Craven Fault which gives the little valley a spectacular headpiece. Gordale Scar, a short distance away, is a ravine where limestone cliffs overhang grandly. Hidden in a valley where rocks as well as trees are lagged with moss is Janet's Foss: a beck seethes over tufa as a fan-shaped waterfall and enters a crystal pool. A mile-and-a-half beyond the Cove, another major geological fault produces yet another change of mood. Malham Tarn, 153 acres in extent, laps and frets in a basin of green slate, being topped up by water from a beck and from springs which bubble up within the Tarn itself.

Malhamdale begins with Bell Busk and ends at the Cove. Beyond the dalehead are the broad acres of Malham Moor, which is not, as one might imagine from the name, a somewhat tedious expanse of peat and heather. The general tones are grey from limestone and green from sweet herbage. The traditional moorland aspect is seen at a peat bog lying west of the Tarn and on the high ground on and around Fountains Fell. The area has long been the resort of archaeologists, who find traces of life from when Mesolithic folk summered here. On Malham Moor, pieces of knapped flint, which were used to tip arrows as well as for more mundane purposes, have been recovered from mole-heaps. Tot Lord, a characterful archaeologist of recent times who frequently visited Malham, kept a dibber permanently in place at the end of his stick so that he might poke and pry wherever moles had excavated. Middle House Farm, tucked away in a secluded area of the Moor, is close to the site of Iron-Age settlements.

Anglians came this way as part of a westward migration; they followed the Aire into Malhamdale and bequeathed to us our names for the principal villages–for Malham, Hanlith, Calton and Airton. Danes introduced the name Kirkby Malham for the settlement where the church was founded. Norsemen of the 10th century settled on the breezy heights of Malham Moor. For some four centuries, this district was owned by Fountains Abbey and Bolton Priory. In the 18th century, the dalehead acquired a conspicuous feature–a crazy pattern of limestone walls on green hillsides below the cove. With hillsides terraced for ploughing, when climatic conditions were right for growing cereal crops, the Malham countryside is seen to have been well used for a long period of time.

Malham village is divided into two parts by the beck emanating from the Cove. The principal bridge, Monk Bridge, dates from 1636, when it was of the packhorse type, narrow with low parapets. It was widened in the following century and periodically repaired. When the bridge was pronounced in need of urgent repair in 1997, a weight restriction was proposed which would have adversely affected farms on the east side, this being the only bridge capable of taking heavy traffic. Eventually, it was decided to shore up the bridge against a time when a restoration was financially possible.

The beck was of special significance after the Norman Conquest, when Malham was divided between the noble families of Percy and Mauleverer who, by a series of grants, transferred almost all to monastic interests. To Bolton Priory came Malham East, who appointed a bailiff and held manor courts here. Accommodation was available for the prior and his friends when they were hunting. To Fountains Abbey came Malham West and also the Moor.

Fountains managed the Moor from a grange at Kilnsey, in Wharfedale, and their village properties were attended to by a bailiff or steward who lived at Malham. The Tarn and its fishery having been granted to William de Percy in the 12th century, he gave them to Fountains Abbey for the good of his soul and the souls of his wife, parents and ancestors. When the Abbey was dissolved, the fishery was maintained by the Cliffords. The village properties came into private hands and the distinctions between Malham East and Malham West were discontinued in the 18th century.

Malham Fair, originally held in the Deer Park, then on the village green, was the precursor of annual sheep sales, held in autumn from about 1920. Of the original fair, a visitor of 1808 wrote:

Cattle and sheep of excellent sorts and in great numbers were exposed for sale in the village by a set of jolly, healthy-looking farmers. On the afternoon, as soon as the cattle and sheep were disposed of, the old people returned homewards: when the young of both sexes from all the neighbouring dales come to Malham and spent the evening in dancing to the music of a village minstrel.

The Lister Arms dates from early in the 18th century, taking its name from a landowning family. *The Buck* inn is of the following century, when Walter Morrison (1836-1921), dubbed 'the Craven millionaire', spent much of his time at Malham Tarn House, which he had inherited from his father on his 21st birthday and referred to as 'my mountain home'. Malham youth hostel was built in 1938 from a design by John Dower, the architect who, as mentioned, lived for a time in Kirkby Malham and prepared the report on which the concept of National Parks was based. An extension, providing an extra 18 beds, was opened in July 1967, by Arthur Dower, brother of the original designer.

Malham Tarn estate came into the ownership of the National Trust in 1946 and Tarn House is leased from the Trust for use as a field centre. Charles Kingsley, intent on getting background information for a book on the Pilgrimage of Grace, stayed at Malham Tarn House in July 1858, and wrote to his wife that the house looked out of fir-woods and limestone scars over a lake which had 'simply the best trout fishing I have ever seen. It belonged to the old monks of Fountains, and will come into the book with the old Percys and Cliffords connected with it'. Keen angler that he was, Kingsley added, 'My largest fish today was 1½ lb. (a cold north-wester); but with a real day I could kill 50lbs.' Surely no stretch of water has been studied more intently than Malham Tarn. For over a quarter of a century it has been viewed by visiting scientists with cool detachment, and by visiting schoolchildren on field courses with a degree of wonderment. Such is the sensitivity towards the environment that a reed bed was planted in 1997 so that nutrients from sewage do not threaten the ecology of the Tarn, a reed bed representing one of nature's most efficient filters. Visiting botanists have special access to the peat bog at the west end of the Tarn; the ground holds traces, in pollen or stumps of wood, of an ancient forest of pine, birch and oak.

20 & 21   *Walter Morrison and Malham Tarn House (before its tower was reduced in height).*

22 *Fountains Hall, built partly of stone from the Cistercian abbey of Fountains, which had great possessions in the Dales.*

Fountains Abbey, the major monastic landowner, had shepherds to attend their flocks, each flock consisting of about 200 sheep kept mainly for their wool. Strictly, Cistercian monks had to forgo all animal produce except fish and they lived mainly on pease, grain and pulses. With increasing affluence, however, some rules were relaxed. A flock of wethers (castrated male lambs) was clearly intended both for wool and flesh. Ewes were milked to provide the Abbey with butter and cheese, so lambs taken from their parents soon after birth were kept in pastures at the Kilnsey Grange and provided with milk from cattle kept for the purpose. When strong enough, the lambs were returned to the farms or sent to other granges. Shearing took place at Kilnsey, the nearest point on the estate to the Abbey.

Priors Rake on Malham Moor was, in monastic times, the setting for a Great Sheep House belonging to Bolton Priory. It was reported in 1290 to be in need of repair, the priory accounts indicating that 14s. was expended, along with 30s. for a thousand boards to be used as part of a slatted wooden floor. The leaders of the flock were provided with bells. Arthur Raistrick has described what he took to be a lean-to shed, probably used for milking. As with Fountains Abbey stock, ewe milk had its goodness locked up in butter and cheese, which was sent to the priory, from where food was sent to men on the estate, the staple being maslin, which consisted of wheat, oats, barley and rye flour. At the approach of winter, sheep were salved to protect them from the bad weather and also, possibly, to kill 'keds' and other insect parasites. The salve, made locally, was a mixture of tar and grease applied to the skins of the sheep in a process known as 'shedding', the wool being parted in strips to expose the flesh and a salver's index finger dipped in the salve to apply it. It was a long and tiring occupation, each sheep taking about an hour.

Visitors to Malham and the Moor today cannot image it as a setting for industry, yet a preserved chimney on a tract of moorland was originally associated with a smelt mill, the premises later being used for 'roasting' calamine, the ore of zinc, which was mined between Pikedaw and Grisedale, beside the old track between Malham and Settle. After being roasted, the calamine was stored in a building at Malham, then transported by horse and cart to the canal wharf at Gargrave. Quite rich deposits of calamine were discovered in the 1790s and the demand for it came from brass-makers. That industry, and a colliery on Fountains Fell, throve for some twenty years.

The tourist trade which dominates life at Malham today began when a few seekers after natural curiosities were attracted by accounts of the natural wonders. At first, there was a trickle of tourists. Malhamdale was not easy of access and even when the railway system was in place, the nearest stations were at Bell Busk, Hellifield and Settle, none of which was especially handy unless you could afford to hire a horse-drawn appliance from an inn at Kirkby Malham or Malham itself. In the days when mill-town folk had limited holidays, trains stopping at Bell Busk disgorged scores, if not hundreds of people who then set off to walk up the dale. Those who set off from Settle then had a long slog over the hills. Walter Morrison, when owner of the Malham Tarn Estate, was met by a wagonette but he invariably waved it away and set off to walk to Langcliffe, thence up the brow to Malham Moor. At times, having called at a local grocer's shop, he carried a ham.

Malhamdale remained a quiet farming valley until after the Second World War. During the war, farmers had co-operated in transporting the milk to a collection point down the dale by horse and trap. Today, when the annual number of visitors is considerably more than 500,000, most of whom travel by car, the tourist route is from the A65 at Gargrave, proceeding via Eshton and Airton. The Dales National Park has provided a car park and information centre at the southern end of the village, where the main road has been widened and the former aspect of Malham greatly altered. Parking elsewhere is not easy, and is prohibited on local roadsides. The best course is on foot, a splendid route being the Monks' Way from Middle House to Arncliffe. Motorists who cross the Moor on their way to Arncliffe go via Darnbrook Farm, where a gate at the bridge must be opened and closed. Beyond the bridge the road climbs, then zig-zags, putting a strain on nervous drivers.

Malham Cove holds the attention of visitors. It is seen from the approach road from the south and comes back into view as tourists reach the start of a footpath which extends to the foot of the Cove and then, in a series of gigantic steps, leads to the pavement on top of the cliff—a pavement whose limestone has been polished by the footwear of countless visitors into a marble-like smoothness. The bow-shaped Cove is generally accepted to have been created by the action of a lively waterfall. Thomas Howson (1861) wrote that

> twice within the last forty years the swollen waters of the Tarn have made their way over the Cove, but the torrent was dispersed in one vast cloud of spray before it reached the bottom; its density and the magnificence of the sight may be imagined from the fact that the spectators could not approach within a hundred yards of the foot of the rock without being drenched through.

Ledges on the cliff mark the division of strata of differing degrees of hardness. The presence of water has encouraged the growth of mosses and lichens which has been perceptively darkened by atmospheric pollution.

A strong flow of water appears from the base of the Cove, and scientists have been absorbed by a study of the underground drainage, which is far more complex than might be thought from surface features. The main point of resurgence is not the Cove, but Airehead Springs, a short distance south of Malham village, where three local becks, plus the spring-water, blend to form the river Aire. Two centuries ago the sight of water pouring from the lip of the Cove was not unusual. Then the stream took a course underground, via joints in the limestone. On one of his visits to the district, Charles Kingsley was asked to explain the dark marks on the face of the Cove and he is said to have replied in jest that they were made by a chimney sweep falling over the cliff and sliding down into the stream. Here was the germ of the idea which led much later to an incident in *The Water-Babies*. Tom, the chimney sweep, meets the babes in the cold, clear water of what Kingsley imagined to be the upper Aire, for he wrote of 'the whole River Aire coming up, clear as crystal, from unknown abysses'. At the base of Malham Cove, the beck issues from a letterbox slit, having passed through 'caverns measureless to man'. Its undermining effect on this cliff will have played a significant part in the erosion process.

Climbers take the hardest ways up this fearsome limestone cliff. The first two successful climbers in modern times spent 58 hours on the task. Their 'hardware' included 85 ringscrews and 12 pegs, quite apart from a large amount of nylon rope. The story of diving in the underground watercourse at Malham Cove began in the mid-1950s with explorations by Ken Hurst, Mike Thompson and their friends, who were aware of the considerable difference in elevation between where water goes into the ground and where it emerges. The small party, each member wearing black suits, small oxygen canister and a 'breathing bag', as used by wartime 'frogmen', managed to dig their way into a bedding plane, a low but wide passage. In the days when bottom-walking was the method of progression, each man had donned a pair of lead boots. At a distance of 60 ft. underground, they were stopped by boulders.

These obstructions were bypassed in the mid-1960s by John Southworth and his friends from the Happy Wanderers Cave

23   *Malham Cove.*

and Pothole Club, who were using the aqualung, an open circuit system invented by Jacques Cousteau and an engineer called Gagnan. The diver breathes from a compressed air cylinder and exhales into the water. The Happy Wanderers reached a point 160 ft. from the cave mouth. Further exploratory work was undertaken in 1976 by Ian Plant, following entry at what became known as Flood Rising, to the right of the main rising. Over the next three years, about 500 ft. of passages were explored using aqualungs with improved cylinders, better suits and lighting equipment.

In 1988, John Cordingley and Russell Carter took up the exploratory work at Malham Cove. Entering by the main rising, they found the passage choked with boulders and sand. A large-scale dig was initiated. By this time, dry suits and large air cylinders enabled several hours to be spent underwater at a time. They excavated about 100 ft. of passage. After reaching a point 800 ft. from the entrance, they were at a boulder-choke which gave them access to the main passage; this has a width of about 15 ft. and a height of 30 ft. The passage is still active and in flood conditions carries a violent current. The limestone is stained a brownish colour underwater because of organic deposits derived from the peat on the moor above. At 1,800 ft. from the entrance, at the end of a round trip of over five hours, almost all of it underwater, the two men reached a hydrological junction, a short distance beyond which is the present limit of exploration.

24   *Gordale Scar.*

Gordale Scar, a more impressive feature than the huge but somewhat bland Cove, is a confined space with 150 ft. cliffs which overhang so much that at one point the gap is only 30 ft. The name Gordale is derived from *gore* or *geir*, an angular piece of land. Gordale is now thought to have been carved by the fierce rush of glacial melt-water at the close of the Ice Age, but another theory is that what was originally a cliff created by the Mid-Craven Fault was eroded back by a flow of water until the stream took an underground course, as at Malham Cove. The resultant cave system eventually collapsed forming a gorge in which the cliffs are close together and overhangs impart to some sensitive visitors a feeling of being menaced.

The gorge was visited in 1769 by Thomas Gray, who had the company of a guide for the comparatively short walk from Malham. Gray saw the beck gushing from an eyehole in rock and seething over tufa. The main horror of the place was the way the rock walls 'slope forwards over you in one black and solid mass without any crevice in its surface and overshadows half the area below with its dreadful canopy'. Adam Walker (1779) saw 'a most threatening cascade' rushing 'through a rude arch of monstrous rocks, and tumbling through many fantastic masses of its own forming'. This was the celebrated tufa, a laminated substance laid down by lime-laden water. Edward Dayes (1763-1804), a celebrated watercolourist and engraver, found that at Gordale

a stupendous mass of rocks forms a ravine, through the bosom of which flows a considerable stream ... Here rock is piled on rock in the most terrific majesty ... add to this the roaring of the Cataract, and the sullen murmurs of the wind that howls around; and something like an idea of the savage aspect of the place may be conceived.

William and Dorothy Wordsworth, visiting the place in June 1807, climbed up a bank of tufa by the waterfalls to near where the main fall appears from an eyehole of rock. They walked across to Malham for tea and, much impressed by Gordale, returned in the evening. William composed a sonnet, which included the lines 'Gordale chasm, terrific as the lair/ Where the young lions couch'. James Ward (1815) was commissioned by Lord Ribblesdale, of Gisburne Park, to paint this mysterious valley. He did so on a grand scale which was accentuated by the presence at the base of wild white cattle (such as his lordship had at the estate at Gisburn) and two stags with interlocked antlers. Ward's effort at painting what many considered to be the impossible may be seen in the Tate Gallery, London.

Frederic Montagu 'of Lincoln's Inn', describing a tour from Bolton Abbey to Ambleside in *Gleanings in Craven* (1838), walked with a guide from Malham to 'Jannet's Cave', now generally known as Janet's Foss, and was repulsed by 'the register of vulgarity, in the shape of names, painted on the rock (it being too hard to cut) by gentlemen in their visits'. It was told to him, 'with the option of believing it–a most necessary proviso–that a member of some family had boldly leapt his horse over the chasm at Gordale. For my part, I do not understand why a man who thus attempts suicide should be termed bold ...' Janet's Foss, at the head of a gorge which has been described as Little Gordale, is distinguished by having a cone of tufa. Janet or Jennet, queen of the fairies, is said to reside in a cave behind the tumbling water. Her name was invoked by parents who did not wish children to venture near the plunge pool.

Weets Top stands on the skyline, offering an impressive view of limestone grass and peaty moorland. Two domed hills, Cawden and Wedber, the latter just beyond Janet's Foss, were originally reef knolls, of the type which are found at various places between Castleberg at Settle and Kail Hill, near Burnsall, in Wharfedale. Cawden Hill was for a long period a common pasture attended by a man who drove the cattle to the village green at Malham for communal milking and then returned them to the hill. Cawden Hill has occasionally burst open, this feature being known in Dales parlance as a 'brast'.

Changes in farming practice have included re-seeding with a rye-grass mix and use of artificial fertilisers to create an early flush of grass. This has happened on the majority of farms, including Lee Gate, at the end of the tarmacadamed road from Malham via Gordale, where modern farm practices have brought into being at over 1,000 ft. a complex of buildings, old and new, small and exceedingly large, which are well-fertilised and yield a fine crop of grass which is ensiled for the cattle. At the adjacent 65-acre New House Farm, Walter Umpleby kept so much to the old ways that in 1996 the National Trust was delighted to be able to purchase the farm and continue his quiet farming routine. The main reason for acquiring New House was to preserve the hay meadows which, in June and July, form a dazzling floral display. The flowers are left to seed before the hay is cut to provide winter feed for the farm stock. In the traditional hayfields of New House Farm are three plants which are nationally scarce, these being limestone bedstraw (*Galium sterneri*), alpine cinquefoil (*Potentilla crantzii*) and blue moor-grass (*Sesleria cearulea*). Other flowers in the meadows of New House Farm are wood cranesbill, great burnet, greater butterfly orchid and melancholy thistle.

Malhamdale lies within the parish of Kirkby Malham, which extends to 36 square miles, consisting of eight townships but with only about 500 residents. It is probable that a church was built in this sheltered, well-watered spot in pre-Danish times, over 1,000 years ago, and the adjacent inn was once associated with it, though it now bears the title of *Victoria*. The church, known for its grand proportions as the 'cathedral of the Dales', was extensively restored in Victorian times but by happy chance, namely a meeting between the vicar and Walter Morrison, retained its old character, the present structure being largely

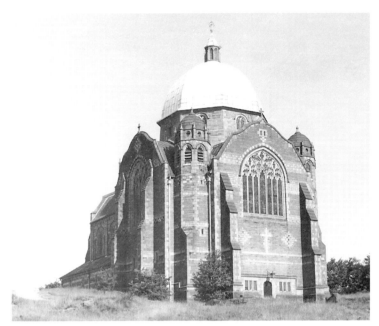

of the 15th century. The six-bedroomed vicarage, formerly the Old Hall (1622), was at one time a workhouse and at another time a cotton factory. Morrison money restored this interesting structure. Although there appear to be three storeys, in fact there are only two. Two rows of windows are found in each of the front bedrooms. A page of the church register bearing what was claimed to be the signature of Oliver Cromwell, witness at a wedding during the Civil War, was stolen in 1972. Cromwell's presence in Malhamdale was connected in part with the fact that one of his principal lieutenants, General John Lambert, was born at Calton, a hamlet on the opposite side of the dale from the church.

James King, a captain in the Royal Navy who died at the age of 31, is commemorated in stained glass at the church. Born locally, at Skellands, King became a distinguished astronomer, sailing with Captain Cook on his last voyage of exploration. In the churchyard is a unique water-grave, marked by a tall marble cross, from the base of which comes a flow of water. The story goes that Colonel and Mrs. John Harrison, of Airton, were separated for long periods because of John's frequent service with the army overseas. With a touch of Victorian whimsy, Helen, the wife, decided that as water had separated them so often in life, so it should in death. She arranged that the streamlet which runs through the grave plot should be the boundary between their final resting places. Helen died in 1890 and was buried on the south side of the stream. John outlived her by ten years. When the grave-digger came to excavate his portion of the plot, the spade struck impenetrable rock. So, after all that, they had to be buried together.

Hanlith Hall, across the valley, has a fine 17th-century doorway, on each side of which is a carved halberd, said to represent the holder of a manor who gained his land through personal service to his lord. A curiosity on part of the village green at Airton is a house with a tiny garden, the house being of 17th-century date. Building in such a place was allowed by Quarter Sessions at a time when houses were in short supply. Much more imposing is Newfield Hall, a guesthouse of the Holiday Fellowship, and, at Eshton, a mansion built by the Wilson family, one of whom, Sir Matthew, became the first M.P. for the Skipton Division.

6

THREE PEAKS

AN ESTIMATED 700,000 VISITORS a year visit Whernside, Ingleborough and Penyghent, which, dominating the landscape in the south-western part of the National Park, have for long been known as the Three Peaks. To John Bigland (1810) the trio was named 'Whamside, Pennygant and Ingleborough'. A couplet recklessly claimed that 'Ingleborough, Whernside and Penyghent/Are the highest hills twixt Tweed and Trent'.

Each peak stands in grand isolation, separated by glacial valleys. Reginald Farrer, writer and plant-hunter, who was reared at Clapham and whose family owned much of Ingleborough, observed that that hill occupied a tract of ground forming a rough triangle. He wrote in *Blackwood's Magazine* (1908):

> On this great triangle, as on a pedestal, stands the mass of Ingleborough, built, like his two neighbours, of shale and grit, with one narrow belt of mountain limestone appearing about a hundred feet from the summit in an abrupt cliff, on which grow the rare plants for which the hill is celebrated.

Whernside, despite being the most elevated, is the least shapely, being the culmination of a long ridge which taunts the walker with false summits before the trig point is eventually reached. The recommended route is from Ribblehead, beside the Settle-Carlisle railway, which is bridged just south of Blea Moor tunnel, then for a while along the old Craven Way to Dent, eventually striking uphill. Until the path was improved the boots of walkers sank in cloying peat. Penyghent, viewed from North Ribblesdale, has a leonine shape, and from the back—from Dalehead, on the Stainforth-Halton Gill road—has the shape of a whale.

On its limestone platform above Chapel-le-Dale, Ingleborough is big, bold and flat-topped, and so placed that it can be seen from afar, even by those who trudge behind the guide across the sands of Morecambe Bay. In his Journal for March 1859, John Ruskin considered Ingleborough

> a really fine mass of hill, the streams in the limestone behaving in the most extraordinary manner, perpetually falling into holes and coming out again half a mile afterwards. Pen y Gent [*sic*] is a fine hill too; and the wind blowing over the whole seemed as if it would blow Ingleborough into Lancaster Bay.

The aforementioned Reginald Farrer commented on the intense fury of the westerlies coming through the wide gap of Morecambe Bay. 'Even the high, stout walls of the Craven Nursery at Clapham did not break the spirit of those westerly winds.'

Young Laurence Binyon, who grew up in the vicarage at Burton-in-Lonsdale, and is annually remembered by the nation as the author of 'Lines to the Fallen', which are recited

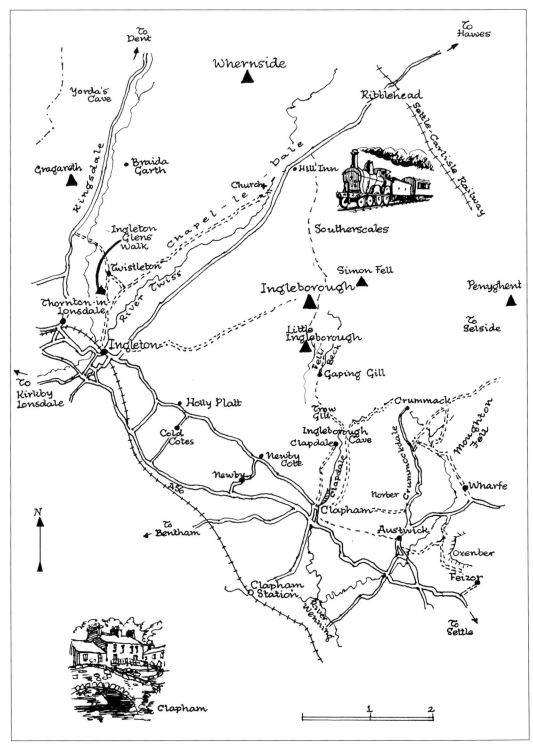

Around Ingleborough.

every Remembrance Sunday, was a poet first inspired by Ingleborough, which he could see from his bedroom window. The first poem he wrote included these lines:

> To a bare blue hill
> Wings an old thought roaming,
> At a random touch
> Of memory homing.
>
> The first of England
> These eyes to fill
> Was the lifted head
> Of that proud hill.

Alan King, an archaeologist who has long been familiar with the Craven limestone country, says:

> It is as densely covered today with freestanding archaeological monuments as any part of the southern English chalklands. This evidence extends from Neolithic cairns and rock shelters to expanses of Celtic field systems.

Of the British way of life on and around Ingleborough in Roman times, King observes:

> The picture is of a thriving arable economy, hemp being grown in the area immediately below Ingleborough on the north-west flank ... The spread of early field systems is almost continuous from Ribblehead to Horton or from Ribblehead to Chapel-le-Dale on the limestone, then along the valley floor from this dale to Ingleton.

King excavated the site of an Irish-Norse settlement between Park Fell and Ribblehead, unearthing the foundations of three buildings with low stone walls of boulders which had supported thatched roofs. One structure was impressively large, being 60 ft. long and internally 12 ft. wide. Coins found in this building dated from the third quarter of the ninth century. He has drawn attention to the complexity of the settlement. Not far from the southern doorway of the long rectangular dwelling rose a burial mound which covered a stone cist containing a leaf-shaped arrowhead. Here were two sites, only yards apart, separated by perhaps 3,000 years of human activity.

The Three Peaks are being 'loved to death'. Pounding boots and cycle tyres, even in places those of motor cycles, have lacerated what used to be a grassy or heathery circuit of 25 miles. The summits of Whernside, Ingleborough and Penyghent inspired little more than literature before the late 19th century, when the hills were known to few others than the farmers and shepherds who tended sheep in these parts. This trio of hills was not linked in popular imagination until two schoolmasters at Giggleswick strolled on a Three Peaks circuit in 1887, their impressive time being 10½ hours. They had originally intended simply to climb Ingleborough after a day's teaching, but with the weather warm and settled they crossed Chapel-le-Dale to ascend Whernside and returned to Giggleswick, just before midnight, via Penyghent. It was the first of many such circuits, walkers attempting to complete the route in less than 12 hours.

In 1925, the Gritstone Club added Fountains Fell and Gragareth to the route, which they completed in just under 12 hours. In 1939 a trio of walkers reached the summits of Whernside and Great and Little Whernside in 17½ hours, and H. Cullingford reported on their gruelling journey in *The Dalesman*, concluding, 'Here's hearty good-luck to all who, after standing on Whernside in the early morn, walk down the last mile to Middlesmoor [in Nidderdale] with the tramp of a lifetime behind them.' A Three Peaks race was followed in 1961 by a cyclo-cross, in which contestants ride their bikes where they can and carry them on the steepest ground, attaining speeds of up to 20 m.p.h. when using the lane on a descent from Penyghent. The record time for the circuit, which involves a total of 5,000 ft. of climbing, is now well below three hours. In recent years, many walkers have 'clocked in' at the Penyghent Café at Horton-in-Ribblesdale and have 'clocked out' on their return, thus becoming members of the Three Peaks Club.

In reinforcing paths with helicopter assistance, the National Park has used alien material, the object being to keep walkers to a narrow strip of durable ground. The tendency in moist places was for walkers to go wider and wider, creating erosion on the grand scale. The Three Peaks Project report for 1986-92 observed, 'Paths in the area had been reduced to almost impassable quagmires, valuable grazing was being trampled underfoot and the special flora ... was being lost.' In 1988, the project was making use of a Swedish-manufactured chemical called 'Solidry' to transform oozing peat bog into solid, durable footpath. A stepped boardwalk from Brackenbottom towards Penyghent was not only an eyesore but very slippery in wet weather. It has been removed and the footpath reinforced, gritstone flags now commonly employed. In August 1997, the unthinkable occurred and a giant mechanical digger violated Whernside, the highest point in the National Park. The digger was photographed for a Yorkshire newspaper with its extended yellow arm and bucket framing the summit of stately Ingleborough. The height of Whernside used to be regarded as 2,419 ft. When the latest round of footpath activity began, the figure had dropped to 2,392 ft. The National Park area management officer remarked, 'After this work, Whernside will be twelve inches higher than before–so you're getting more of Yorkshire.'

The Three Peaks are the sentinels of the western dale-country. Ingleborough, 2,373 ft., takes centre stage, even when viewed from the east. J.B. Priestley, who was an enthusiastic artist when he was not writing, painted a view of the mountain from near Gearstones and regarded the picture as one of his best works. Ingleborough bobs into view from surprising places such as the ridge leading to Great Shunner Fell, above Wensleydale. Binyon was right when he associated Ingleborough with blueness. The hill is often blue-grey under its own special cloud.

WHERNSIDE

The name of this hill is associated with querns, the stone presumably being suitable for making those vital domestic objects used for the grinding of grain. As mentioned, Whernside is not so much a peak as a ridge. It lies within the Yorkshire Dales National Park but North Yorkshire shares it with Cumbria. Neatness is imparted to the crest of Whernside by the gritstone wall, built of local materials which are eminently suitable for walling. The hill is distinctly plain, flanked at either end by moorland.

Those who follow the line of fingerposts from Ribblehead find, at an elevation of 2,000 ft., three tarns which for years had a nesting colony of black-headed gulls. The colony was established about 1914, when there was an infestation of caterpillars. William T. Palmer wrote of Whernside's 'bogs of fire', or

> peaty quagmires which, on disturbance, send up a blaze of blue. The peat is permeated with some luminous fungi or mycelium which is quite normal in appearance by day. I have carried the glow for miles before the earth was shaken off my boots or washed away when walking through wet grass and streams.

Whernside is a splendid viewpoint, not least for Ingleborough, to the south. Move about a little and look north-west, beyond Gragareth, for a glimpse of the Lakeland fells, which are like a tented settlement on the horizon. Cross Fell, the highest of the Pennine hills, is observable at a distance of 30 miles, especially when sunlight gleams on its winter snowcap. Dentdale stretches away to the north-west and leads the eyes to a contemplation of the Howgill Fells. In the 1930s, the summit cairn was demolished by the Ordnance Survey and replaced by a concrete trig point. Among the objectors was C.J. Cutcliffe Hyne, a novelist who had settled at Kettlewell. He pressed for the cairn to be restored, which it was. The so-called 'Cleopatra's Needle' was obscured by the stones which had formed the old cairn. An unusual Ordnance Survey experiment at the time was to communicate between Whernside and York Minster by heliograph.

INGLEBOROUGH

Ingleborough is buttressed by Little Ingleborough, Park Fell and Simon Fell. The 2,000 ft. contour which encircles the group is some five miles in length and sprawls in a triangle bounded by North Ribblesdale, Chapel-le-Dale and the A65 between Settle and Ingleton. The main feature of the flanks of Ingleborough is bareness. If there is a tree, such as a thorn or rowan, it is almost certain to be growing from a pothole, where it is out of reach of the sheep. Four townships, namely Austwick, Clapham, Horton-in-Ribblesdale and Ingleton, have a share in the commonland, and sheep from the various farms usually know their own 'heath', which is where as lambs they were suckled. They also know their way down to the farm, as a young man discovered when, taking up a job on the Clapham side of the hill and being sent out to gather sheep, he was lost in fog. He got back home by following the sheep he had been sent to collect!

The summit plateau, which extends to 15 acres, is often buffeted by a strong wind and it is with relief that on reaching the summit a climber finds there is a windbreak, as well as an indicator from which to identify natural features round about. The most popular approach is from Storrs above Ingleton, walking via Crina Bottom, which was formerly a farmhouse. Those walking from near the *Hill Inn* pass an area of limestone pavement at Southerscales and ascend the Yoredale strata on a boardwalk which protects the vegetation from damage. The longest, most fascinating ascent is from Clapham, through the woods and dry valley to Trow Gill, beyond which lies the yawning hole known as Gaping Gill. The footpath from here to Little Ingleborough has been well defined by booted feet, and before long the visitor is on the main hill.

26 *Ingleborough, viewed from a stretch of limestone 'pavement'. The crevices, known as grykes, hold a variety of plants.*

The shelter and view indicator on the summit were erected by the Ingleton Fell Rescue Team to mark the coronation of Queen Elizabeth II. The cross-shaped walls are five foot high and radiate twelve feet from the centre, stretching to the cardinal points of the compass. In view, from the rim of the plateau, are the Lakeland fells, with solitary Black Combe in the south-west. Also in view are the Howgill Fells and Pendle. When the air has clarity, the green mass of Snaefell has been seen rising from the Isle of Man.

On part of Ingleborough's broad summit are the remains of an Iron-Age hill-fort constructed by the Brigantes, the site being encompassed by a stone rampart nearly two-thirds of a mile in length. The Royal Commission's report on the Ingleborough hill-fort refers to the highly unusual construction of the rampart wall, which is of gritstone, the rear face being formed of orthostatic blocks and the outer face having a drystone construction. Arthur Raistrick linked this hill-fort with the Brigantean patriot Venutius, a former husband of Queen Cartimandua who stood out against the Romans when she, literally, embraced them. Yet the hill-fort on Ingleborough must have existed for a considerable period before the Romans arrived.

The Rev. John Hutton, who ascended Ingleborough around 1780, summed up the experience of many who have climbed the hill since his time when he wrote:

> Though we had many a weary and slippery step, we thought ourselves amply repaid when we got to the top, with the amusement we received in viewing the several extensive and diversified prospects ... Of late years it has never been frequented by any except shepherds ... and the neighbouring country people, who resorted to the horse races which were formerly annually held on its top.

The once rich community of alpine plants was destroyed by botanical visitors, who began to arrive as early as the 17th century. The high crags of The Ark, on Ingleborough, have been the hunting ground of plant-collectors from the time of John Ray, who travelled this way on horseback in 1677 and jotted down the first English record of the purple saxifrage (*Saxifraga oppositifolia*) which, much later, Tom Hey suggested should be renamed 'Ingleborough Beauty'. Light fingers still clutch at purple saxifrage which, to quote the Victorian historian Speight, 'may often be seen bursting into life and beauty while the snows of winter still linger about the hoary head of the mountain'.

A circular tower, complete with battlements, was built on the eastern side of the plateau on the instructions of Hornby Roughsedge, a Bentham mill owner, when he became Lord of the Manor of Ingleton in 1830. It was intended primarily as a shooting 'hut'. On the opening day sports were held, including a race around the summit plateau which was won by colliers from Clapham and Ingleton. Beer and other refreshments had been carted up the hill but an argument broke out and inebriated men damaged the tower. Mr. Roughsedge left Ingleborough in a huff and refused to have the tower repaired. It was wrecked irreparably. Wind, rain and frost completed its destruction and now there is just a heap of stones to mark its former presence.

When Victoria celebrated her Jubilee in 1887, a beacon was kindled on Ingleborough, and according to Speight the glare was seen from the west of Leeds, some 40 miles away. He also noted that 'upwards of 60 fires were visible from the tabular summit'. At one time, horse races were organised. There was even a plan to make an electric railway.

Ingleborough is a 'hollow' mountain, the limestone being honeycombed with natural shafts and passages. The mightiest of these underground systems, Gaping Gill, a 340 ft. deep limestone shaft leading into a chamber on the grand scale of a cathedral, engulfs Fell Beck, which drains much of the eastern slopes of Ingleborough. In all but the driest conditions the stream spills over the brink of the chasm and is dissipated in spray on a rocky ledge 190 ft. down, before continuing its descent to the pebbly floor of the main chamber. The water which courses through Spout tunnel enters the main chamber where it has an uninterrupted fall of 310 ft., making it the highest unbroken waterfall in Britain. Extensive passages extend from the main chamber, some of them having calcite formations.

The main shaft of Gaping Gill was first descended as long ago as August 1895, by Edward Alfred Martel, a diminutive Frenchman who used three rope ladders, each 100 ft. long, joining them together to plumb the depths. Edward Calvert, a member of the Yorkshire Ramblers Club, had been planning a descent. He reached the floor of the main chamber in the following year—and triggered off a spate of pot-holing by fellow members of the club who sustained their enthusiasm until virtually every open shaft had been descended. Today, there are several points of access to the Gaping Gill system, and abseiling is fashionable, but twice a year, when pot-holing clubs meet at Gaping Gill, descents take place in the old-fashioned way—by winch, cable and bosun's chair. No charge is made for the descent but payment is requested for the return journey! In 1941 Bob Leakey initiated cave-diving in the Dales and found a new way into the Ingleborough system when he negotiated a short stream cave, with no pitches, which ended where the roof went below the water. Bob is said to have stripped and gone in feet first. He could feel air space. Bravely committing himself to diving through, he located a syphon, drained it by digging away a shingle bank, and became the first to explore the wet crawl known as Disappointment Pot.

The most notable achievement was the strenuous exploration, spread over many years and completed in 1983, of the course taken by the beck between Gaping Gill and Ingleborough Cave, a distance of some one-and-a-half miles. Ingleborough Cave, one of the three main show caves of the Dales, had been discovered when the Farrer family (see pages 58-60), intrigued by a well-known short gallery at the base of a limestone cliff in Clapdale, broke down a stalagmitic barrier, thus draining an impressive cave with a large and varied assembly of calcite formations; from a huge stalactite, soon referred to as the 'Sword of Damocles', to 'curtains' glistening in the light of the explorers' lamps.

PENYGHENT

The Celtic name Penyghent is said to mean 'hill of the winds'. J.H.B. Peel, in his book *Along the Pennine Way*, thought of it as 'hill of the border', which indeed it was in the days when the English-Scottish border was close at hand. On Saxton's map of Yorkshire (1577) it was spelt 'Pennygent', much more distinguished than the 'Penigent' of Dr. Thomas Dunham Whitaker, in his *History and Antiquities of Craven* (1812). Whitaker relates that a Mr. Wilson, curate of Halton Gill on the other side of Penyghent, wrote a fanciful story called 'The Man in the Moon', in which one Israel Jobson, a cobbler, climbed to the summit of Penyghent and, using a long ladder, reached the moon.

Walkers who are tackling the Pennine Way from the south have covered a third of the route when they arrive at the top of Penyghent. The hill has, like Ingleborough, a weather-worn appearance. Its gritstone capping is heavily weathered. Deep grooves which began to form in the side of the hill following a severe cloudburst about 1930 are 10 ft. deep and twice as wide. Penyghent retains snow longer than the other peaks. When viewed from the river bridge at Settle, the fell, which resembles an upturned pudding dish, stands proud of its neighbours and may be dusted with snow as late as April, when the dale is awakening to spring. Patches of snow have been found in the gullies in June.

The most commonly used approach to Penyghent is from Horton-in-Ribblesdale, passing near Hull Pot, where the beck leaps into a limestone amphitheatre. Even better, for those who prefer an easier route, is the walk from high-lying Dalehead, beside the Stainforth-Halton Gill road. A firm track, with boards spanning a particularly wet area, leads directly

27   *The nose-end of Penyghent, North Ribblesdale.*

to the nose-end of the fell, which used to be intimidating but has now been provided with a stone staircase to a point where the path resumes in a big zig-zag to the high crags. The walker is now within an easy distance of the triangulution station marking the summit.

W.T. Palmer, who knew Ribblesdale well, wrote:

> The hills have a bare monotonous aspect, yet far down in the deep dale Penyghent's true summit lies at its southern cairn. The view is not as extensive as that from Ingleborough but the prospect is fresh and interesting. A visitor might stumble on lumps of inferior quality coal. Evidence of early coal-working can be found on the mountain and more profusely on nearby Fountains Fell, which sweeps away to the east and is littered with old pits.

CLAPDALE AND REGINALD FARRER

Until the early part of the 19th century, Clapdale was a wild little valley, difficult of access. In 1833, the lower end was dammed on the instructions of James William and Oliver Farrer. The dam, with an earth core, transformed the appearance of the valley and led to the creation of Ingleborough Lake, the overflow from which proceeds as a series of rapids under ornamental limestone bridges to plunge with a roar at the head of Clapham village, providing drinking water for the community and electricity to light the streets at night and provide power for a few selected homes.

Reginald Farrer (1880-1920), the brilliant son of James Anson and Elizabeth Farrer, wrote:

> Ingleborough Lake lies high above Ingleborough House, in a long winding gully of the hills that used to be one of the characteristic ghylls of this country, until one of my ancestors was lured by degrees, on the first pretence of making a few fishponds, into so damming up the stream at the valley's exit as to make the whole glen one broad long lake.

From March to May, the rhododendrons planted at the side of a gorge immediately above the lake sustain a feast of colour, mainly pink and red. Any white blossoms are clearly delineated against a mass of dark glossy leaves.

There are bamboos, too, and these came first. Writing in 1909, Farrer wondered whether the waterfalls, in their glen, would be so vehemently English in their liveliness as to swear and scream at the alien loveliness of the bamboos; 'or whether, seeing that the bamboos are no strangers to the adornment of waterfalls in Japan, they may be kind and admit the newcomers to a share in the picture they present'. He had the bamboos planted 'without quite having succeeded in allaying my qualms'.

The damming of Clapham Beck was part of a grand plan of transforming the Clapham district. The Farrer family virtually rebuilt the church in 1814, and converted a farmstead into a shooting lodge, thence into a neo-Classical mansion which became known as Ingleborough Hall (1820-30). A craggy landscape was softened by the planting of many trees, including holly oak from the Mediterranean, red oak from eastern North America, Spanish chestnut, and Japanese maples, both red and yellow. Here too are Weymouth pine, western hemlock and European silver fir, quite apart from hardy natives like yew, holly, Scots pine, ash and hazel.

Bridges were made and carriageways introduced. The Farrers could be driven from the Hall, over Thwaite Lane, where tunnels preserved the old right of way, and into bosky Clapdale, where the family and their friends might admire the lake, linger at a limestone grotto and, if they felt particularly adventurous, enjoy the delights of a dry valley beyond. When the hall passed from the ownership of the Farrers it became a special school for bronchial and asthmatic children from West Riding towns and, subsequently, an Outdoor Education Centre. Those who stay here marvel at the way in which Dent marble, a highly fossilised and dark limestone from the head of Dentdale, was polished and positioned as pillars and for decorative effect in some of the rooms.

Reginald Farrer, born at the family's London house, was raised at Ingleborough Hall at a time when the gardens were being developed–largely by his mother. He soon had a good knowledge of botany. Farrer, having a hair-lip and a shy disposition, spent much of his time on his own, being an avid botaniser and climber of trees. In December 1979 the 90-year-old Hon. Mrs. R. Wood, a great friend of the Farrers, jotted down some memories of Reginald Farrer as she had known him when, as a small girl, she visited Ingleborough Hall.

Reginald was ten years older than her. It was explained that he could not talk normally and that she must not show any surprise or it would hurt his feelings. 'I was rather a precocious little thing and duly took Reginald's queer voice and look without showing I noticed anything!' It seems that until he was well on in his 'teens, 'only his mother understood what he said. Reginald had a great love of his mother. The first money he earned as a writer, when he was in his twenties, was spent buying her a necklace. This bond was naturally a source of jealousy for Reginald's younger brother, Sidney.'

28 *Reginald Farrer (1880-1920). Courtesy of Dr. J.A. Farrer.*

29 *Rhododendron watercolour by Farrer which he completed in July 1920.*

On leaving Oxford, Reginald began to explore the alpine areas of the world, beginning with the Alps themselves and eventually making daring explorations to the high peaks of Asia. Farrer introduced to Britain no less than 24 varieties of rhododendron. He is considered to be one of the founders of rock-gardening, planting up the limestone cliffs beside Ingleborough Lake and eventually creating a new garden in the grounds of the Hall. His observations about plant-collecting and rock-gardening, in vivid prose, survive in the several books he wrote. What he described in *My Rock Garden* (1907) as his 'best friend' among English flowers, *Primula farinosa*, is 'such a gallant little thing', being

so fragrant, and so dainty, and altogether so lovable ... A curious characteristic it has, too, which shows how it still remembers the alpine and glacial period. For in the high places it hurries eagerly into bloom, as early as it can, like a true alpine, anxious to get its flowering over safely in the brief flash of summer, before the glacial winter descends again; while in the valleys and on the rich railway cuttings it makes no such hurry, but takes its own time about blossoming.

At the age of 33, Farrer completed the writing of what is possibly his most influential work, *The English Rock Garden*. He died, aged 40, after he contracted diphtheria while on a plant-collecting expedition in a remote part of Burma, where he was subsequently buried. At Clapham, his deeply grieving mother arranged for a memorial, in the form of a stone column and ball surmounted by an angel. The angel was incongruous to those who knew Farrer, for he had become a Buddhist. His passion for the exotic led him to own a succession of Siamese cats, to some of which he dedicated books. The Reginald Farrer Trail, through the woods, was established in 1970 to mark the 50th anniversary of his death. Details are available from the Information Centre at Clapham.

KINGSDALE

Kingsdale, tucked away between Gragareth and Whernside, is approached by road from Thornton-in-Lonsdale, near Ingleton. The road, which used to degenerate into a track just beyond the last farm, was tarmacadamed throughout its length some forty years ago as an experiment in laying a hard surface in peaty terrain. The road attains an elevation of 1,552 ft. on its way to Deepdale ['Dibdil'] and Dent Town. When the route was still a rough track, flagstone from a quarry at the top of Dibdil, and Dent marble from a quarry called Binks, were transported over the top and through Kingsdale.

Despite a romantic notion, expressed in the 1930s, that Kingsdale is 'the valley of the Vikings', the name almost certainly means what it says. This was 'the King's Dale', a valley inherited by Henry VII from his mother. It descended to Henry VIII, who later gave it to one of his illegitimate sons. It was then part of the Barony of Kendal. A possible alternative explanation of the name is 'Cow Valley', since on a late 17th-century map it is referred to as Kinesdale. In Kingsdale, the local people used to say, there is a white side and a black side. Kingsdale Head farmstead is on the white or 'sunny' side and Braida Garth occupies the more fertile black or 'money' side. The land is divided up into meadows, pastures and allotments by 25 miles of drystone walls.

In a limestone area, where underground drainage is common, the canalised beck which takes a straight course down the valley rarely contains water. About 12,000 years ago, at the end of the Ice Age, a lake had formed here. After it was drained, the beck meandered across the old bed and remains of its loops can still be seen. About 1820, when Thornton Fell was enclosed by Act of Parliament, Kingsdale Beck was ordered to be straightened. The farmers who received awards of land beside the beck had to maintain this straight line. Edward Batty, who farmed Braida Garth, claimed that the floor of Kingsdale is 'full of old beck courses'.

Sheep were the principal occupants of this little dale. Last century, they were of the 'Scotch' breed, which tended to be short in the leg and grew 'ower much' wool, which dragged on the ground, making it difficult for them to get out of snowdrifts. After the First World War, the farmer at Kingsdale Head introduced the Swaledale breed and, later, 'Dales-breds', which was a type fixed by farmers in Wharfedale and North Ribblesdale and well suited to a limestone landscape.

Kingsdale used to have abundant heather. Shooting parties arrived by wagonettes hired from the inns of Ingleton. The Braida Garth party stayed for a long weekend, from Friday to Monday, and local lads were employed as beaters. By day, they shot grouse, rabbit and partridge. At night, the sportsmen chatted, wined and dined, and danced in the big attic, a piano being available to accompany the quadrilles and waltzes, lancers and shottische, which were popular dances in late Victorian times. Another time, the attic was cleared and part of it covered with turves so that a 'mains' of cockfights could be held, with much laying of bets. The gamecocks were collected at Ingleton a fortnight before the main, to allow for training and feeding the birds with special nutritious food.

At Keld Head in 1945, Graham Balcome undertook the first properly equipped cave dive in the Dales. He was using homemade equipment, a form of dry suit and strange hooded affair with small glass plates for the eyes. He had a simple form of re-breather.

CHAPEL-LE-DALE

Chapel-le-Dale, a fancy name for an area which was called Ingleton Fells, alludes to a tiny kirk. This fascinating dale has a large railway viaduct at either end. Ribblehead viaduct is the focal point in the east, and to the west, where the homes of Ingleton snuggle in the Greta gorge, a viaduct (no longer used) was built by the Little North Western Railway on a branch line between Clapham and Lowgill. At one time, two companies operated the line and Ingleton had two stations, changing passengers having to cross the valley which lay between them. Trains brought a host of visitors to the village, and many did the Glens Walk, on paths and bridges painstakingly made in 1885 to open up what had been two secluded gills with their many picturesque waterfalls. The most impressive feature is Thornton Force, over which the Twiss pours as a waterfall of 46 ft. Geologists enthuse over the cliff itself, which is an Unconformity, the upper part being formed of the horizontal beds of Carboniferous lime-stone and the lower part some vertically-bedded slates of Lower Ordovician origin. Between the two beds are pebbles and boulders, part of a beach, formed 300 million years ago.

Weathercote Cave, Jingle Pot and Hurtle Pot are 'windows' into the underground course of the river, which is not far below the surface and has its point of debouchment

30   *Thornton Force, Ingleton Glens.*

at a lip of limestone called God's Bridge. Weathercote Cave, which is not open to the public but whose features are well-known through paintings and photographs made since the days when Turner painted a rainbow in the spray, is where Chapel Beck flows out of one bedding plane cave, down a major joint and into a lower cave. The waterfall appears from behind a wedged boulder, Mahomet's Coffin, the water then taking a 77 ft. leap into a cloud of spray. Early tourists marvelled at the presence of a dark type of trout in the lake at the bottom of Hurtle Pot and elsewhere.

The story of White Scar, one of relatively few Dales show caves, is mainly that of Christopher Francis Drake Long (1902-1924) who, showing either extreme bravery or a lack of caution, discovered an extensive cave system and made an initial solo expedition, shuffling full length through a passage with only inches to spare. Long, the son of a York doctor, was at Lancing College when he had his first taste of the underworld. He was on holiday with a school friend, John H. Churchill, and they joined visitors to the Cheddar Caves in Somerset. Hearing that the Marquis of Bath, who owned the caves, drew £1,000 a year in rent, he determined to find and develop commercially a cave of his own.

The two men visited caving areas in Somerset and the Peak District. While on a first vacation from Cambridge in December 1921, they entered Stump Cross, a show cave on Greenhow Hill, in the Yorkshire Dales. The following Easter, Long organised a party to stay in and explore Stump Cross, returning in summer, when the cave system was surveyed. In August 1923, while staying at Ingleton, Long and Churchill walked across Twistleton Scar, above Chapel-le-Dale, and noticed a flow of water from a cliff on White Scar. They explored the stream passage for 1,200 ft. So constricted was the passage that they had to hold their heads sideways in order to breathe. Then, and on successive trips that month, they toured what is now White Scar Cave as far as the lake.

Long had found his potential show cave–half a mile of stream passage, with stretches adorned by fine calcite formations. Captain Geoffrey Swift, a York solicitor, gave the young men commercial backing. The low wet crawl was avoided by employing out-of-work coal miners to drive a level. Long had a breakdown in health in 1923 and his life was brought to an end on 8 September 1924 when he appears to have accidentally taken an overdose of the chloral hydrate he took for the symptoms of the manic-depressive psychosis which he showed.

7

NORTH RIBBLESDALE

THE TOPMOST REACHES of Ribblesdale consist of a large marshy area, where drumlins are numerous and produce the 'basket of eggs' effect. The sides of the dale are rimmed by limestone pavements, bone-like in their hue and appearance. The River Ribble runs for 56 miles from High Craven to the Irish Sea near Preston. Michael Drayton, a writer of quaint verse about watercourses, proclaimed in the *Polyolbion* (1598) that the Ribble rose 'from Penyghent's proud foot' and that the mountain was 'my proud sire [which] in height of all has pride'. He continues,

> And Ingleborough, too, of that Olympian brood,
> With Pendle, of the north the highest hills that be,
> Do wisely me behold and are beheld of me.

Cam Beck, a principal feeder of the Ribble, has its source near remote Cam Houses. Gale Beck, the longest tributary of the Ribble emanates as a spring on Wold Fell. The Ribble Way starts perversely on the Cam End side of the road, from which it is approached through a peaty wilderness. The upper dale, meeting place of several valleys, and several keen winds, was regarded as somewhat dreary by strangers. The historian Thomas Dunham Whitaker (1812) considered that 'the beauties of Ribblesdale might be said to expire at Horton—and very abruptly, for at Stainforth a little below is all the verdure and cheerfulness of a Craven valley'.

Torfin was the pre-Conquest owner of the upper dale, which then had a frontier status, being the last flourish of England at a time when land to the north was part of Scotland. It has been suggested that the name Ribble alludes to this border status, which ended in 1092 when William Rufus wrested what is now Cumbria from the Scots. Torfin was succeeded by Roger de Poitevin, who was related to the Conqueror and was granted large tracts of land in the north-west. The Scottish presence was felt again in 1189 when, for a time, Cumbria was recovered by the Scots and Ribblesdale was ravaged. Future raids from the north took advantage of the north-south valleys of Eden and Ribble.

Through grants made by pious Norman lords, Furness Abbey became a major land-owner. Jervaulx Abbey, in Wensleydale, had territorial rights to some of the valuable pastureland. Fountains, near Ripon, held land which had been secured by a number of small grants. Part of Horton was owned by the nunnery of St Clement in York. There were many disputes between religious houses, an instance being that of 1330, when the Abbess of St Clement had to pay compensation to Furness following the trespass of 30 cows and nine bullocks on the major abbey's land at Birkwith.

Col. John Byng, subsequently Lord Torrington (1743-1813), who toured the Dales in June 1792, approached Ribblehead from Wensleydale, over Cam End, which he referred

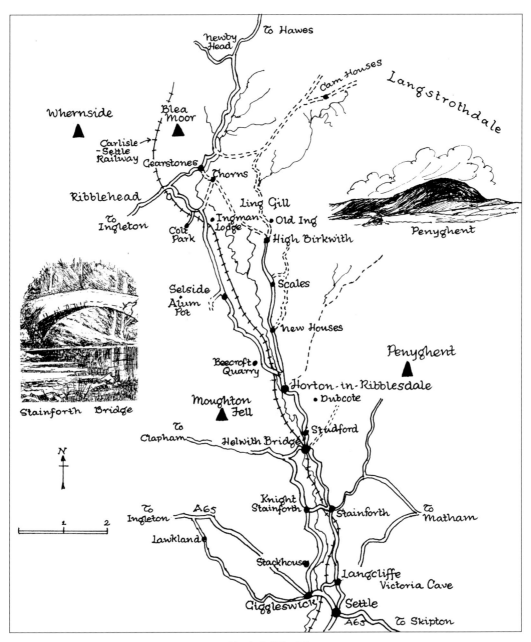

North Ribblesdale

to as the 'Mountain Cams'. After fording Gale Beck, he was led by a farmer to *Gearstones*, an inn-cum-farm on the turnpike road between Lancaster and Richmond. Byng described the inn as being 'the seat of misery in a desert'. One of two annual fairs for Scotch cattle was being held on the common and 'at the conclusion of the days of squabble, the two Nations agree in mutual drunkenness'. The premises which went under the name of an inn were thronged by buyers and sellers, 'most of whom were in plaids, fillibegs, etc.'.

Gearstones was indeed the setting twice a year of fairs for horses and grain as well as for cattle. The last of these fairs took place in the early 1870s, at which time the construction of the Settle-Carlisle line was radically changing the appearance of the district and led to the economical transport of stock and provisions over large distances. Byng's account of a night spent at *Gearstones* does provide an insight into the conditions faced by those 'gentlemen of taste and leisure' who, in the late 18th century, arrived in the Ingleton district, keen to see the caves about which written accounts were circulating.

> The stable did not afford hay. My friend, who knew the house, forced his way thro' the lower floor, and interned himself in the only wainscotted bedroom, up stairs, where at length procured some boil'd slices of stale pork, and some fry'd eggs; with some wretched beer and brandy–to which my hunger was not equal; and from which my delicacy revolted. When our room was invaded by companions he call'd out: 'This is a private chamber'.

Much later, the Farrers of Clapham, owners of Ingleborough Estate, which stretched over Ingleborough and on to Cam Houses, had a fine shooting lodge at Gearstones, with facilities for visiting gentlemen who arrived at Ribblehead by train to be conveyed there by horse-drawn vehicle. The lodge is now a centre for visiting schoolchildren.

The commonland at Ribblehead was 'stinted', to regularise and not overuse the grazing, various numbers of stints being allocated to the local farms. The annual meeting of the holders of stints, or gaits, was once held at Gearstones Lodge on the afternoon of the first Thursday in March, and among the rules devised for the use of the land was a declaration that not more than two gatherings (of sheep) shall be allowed at clipping time. One gathering would be for geld sheep or wethers (stock not in lamb) and the other for ewes in milk. 'Should there be any sheep after such second gathering which for any reason will not clip, they shall be kept in the inland (enclosed ground) until they are fit to clip and not go back on to the Moor until they have been clipped.'

31 *Driving Swaledale-type sheep and their lambs at Old Ing, North Ribblesdale.*

It was decreed that the gait-holders shall keep in repair and make up all the fences which surround the Moor as allotted to each gait-holder,

> ... and it is agreed by the respective gait-holders that the lower or most southerly portion of the fence against Skelside on the west of the moor shall be repairable by Winterscales, the middle portion by Gunnerfleet and the upper or most northerly portion by Ivescar, the various lengths being in proportion to the number of gaits which run with each farm. All sheep, including shearlings [animals clipped once] shall be taken off the Moor for one month during tupping time. All lambs shall be taken off the Moor by the 12th day of August, a few days' grace being allowed if necessary, and after that date any lambs left on the Moor shall be counted as half stint until dipping or tupping time, that is, until about the middle of October.

Stocking the Moor with cattle by any gait-holder would be limited to one-fifth of the stint allotted to any farm, and cattle would be allowed on the Moor for only one month after the sheep have been brought in, a few days' grace being allowed if necessary. Finally, no gait-holder would be permitted to turn more than one horse on to the moor.

In 1938, formal notice was made under the Game Act, 1831, by Sidney James Farrer, of the Ingleborough Estate, to the Sessions of the Peace for the West Riding with regard to the gamekeepers employed, this being necessary in case they had to apprehend anyone for illegal angling or the taking of ground game. The gamekeepers were George Murray of Clapham, Thomas Brennand of Butterfield, Keasden, Thomas Campbell of Austwick, John Carrick of Gearstones Lodge, Ribblehead, and Thomas Murray of Winshaw, Ribblehead.

Newby Head, a farm close to the watershed, was once an inn at an elevation of 1,500 ft. It was used by travellers and also locals. The farmers, shepherds and gamekeepers gathered here twice a year for a 'shepherds meet', theoretically (as in Lakeland) to return stray sheep, but it was also an excuse for much drinking and singing. Silver coins were placed on a tray by those taking part and drinking went on until the stock of money was exhausted.

At the head of North Ribblesdale becks have deeply scored the landscape. Ling Gill, named after the commonest local species of heather, has a single-span bridge which was part of the old road up the dale linking Hawes with Settle and well used by packhorses. The original stone bridge was repaired in 1765 at 'the charge of the whole West Ridinge', as an inscription notes. The Settle Rural District Council carried out repair work in 1932. Thorns Gill, which was carved out by Gale Beck, is crossed by a single-span packhorse-type bridge with no parapets to hinder the progress of laden animals. Most recently it was repaired by the Yorkshire Dales National Park Authority. The right of passage across the beck was assured, though until recently no public access existed on the flanking land.

Ribblehead is a meeting place of the winds and a blast of over 100 m.p.h. has been recorded. The railway station, once used for weather recording, coded messages being sent to the Air Ministry at regular intervals, recorded a wind of 92 m.p.h. in November 1961. The average rainfall of 70 inches was greatly exceeded in 1954, when 104 inches were recorded. Five inches fell on a single December day.

Ribblehead is dominated by the works of the Midland Railway Company, who from 1869 until 1876 were constructing a finely engineered, all-weather line from Settle to Carlisle, intent on having a direct share in the lucrative Scottish traffic. They had hitherto reached an agreement of sorts for Midland passengers and goods to be accommodated on the Lancaster-Carlisle route, which was operated by a rival company. Ribblehead viaduct, 1,328 ft. long, is imposing in its grand setting of fells. The highest part of the structure is just over 100 ft. The decision to make 24 arches was taken in January 1872, almost two years after the first rails had been laid by the contractor, William H. Ashwell. The chief

32 & 33 *Constructed by the Midland Railway between 1870 and 1875, Ribblehead viaduct is 440 yards long and 104 feet high. It has 24 arches and is the longest viaduct on the Settle and Carlisle line. In illustration 32, above, on the right of the picture, can just be seen the only known photographic study of a 'shanty town' of the late 19th century.*

engineer, John Crossley, delayed until he was quite sure of the ratio of navvies, employed in dumping material for embankments, to masons, who would be responsible for placing the big blocks of dark limestone quarried from nearby Littledale. At one stage an 18-arch viaduct had been considered. The viaduct catches the visitor's eye. The long and steep embankments are also impressive.

The viaduct was constructed from north to south, the best stone being exposed in the bed of the Littledale beck, from which water was diverted to allow for excavation. The limestone having been deposited in layers, not too much dressing was needed. Freeze-thaw action on the structure after completion meant that blocks were apt to crack. An on-site brickworks produced the bricks needed for lining purposes, both here and in Blea Moor tunnel to the north. Shale was mixed with clay then baked in one of 10 ovens, which could produce 20,000 bricks each day if necessary but rarely worked to full capacity. The local bricks proved in the long run to be unsuitable, and more hardy types–Staffordshire blues and Accrington reds–were subsequently imported.

The Settle-Carlisle has a devil-may-care attitude towards the landscape, and on the fells is marked by an impressive succession of embankments, cuttings, viaducts and tunnels. The early years of operation were busy and lucrative, the peak being reached before the Frist World War, when there were few motor vehicles. It was especially busy in the Second World War, after which it became shabby, under-used and run down as a prelude to closure. Steam traction gave way to diesel-hauled trains in the early 1960s. By 1970, the only stations open were those at Settle and Appleby. Dalesrail, a monthly passenger service brought about through collaboration between the National Park Authority and British Rail, revived some of the line's lost fortunes and created a demand for seats on what was soon being referred to as the country's most scenic railway.

There was an enthusiastic response to the advent of 'steam specials' in 1978. Eventually, the passage of each special train was being observed by a thousand or more railway enthusiasts, almost all of them with cameras. Then began what one critic referred to as 'closure by stealth', the slow changing or rundown of services. In June 1981, the tide turned with the creation of the Friends of the Settle-Carlisle Line, and a long fight with British Rail to retain the line was begun. A proposal in 1983 to close the line between Ribblehead and Appleby would have destroyed its original purpose, creating in effect two branch lines serving local quarries, and the idea was abandoned.

British Rail then expressed fears about the state of Ribblehead viaduct and an inflated figure was given for the cost of repairs. At the last moment, in an announcement in Parliament which took everyone by surprise, the government refused permission for the line to be closed. British Rail, to its credit, then applied energy and money to repairs, notably to the major viaducts. The Settle-Carlisle now has conservation status and the stations which remain open look smarter than they did when the railway was fully operating. In 1998 the main building at Ribblehead station is being restored; a new 'down' platform has been provided so the station can be fully used.

Colt Park, 1,100 ft. above sea level, is a survival of the old type of woodland, a limestone pavement with a scattering of ash trees which, though relatively small, include some with an estimated age of 300 years. The grikes of the pavement contain remnants of the old woodland flora, protected here both by a dangerous habitat and by a substantial boundary wall built to deter invasion by sheep. Some 200 plant species have been recorded. A profusion of trees, moss and ferns, which generates a feeling of mystery, even enchantment, is explained by the extra humidity given off by the trees. The grikes offer both shelter and shade. The moss flora is luxuriant in the relatively clean air of the upper dale. Once the mosses have a foothold on the clints there is scope for other plants, grasses, herbs and wild flowers to root. When there is a prolonged drought, which in one period was an almost annual occurrence, the soil on the surface of the pavement is so thin that everything is killed. Surviving fragments in nooks and crannies, or seed which has been deposited, make a fresh start.

Visitors to Colt Park with permits from English Nature are advised to move gingerly across the natural blocks–clints. In springtime the wood is full of wild flowers, abounding in primrose and wood anemone, but also sustaining globe flower, lily of the valley, whirled Solomon's Seal, and yellow Star of Bethlehem. The prickly sedge which grows here is nationally rare, being known at only five locations in Britain. The wood contains baneberry, a plant peculiar to limestone pavement. East of the river, Newhouse Tarn, a trout preserve, belongs to Manchester Anglers, who acquired the fishing rights over 14 miles of water from Ribble's source to Helwith Bridge. This famous club collected trout spawn from the becks following the spawning season at the back-end of the year and had their own hatchery, thus keeping up a good stock of fish.

Horton, the 'Hortune' of Domesday Book, began as a farmstead on muddy land by the river and is now long and drawn-out. The church, which was not altered appreciably during the Victorian mania for rebuilding churches, is dedicated to a north-country saint, Oswald, and has a piece of stained glass, which may have come from Jervaulx Abbey, showing the mitred head of Thomas à Becket. An account of the evolution of the parish, its life and industry, compiled by the Horton Local History Group, described the community as being one of

> independent people feeling no need for individual leadership but making a satisfactory life for themselves in what has always been a relatively isolated situation ... The parish church is not embellished with the richly carved tombs of mighty or influential overlords, but is set in a yard full of modest gravestone recording ordinary lives.

Along the side of Moughton Fell are immense quarries, one for limestone, others for flagstone, which is broken up to a size suitable for surfacing roads. Beecroft Quarry is a vast white cliff above a turquoise lake, a big hole used by quarrymen to reach the underlying flagstone having filled up with water. A Dales tycoon prominently associated with Beecroft Quarry and with another huge enterprise at Skirethornes, in Wharfedale, was John Delaney (1846-1921). An Irishman, he was born during the Great Hunger. His father, an estate agent, was murdered by rebellious smallholders and a sister brought John and the rest of the family to Stalybridge in Cheshire. Delaney eventually found employment at Christie's Mill at Settle and became an overlooker. In 1870 he married Annie Calver, a Lancashire weaver, the marriage being solemnised at Langcliffe church.

Delaney had enough energy to develop sidelines. He traded in various commodities, especially in coal, which was available in limitless quantities after the southern reaches of the Settle-Carlisle railway made available imports from the deep mines of the Yorkshire coalfield. Requiring £40 to buy a horse and cart with which to deliver coal, Delaney was refused the loan by local banks, so he went to a Quaker banker in Sheffield and received not only funds but advice on the development of his interests. He became a member of the Society of Friends in 1876 which incidentally, was the year the Settle-Carlisle was opened for passenger traffic, freight trains having been running for a year to bed down the track. Delaney left Christie's when he received an ultimatum from the manager, who was perturbed by his several business interests. Buying a small general store at Langcliffe, Delaney left Annie to look after the business and their daughter while he studied geology at Manchester University so that he might develop his interest in limestone, the quarrying of which could be allied to the development of vast new steel mills at Sheffield and elsewhere.

He opened Beecroft Quarry, using the railway to bring in coal and take out lime, and became the district's main distributor of coal and owner of over 1,000 private railway wagons, some of which, bearing his name, were to be seen in North Ribblesdale until the Second World War. He became a millionaire but never lost the common touch. When a workman asked for a day off, and the reason for this was requested, the man replied, 'I'm getting married then and I'd like to be there'. On his death, Delaney was interred in the graveyard of the Quaker Meeting House at Settle.

34 *John Delaney, who made a fortune in deals with lime and coal in North Ribblesdale.*

A large exposure of Horton Flags, which are of Silurian age, occurs at Helwith Bridge, being present as steeply-dipping folds. A number of small quarries existing in 1774 were mentioned by those promoting the idea, which never developed further than an idea, of cutting a branch canal to Settle. At Arcow Wood an old flag quarry has been excavated by modern means to a depth of some 200 ft., the quarried material being used for roadstone. Certain use of Horton Flags dates from the early part of the 18th century when they were incorporated in the structures of farmhouses, providing, for example, benks in larders, the smooth flag being easily cleaned and, remaining cold, having food-keeping qualities. Flags were used for softwater cisterns, and as boskins, or divisions between cattle stalls, in shippons. Horton Flag was last quarried as such, then sawn up into useful pieces, in the 1920s. It is now blasted from its bed and crushed as roadstone or as aggregate for concrete.

The Helwith Bridge slate-mill, where the sawing took place, is now marked by a pile of rubble on the river bank near the bridge. It was constructed in the 19th century and drew its power from the river Ribble via a mill-race formed of slate, the natural fall on the site of the mill providing a weir below which the tail race of the wheel emptied itself. The building measured 44 ft. along the river side and some 28 ft. along the land side which was open to the elements. The river turned an iron and wood undershot wheel, the drive being taken by cast-iron bevel wheels to a vertical shaft housed in a stone 'chimney' with a set of bevel wheels at the top. These turned the 14 ft. horizontal shaft of the main drive; four sawing benches, each equipped with eccentrics and their straps, cut the slate blocks as required.

The blades of the saws were plain steel in a wooden frame tensioned by a rod at the top of the two vertical legs. Sand and water formed an abrasive. The slate blocks were held in position by their own weight on a slate saw-bench. An adjustable horizontal bar acted as guide to the oscillating saw-frames, a bar between the eccentric straps and the frames providing the movement to the saw-blades. A polishing machine was also installed. When the mill was dismantled, the vertical drive shaft was put to use as a quarry toilet. The wheel itself was removed to Horton-in-Ribblesdale, where it was set beside a beck to generate electricity in the first electrification scheme in the village.

Stainforth, 'the stony ford', is in two main parts, the major one had a medieval connection with Salley or Sawley Abbey in the Ribble Valley below Gisburn. The other, Knight Stainforth, had connections with the mighty Tempest family. A beck from Malham Moor, in the east, makes two great leaps as Catrigg Force, the total fall being some 60 ft. Stainforth has an important road link with Halton Gill, in Littondale, the road extending between Penyghent and Fountains Fell. The Pennine Way ascends the fell from this direction by a track once used by those mining coal using bell-pits, many of which are to be found on Fountains Fell, where the colliery was in use from 1790 to 1860. The coal was used for calcining ore produced by a calamine mine on Pikedaw, between Malham and Settle, for lime-burning, and also for domestic use.

The two Stainforths, once connected by a ford which was liable to be impassable because of flooding, were provided with a bridge by Samuel Watson, a Quaker who lived at Knight Stainforth Hall. Like many another Quaker, Watson was cruelly persecuted and languished for a while in prison in York. While speaking at the steeple-house (church) at Giggleswick, one freezing winter day, he was attacked, his head striking the seats, and was then thrown out of the building. He was fined a swingeing £120 for attending forbidden religious meetings. In settlement of the fine his cattle, valued at £150, were seized.

Salmon still run up the Ribble passing under Watson's bridge. The salmon's task is made easier at Stainforth Foss by a modification to the rock. After much wrangling with the Dales Park planning authority and the expenditure of a few thousand pounds, the river

35   *A garden party at the home of the Wilkinsons, in Hellifield. At the rear of the group is Edward Elgar, who in his young days was friendly with a Giggleswick doctor, and also (for a short time) with one of the daughters of Squire Wilkinson.*

authority sculpted the rock in an inconspicuous way. A famous composer was fond of 'potted trout'.

As a young musician dreaming of making his way as a composer, Edward Elgar visited the riverside at Stainforth with his Giggleswick friend, Dr. Charles William Buck, whom he had met at a BMA conference in Worcester in 1882. Buck, who was attending as a doctor, was persuaded to bring his cello and play in an augmented orchestra mustered by Elgar, who had a photograph of Stainforth Bridge at his Worcestershire home. (The bridge was given to the National Trust in 1931 by the Maudsley family.)

What appears to be a natural limestone cliff between Stainforth and Langcliffe was, within living memory, a quarry face. A Hoffman Kiln was built at this quarry, and operated from 1873 until 1931 and from 1937 until the outbreak of the Second World War. It is a rare survivor of a type devised for the continuous burning of limestone, the stone being stacked in chambers and, once incinerated, loaded into railway wagons in a siding from the Settle-Carlisle railway. The first company to use the Hoffman principle for lime-burning in Yorkshire was called Ingleton Patent Limeworks. It was noted by the *Lancaster Guardian* in 1872: 'Since these new kilns came into operation, there has been such a demand for Ingleton lime that the firm could not meet it and were under the necessity of abandoning the trade method of soliciting orders.' An immense kiln would be constructed 'not far from the old paper mill near Stainforth'.

The old company was dissolved and another, The Craven Lime Company Ltd., was formed. The founders, John Clark, Michael Wilson and a man called Thistlethwaite, had begun lime-burning in a small way near Austwick, then at Giggleswick Scar. Success in business led to the opening out of the quarry at Mealbank, Ingleton. The right to Mr. Hoffman's patent 'for lime burning within a limited area' was acquired. The kiln built at Langcliffe was 150 ft. long and 48 ft. wide, with 16 chambers, each capable of holding 100 tons of stone. It was surmounted by a chimney over 200 ft. high, 22 ft. wide at the base and 11 ft. at the summit, consisting of 200,000 bricks, almost all of them red brick, the exceptions forming the date 1873 high on the structure.

The kiln had a large number of flues, one account giving the total as 44, which ran from the chambers into a narrow arched passage known as the smoke chamber, 'in which there is an apparatus for increasing or diminishing the draughts of the flues', so it was possible to draw on the fires and keep the system in operation. The Hoffman Kiln was built close to the Settle-Carlisle railway, then still under construction though the southern section was completed, and lime was despatched on new metals from the quarry to the Bradford district. Stone arrived at the Hoffman in pony-hauled kiln-carts or bogeys which had open sides. A tally system identified the bogeys filled by particular workers and the weights were totalled on a Wednesday so that wages could be paid on Friday. Coal was delivered by rail and lifted to the top of the kiln by an ingenious system which used a water tank as a counterweight. Men packed a chamber with a large variety of block sizes, positioning the stone so cleverly that it resembled a drystone wall. Cavities were left in appropriate places so that when the coal was poured down from above there would be even burning. When the fire had passed by, the sealed chamber was opened and lime removed. That which had been stacked against the coal was hard and dark, and was consigned to the steel works. Elsewhere the lime was 'satin white', a term derived from a type of paper in the production of which it was used. This lime was ideal for paper-making, sugar-refining, the manufacture of chocolate, tanning of leather and the softening of water. A good piece of lime, if dropped on a hard surface, 'rang like the best China'.

The basic kiln remains almost complete, but the chimney was demolished, the covered area on top has gone, and grass now grows on the flat top of the kiln where once bogeys delivered coal, and where a small stack of new bricks stood ready in case part of the kiln collapsed. The railway docks beside the kiln are now partly filled with water which has drained from the silent quarry.

Langcliffe was mentioned in Domesday Book, but the old village was forsaken for the present village, half a mile or so away. Little is known of the circumstances, but it may have been a consequence of Scottish raids. Langcliffe Hall, long the home of the Dawsons, was visited by Sir Isaac Newton, a great friend of William Dawson. His poem in Latin, 'In Praise of Langcliffe', is quoted in Whitaker's *Craven*. Geoffrey Dawson, who inherited the Langcliffe estate in 1917 and died at his London home in 1944, was a celebrated editor of *The Times* for almost a quarter of a century. He changed his surname from Robinson to Dawson in order to inherit Langcliffe, which was owned by his mother's family. Born in 1874, Geoffrey spent his formative years at Overdale, Skipton, and was fond of visiting two aunts at Langcliffe Hall. After his education at Eton and Oxford, he joined the colonial service and became private secretary to Lord Milner, the British High Commissioner for South Africa. Milner's patronage led to his becoming editor of the *Johannesburg Star* in 1905. He became a correspondent for *The Times* and, meeting its owner, Lord Northcliffe, during a visit to London, he was invited to join the editorial staff of 'The Thunderer' in London. In September 1912, Geoffrey Robinson, aged 37, became editor.

He maintained his links with his Dales estate, though when he visited Langcliffe he had to endure his aunt's intolerance of the telephone; she would not have one in the house. If Dawson's London office wished to communicate with him a call was made to Settle and a message passed on by runner. He sometimes telephoned London from Bowerley, the nearby home of friends. He resigned as editor after a disagreement with Northcliffe in 1919, but, following Northcliffe's death in 1923, the Astor family, who now owned *The Times*, invited him back. He edited the newspaper for the next 18 years. Geoffrey Dawson and Dr. Blunt, Bishop of Bradford, applied the pressure which led to the abdication of Edward VIII in 1938. Dawson retired in 1941 and died three years later, his burial place being at Langcliffe. The great and the good attended a memorial service at St Paul's in London.

Settle, now bypassed, has an attractive central area. Dominating the town is a limestone knoll called Castleberg. The market place, with its stone cross, is the setting for the Shambles, a curious block consisting of a basement, a row of shops (formerly slaughterhouses, hence the name), and above that a terrace of two-storey cottages. A quaint Town Hall built in a style which has been called 'Jacobean-Gothic' stands nearby and a variety of 17th-century buildings are ranged around. Settle is proud of its market place, especially on Tuesday, market day, when canopied stalls sprout like mushrooms in a meadow. Part of a distinguished 17th-century house known as The Folly has now been acquired as a Museum of North Craven Life.

36 *Settle Market Place, ready for a livestock market, photographed by C.W. Buck, Elgar's doctor friend, who lived at Giggleswick and, for a time, in the large building in the background of the photograph. The friendship between Elgar and Buck began in the 1880s and continued, mostly by correspondence, for just 50 years.*

37   *Giggleswick Post Office which, like many in the Dales, is also a well-filled shop.*

Giggleswick, the older of the two places and the setting for a church with a far-flung parish, acquired its present elegant appearance when those with means and pretensions moved here. Settle did not become a separate parish, with its own church, until the 1840s. W.T. Palmer wrote of Giggleswick:

> The beauty of the village is apparent to everyone who has eyes to see and a soul to drink in its charm. A spell of antiquity pervades Giggleswick, with its old-time stone cross, remains of stocks, lych-gate, church under stately elms, babbling brook and crystal waters. The rows of antique cottages with ... deep mullions ... over which the richly-hued Virginia creepers droop and festoon, are worth going far to see.

Anyone who travels along the A65 between Long Preston and Settle, sees the Ribble performing a series of meanders which are like a doodle on the map. After heavy rain or a sudden melting of snow on the high fells the river swells into a lake and teems with geese, swans and ducks. At the Deeps, the river flows slowly between sandy banks. Then, just below Cow Bridge, the Ribble regains its old buoyant character, being fast and shallow. Soon, what has been a Yorkshire river crosses the border into Lancashire.

8

SEDBERGH, DENT AND GARSDALE

PRIOR TO 1974 Sedbergh was in the West Riding of Yorkshire and councillors on business had to travel to the county town of Wakefield. Now it is in Cumbria, though both the town and the Howgill Fells remain in the Yorkshire Dales National Park. It has been customary to refer to Sedbergh as 'isolated', but this description became outmoded when the M6 extension was built, passing within five miles of the town. Sedbergh, the home of some 2,000 people and the largest place in the Park, has a varied life of its own, though most workers commute to Kendal, 11 miles away.

It lies at the convergence of three river valleys, the Rawthey, Clough and Dee. The Lune is just two miles to the south-west. Sedbergh is backed by Winder, one of the Howgill group of fells–big, rounded, wall-less hills, with their own shadow pattern, which rise to the high ground of The Calf, at 2,200 ft. Nothing in the National Park can be compared with the slaty Howgills, which are separated from the Carboniferous rocks of the Dales proper by a geological fault. When the Howgills are snow-clad and the air is clear, they stand out from a great distance. Wordsworth wrote of their 'naked heights' and another even more imaginative visitor likened their smooth forms to a herd of elephants which had lain down to sleep.

38 *Sedbergh, backed up by Winder, one of the Howgill Fells.*

The Howgills, which are named after the small and secluded settlement of Howgill in the Lune Valley, have hidden places, one such being Wandale, which is connected by a narrow ribbon of tarmac with Ravenstonedale and is otherwise approached on footpaths: a green track once serving several farmsteads which are now deserted, and another, from the Sedbergh-Kirkby Stephen road, climbing a brant (steep) fellside by a zig-zag route which is a blend of grass and moss. In Wandale is the big old farmhouse of Adamthwaite, complete with a spinning gallery. Wandale has enough woodland to attract nesting buzzards. Other notable birds of the Howgills are peregrines, whose chattering calls are heard when their nesting area is being violated. Cautley Spout, at the craggiest part of the Howgills, is where several waterfalls combine and rush down a hillside for about 600 ft. The croak of the raven is heard above the gurgle of the water.

The derivation of Sedbergh has been hotly debated, but the popular explanation is *setbergh* or 'flat-topped hill', referring not to the Howgills but to sprawling Baugh Fell, to the east. At each approach to Sedbergh a river is crossed by a narrow bridge. A Norman motte and bailey stood on Castlehaw, a wooded knoll. Sedbergh has remained compact, with one of the tiniest market places imaginable and a charter dating from 1251. One of the joys of visiting the town is to explore the little yards leading from the main street—yards in which houses were packed and where upper storeys protruded as spinning galleries, which was also a feature of the old Dent Town. The textile industry flourished in the 17th, 18th and early 19th centuries, the local watercourses providing the power to turn the wheels of machinery for processing wool at Hebblethwaite Hall and cotton at Birks, Millthorpe and Howgill. Sedbergh was also a major centre for hand-knitting, which flourished in other north-western dales, especially Dentdale.

On Wednesday the area near the church holds a cluster of stalls. The market cross and steps were removed in the 1870s and the stone ball from the top of the cross can now be seen at Brigflatts Meeting House, a mile or so out of town just off the road to Kirkby Lonsdale. The town has a variety of shops, most of them owned by firms of local origin rather than national renown. In the early morning the smell of newly baked bread pervades the main street. After an unsuccessful attempt to cobble this thoroughfare, it was re-macadamised, given one-way status, and provided with broad pavements. Being on the A684 Kendal-Northallerton road, an important low-level route through the Pennines via Garsdale and Wensleydale, the town is a focal point for a widely scattered community of hill farmers. One of their regular gathering places is the auction mart founded by the Harper family in 1903. Visitors head for a refurbished National Park Centre. An antiquarian bookshop run by the Hollett family has a prime position in Finkle Street, opposite the church. St Andrew's at Sedbergh, an architectural focal point, was restored in 1886 yet manages to retain traces in its fabric of almost every architectural style back to Norman times, work of this period being seen at the base of the tower. Behind the altar is an unusual example of stained glass, being one picture spread over three windows. The subject is Christ meeting the disciples by Galilee.

Sedbergh School, which has 400 students on the roll, evolved from a chantry school founded in 1525 by Roger Lupton, a native of the parish who became canon of Windsor and Provost of Eton. The original chantry was endowed with scholarships and fellowships at St John's College, Cambridge. Sedbergh became a free grammar school in 1552 and was rebuilt in 1716, the elegant schoolhouse of that date now being used as a library. The school assumed its present form as a public school in 1874. The chapel is a fine example of High Victorians. The futuristic Queen's Hall, which is also used by local organisations, was indeed opened by the Queen when she presented Sedbergh with a new coat of arms.

On a Tuesday in March, the Wilson Run, a 10-mile cross country race, takes place, continuing a tradition which began with a steeplechase in 1881. It is named in honour of Bernard Wilson, who encouraged scholars to explore the countryside round the town. Strategic points on the course include Baugh Fell, Whinny Gill, Muddy Slide, Spectators' Hill and Danny Bridge. On the evening of race day a grand concert is held at the school, and all the boys who finished the course are called up on to the stage. The company then sings a song entitled 'The Long Run'. Two extracts from another of the Sedbergh School songs reflect pride in the local area

> ... ours the mountain fastness,
> The deep romantic ghylls,
> Where Clough and Dee and Rawthey
> Come singing from the hills.

And, from the chorus–

> Its Cautley, Calf and Winder
> That make the Sedbergh Man!

There is pride, also, in the places of worship scattered around this frontier district. St Mark's, Cautley, designed by Victorian architect William Butterfield, is in marked contrast with Cautley Chapel, the spiritual home of local Methodists built at the roadside between Sedbergh and Kirkby Stephen. The chapel (of 1845) is small and yet its simple furnishings give an impression of space. Other diminutive Methodist chapels in the Sedbergh area are Fell End (1861), Ravenstonedale and Garsdale Street Chapel (1841), the last named having scarcely changed since its construction. The seats are painted, box-like and tiered, giving easy eye-contact between preacher and worshipper. Firbank and Brigflatts, centres of Quakerism, maintain a tradition of worship and witness which began in the mid-17th century with the arrival of George Fox at Firbank in 1652. He spoke out-of-doors, at a rock which is called Fox's Pulpit, and held the attention of about 1,000 'seekers' for three hours. Brigflatts (1675), two miles from Sedbergh, is the oldest Meeting House in northern England.

There are strong links between the north-west corner of the Yorkshire Dales National Park and Liverpool. Many Dales families moved to the city during its expansion and, by becoming cow-keepers, ensured that local families had a good supply of fresh milk. The most ambitious of these cow-keepers hoped to make money quickly in order to return to their birthplace and buy farms. Some of the emigrants grew to like big city life, however, and their descendants occasionally drive out to the western dales seeking family connections. A member of the Handley family who grew up in the city was Tommy Handley of ITMA, a famous radio comedy programme.

The cow-keeping period began in about the 1860s, when the first families from the Dales, from Bowland and from Westmorland relocated themselves. The heyday was just before the First World War, after which a steady decline set in, affected in later years by a tightening up of municipal health laws, by refrigeration and improved transport, and by the growth of big milk-retailing companies.

In 1900 some 4,000 head of cattle were being kept within the Liverpool boundary, providing fresh milk daily to the citizens. The city had swamped the nearest farmland and was virtually cut off from rural areas by the Mersey. Cow-keeping was profitable but the working day long and arduous, the animals being milked as early as 5 a.m., the first daily milk round taking place from about 7.30 a.m., and the afternoon milking occurring from about 3 p.m., this being followed by yet another milk round extending into the evening.

Each milkhouse had its dairy shop, which remained open until 8 p.m. or even later. In about 1910, the Metcalfe family, who had migrated from Garsdale to a milkhouse at Fazakerley, owned one of the first motorised milk delivery vehicles in Liverpool.

Dent is tucked away among the fells. An old saying advises a hungry person to 'do as they do in Dent—chew bent [a coarse type of moorland grass]'. Robert Southey (1774-1843), in *The Doctor*, referred to 'the terrible knitters o' Dent', the word 'terrible' in this connection being a compliment. Hand-knitting, an offshoot of the Dales textile industry, led to the folk of Dent—children too—spending any spare moments knitting gloves and stockings. Army fashion created such a big demand for knee stockings that during the Seven Years War (1756-63) agents representing the army toured Dentdale and neighbouring valleys buying up large quantities of stockings. Whernside Manor, originally West House, was enlarged and renamed by the Gill family of Deepdale, whose money was augmented by income from Jamaican plantations. There is a persistent story that in the late 18th century, some black plantation workers were brought to the dale to work as servants in the house.

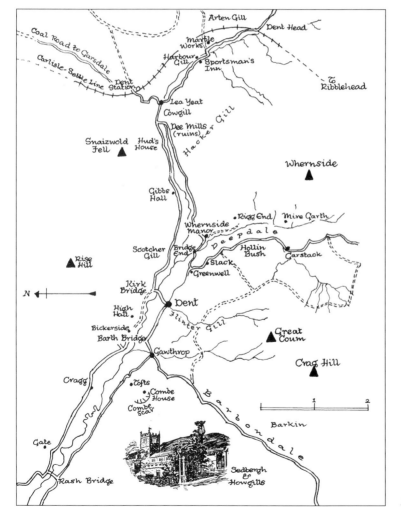

Dentdale and Cowgill.

Dent is in the valley of the river Dee, the topmost part of the dale being in the parish of Cowgill, where there are far more sheep than people. The dale has a hemmed-in feel about it, three of the four roads connecting it with the outer world having the character of mountain passes. Little fellside farms are blotches of white against green meadows, the porches and frontages of the old buildings having been painted white in the Old Lakeland fashion.

At Dent Town the main street has retained its cobbles, which look quaint but can be hard on the feet. The Dent recalled by Samuel Taylor Coleridge, a visitor of the Romantic Age, was

> ... a town of little note or praise;
> Narrow and winding are its rattling streets,
> Where cart with cart in cumbrous conflict meets.

St Andrew's Church is notable for its 17th-century woodwork and examples of the so-called Dent marble, a dark form of limestone. Propped up against the corner of one building, and looking like a large coffin because there is an inscription upon it, is a piece of Shap granite commemorating Adam Sedgwick (1785-1873). The boulder is a fountain in disguise. Sedgwick, a native of Dent, in which valley his family had lived since the 13th century, was reared and given his first schooling in the Grammar School which stood in the churchyard. He went on to Sedbergh, then to Trinity College, Cambridge, was ordained and had the course of his life changed in 1816 when he became acquainted with the Geological Society of London. Now he applied his considerable intellect to a relatively new science. He did so with distinction.

Sedgwick identified, explained and named the Dent Fault, which separates the Carboniferous deposits of the upper dale from the slaty rocks of the lower valley. He conducted research in the Lake District and Wales, identifying and naming the different strata. He became Woodwardian professor of geology at Cambridge and was on friendly terms with Victoria and her consort. The breadth of his mind is indicated by his friendship with William Wordsworth. Sedgwick kept his native dale in the forefront of his mind and visited it whenever it was possible, on horseback or by post-chaise up the Lune Valley and through what was then wild little Barbondale.

Arriving in Dent in 1815, he brought news of the successful outcome of the Battle of Waterloo, clambering on to a mounting block in Dent to read the official announcement of Wellington's victory. Sedgwick's great legacy was his printed recollections of Dent history and lore. These were penned following an obscure controversy with the Rev. Joseph Sumner, curate of Cowgill, over the spelling, meaning and history of Kirthwaite, or Kirkthwaite, in the upper dale, of which Cowgill forms a part. Sedgwick, supported by the Queen and the Prime Minister, triumphed and on 30 June 1837 it was he who laid the foundation stone of Cowgill (not Kirkthwaite) chapel. A photograph of Sedgwick as an old man shows him to have had a rounded, seamed face, a good head of hair and a pair of bright eyes.

The dale round the little town contains good alluvial soil. There are hedges rather than drystone walls. The main colonists, from the ninth century onwards, were the Irish-Norse, arriving from the west. They were pastoralists who felt uneasy in a crowd. There grew up in Dentdale a robust, independent-minded community—a people who, when the Dissolution of the Monasteries occurred, supported the rebellion which became known as the Pilgrimage of Grace (1539). Dent folk gave a thoughtful hearing to George Fox when he tried to bring a breath of spiritual fresh air to their district. Many dalesmen, resourceful and independent by nature, owned their own homes and some land and were proud to call themselves 'statesmen'.

39   Midland Railway architecture. This building on the 'down' platform at Dent is now in private hands and has been sympathetically restored.

The Settle-Carlisle railway operates on a ledge cut from the lower slopes of Great Knoutberry, a 'knoutberry' being the cloudberry, and the station is situated on the hillside, at an elevation of 1,100 ft., some 600 ft. above the valley and over four miles from Dent Town. Even more conspicuous than the main station is the stationmaster's house, at a slightly higher elevation than the main station building. Both properties are now privately owned. The Midland Railway Company's deference to the elevation and Pennine weather led to it having its walls slated on three sides and to the installation of double windows–two windows, side by side–representing an early form of double glazing. A former stationmaster cured winter draughts by waiting until there was a frosty spell and spraying the house with water from a hosepipe. Dent was closed for goods traffic in October 1964, but passenger facilities, removed in 1970, were subsequently restored. The station buildings are in an excellent state of conservation. The signal box, installed in 1891 with a 20-lever tumbler frame, was closed in 1981 and the wooden structure was eventually 'put to the torch'. Sprinter trains stop at Dent to pick up or discharge passengers and the line is used by a variety of freight traffic.

In 1967 Arthur Raistrick wrote:

> We might think that, except for the distant sight of the expresses roaring across the high fellside at the dalehead, Dent had never heard the sounds of industrial life. Though never on an urban scale, Dent has had its close acquaintance with industry ... Marble quarrying, cutting and polishing, coal mining and textiles have all had their share in the life of the dale, but their harshness has been ameliorated and their traces do not obtrude.

On Knoutberry itself are to be found evidence of partly completed grindstones, even a gatepost, cut straight from the rock, on which work stopped abruptly when a flaw developed.

The track up Flintergill, once extensively used by packhorses heading for Ingleton, was incorporated into the Occupation Road in 1859, at the time of the Enclosures, which were quite late in this part of the Dales. The full name of the lane is Flintergill Outrake. It is quite well wooded, the trees including sessile oak and, higher up, some wych elm, the leaves of which were once collected to be fed to farm stock. Green Lane, to which the track up Flintergill leads, is a broad green road. Its core is an old track once used by packhorse traffic which was preserved to give access to the big fields created on enclosure. From these upland acres have been taken a brittle type of coal, large slabs of sandstone which proved suitable for roofing purposes, and also the dark, well-fossiled limestone known as Dent marble.

I *Addleborough from Howgate, Askrigg, Wensleydale.*

II *Hawes and Abbotside Common, from Wether Fell, Wensleydale.*

V Above left. *The* Moorcock Inn, *at the head of Wensleydale.*

VI Above right. *Weets Cross above Malhamdale.*

VII Below. *The inflow stream at Malham Tarn.*

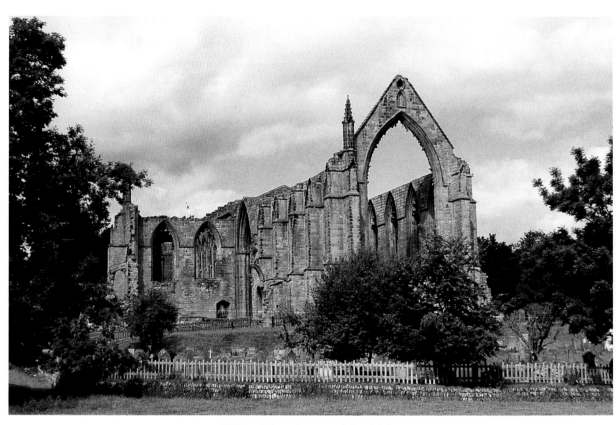

VIII *Bolton Priory in Wharfedale.*

IX *Fountains Abbey near Ripon, North Ribblesdale.*

X Above left. *The Strid, Wharfedale.*

XI Above right. *Kilnsey Crag, Upper Wharfedale.*

XII Below. *Muker in Upper Swaledale.*

XIII *The Cross Keys and Cautley Crag, between Sedbergh and Kirkby Stephen.*

XIV *Former railway workers' cottages, Garsdale.*

XV   *The Folly at Settle.*

XVI   *The lead mining museum at Earby.*

XVII *One of the Buttertubs, between Wensleydale and Swaledale.*

XVIII *Giggleswick Scar, North Craven.*

Between the railway stations of Dent and Garsdale is the Coal Road, named after the coal produced at the numerous bell-type pits which were driven into the Yoredale rocks to mine a somewhat brittle coal that was sent to the farms and cottages first by packhorse, then by horse-drawn carts. Some was burnt locally in lime kilns producing cob-lime, which was used domestically or spread across acid land to sweeten it during land improvements in the 18th century. Tarmacadamed now, this route undulates like a ride at a fairground. From the high vantage point a motorist looks across the bare ridges of the Pennines or across the new conifer forest planted near where the Settle-Carlisle railway extends from Dent Station, through Rise Hill tunnel, to Garsdale.

Cowgill, the parish of the upper dale which Adam Sedgwick had in mind when he wrote his *Memorial*, begins some three-and-a-half miles above Dent Town, where a beck joins the river Dee. In dry spells the Dee offers the sight of expanses of water-smoothed limestone. In 1837, Sedgwick laid the foundation stone of the chapel at Cowgill, dedicated to St John the Evangelist, which was consecrated by the Bishop of Ripon in October 1838. In 1869, some thirty years after the consecration of the church, an Act of Parliament was passed to give 'an Award of a District to Cowgill Chapel'. Short and to the point, this Act restored to it the old name of Cowgill.

Scattered around the head of the valley, and in the gills, were quarries from which, from the middle of the 18th century, and especially towards its end when the work was better organised, was cut Dent marble. This is everywhere exposed in Arten Gill. Professor Versey of Leeds University, who led many an expedition to the high Pennines, was fond of breaking a piece of marble and inviting a student to sniff the peculiar kerosene-like tang which had been released. There is no need to face the midges of Arten Gill to enjoy the special beauty of Dent marble. Memorials in Dent church are made of it. So commonplace were marble products that the surrounds of fireplaces in waiting rooms of north-country railway stations were 'marbled'.

Arthur Raistrick distinguished between three types of 'marble' which were quarried, polished and exported for decorative work: one is a very dark colour, black when polished, contains abundant fossils, mainly corals, and is often of large size; another 'black marble' is almost free of fossils; a third variety has a grey background, with an abundance of fossil crinoids, 'sea lily' stems and fragments. The limestone lay in beds of varying thickness and could be broken free using levers and wedges. Explosives were not necessary. After a period when hand-sawing was carried out, water power was employed, as at the High and Low Mills in Arten Gill. The remains of the High Mill, originally used for textiles, are detectable just below Arten Gill viaduct.

A visit by a Tynesider to Arten Gill in 1835 led to the development of the celebrated Armstrong engineering works. William George Armstrong, a young man articled to a solicitor, and his new wife, the former Margaret Ramshaw, spent their honeymoon in the Dent area and ventured into Arten Gill. It had been his intention to do some angling in the river Dee. Armstrong appears to have had some prior knowledge of the marble works, and was impressed by a large waterwheel enclosed in a two-storey building which provided the power for sawing and polishing. He calculated that the set up was wasteful, using only about a twentieth of the available power of the beck; hydraulic power was the thing. Back in Newcastle he became preoccupied with hydraulic machinery. In 1838, he prepared a scientific paper on the subject, from which—with other experiments—grew the enormous engineering works.

At the time the Armstrongs were in the district, polished marble was being taken by various means from works at the head of Dentdale to where it might be transported to market by carriers, canal barges, even ocean-going ships. Dent marble was consigned to the warehouses of Darlington and London. Local builders maintained a steady demand for the stuff which was, of course, much cheaper than importing marble from Italy. In its heyday the industry was despatching slabs for monuments and fireplaces, and it benefited temporarily from the arrival of the Settle-Carlisle, which provided cheaper transport. However, in a short time, Italian marble was in fashion. The last wave of activity at the head of Dentdale was polishing rough slabs from Italy for a trade no longer demanding the home product. Before the end of the 19th century the quarries had been closed.

The lofty piers of Arten Gill viaduct consist of Dent marble. About 50,000 tons of dressed stone, some of the pieces weighing more than eight tons, were transported to the staging in tramway bogies. A 'steam traveller' operating on tracks laid on wooden scaffolding lifted the blocks and deposited them exactly where they were needed. They were given extra strong bonding by a 'cement' devised by the resident engineer, John Crossley, who recommended a mixture of lime and burnt clay. The Midland historian, F.S. Williams, wrote after a visit during the construction period, 'The viaduct is built of the same sort of stone as that which, when cut and polished at Mr. Nixon's marble quarries close by, is known by the name of Dent marble.'

Deeside House, built as a shooting lodge in the 19th century, has been a youth hostel since 1944, attracting between 4,500 and 5,000 overnights per annum. Standing four-and-a-half miles from Dent Town, with a sheltered situation beside the Dee, here spanned by a narrow stone bridge, its white-washed walls gleam among the summer greens. So white is the house in appearance it belies its bulk. Some of the youth hostellers use Deeside Lodge as a base for local walks, including an ascent of Whernside. Caving weekends are organised by the warden, and parties visit underground systems with quaint names such as Ibbeth Peril, Calf Holes and Katnup, as well as Upper and Lower Churn, Birkwith and Great Douk.

With a gamekeeper attending to the lodge and the servants having gone ahead with enough food and drink for a regiment, the Bentincks of Underley Hall, near Kirkby Lonsdale, had none of the irksome jobs which befall less affluent folk. Everyone would be aware of the passage to their dalehead property. Fine horses and iron-shod wheels of stately carriages clattered over the cobbles of Dent Town and raised dust on the updale road whose flanking hedges gave way to drystone walls as the valley narrowed and began to show its ribs of stone. Another famous updale building, *The Sportsman's Inn*, a three-centuries-old listed building, has its sporty flavour imparted by the mounted head of a red stag.

The Methodist presence was felt not only in Dent Town but also in remote little Deepdale, where in 1889 the Primitives opened a small roadside chapel, having paid for its construction leaving £3 8s. 3d. in hand. The 'Prims' had the makings of a society in 1861 and appeared on the Plan of Middleham Circuit in 1873. The chapel site was purchased from Lord Bective, of Underley Hall, for £10, the cost of the chapel and a lean-to for a vestry-cum-Sunday School being £159 0s. 5d. The first trustees were two flag merchants, a mason, three farmers, two farm workers, two provision merchants, two drapers, a carter and a brush dealer.

Garsdale, locally known as 'Gasd'll', is a trough between Baugh Fell and Rise Hill, its river being the Clough, a tributary of the Rawthey. Baugh Fell, a sprawling fell, acts like a great sponge, releasing water gradually. There is an East and a West Baugh Fell, shaped and joined–as Harry Griffin, the Lakeland writer, once noted–like the two halves of a black pudding. When, in 1889, the Clough was swollen by the run-off of four-and-a-half inches of rain which had fallen on Grisedale near the head of the valley, three of the seven county bridges were destroyed and the rest were damaged. The torrent entered a number of houses and swept away walls and trees.

Garsdale and Grisedale.

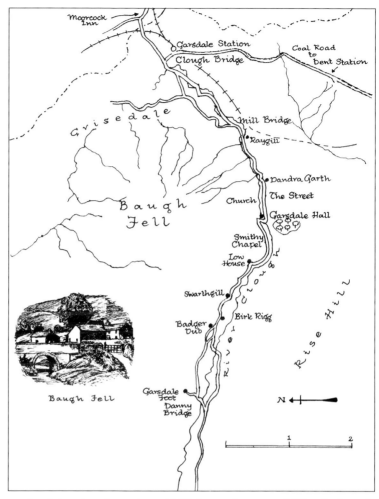

Baugh Fell

The most fascinating reach of the river has, since 1985, been designated 'The Sedgwick Trail', 200 years after the birth of Adam Sedgwick, the aforementioned native of Dent who became Cambridge professor of geology. The trail begins at Danny Bridge, near where the Dent Fault crosses the dale. Wooden posts mark the points of special interest, the numbers on the posts referring to a leaflet available from the Information Centre at Sedbergh. A visitor traces the Great Scar Limestone of Carboniferous Age (340 million years old) to where there is an upfold or anticline created by pressure along the fault, against which the limestone ends, the adjacent rock being the Brathay Flags of the Silurian Age (425 million years ago). The change from limestone to flagstone is reflected in the vegetation along the banks, the sweet limestone soil holding a stock of plants such as wild thyme and the flagstone area supporting heather and sphagnum moss.

A stranger who passes through the dale is immediately impressed by the number of places of worship. St John the Baptist Church was rebuilt in 1861 on land just east of the burial-ground of a former chapel which Wordsworth had described as 'a lowly house of prayer in a charming little valley'. The tradition of worship in the dale began in Norman times when lands were conveyed to the canons of Easby Abbey at Richmond for the support of a chaplain 'who shall celebrate divine service in the chapel of St John the Baptist for ever'. Methodist chapels proliferated. After the unruly miners of Cotterdale had been Christianised by Primitive Methodists in the 1830s, the evangelists switched their attention to Garsdale, where the Street Chapel was built in 1841. The interior has the original painted box-like tier seats and a 'penitent form' where a preacher invited members of the congregation to make public confessions of their faith. Today, services are shared between Street Chapel and Low Smithy, a chapel founded by Jonathan Kershaw, whose fervent evangelism led to his being dubbed 'Apostle of the Dales'. The original chapel, of 130 square yards, cost the 'Apostle' the then princely sum of £5. The premises were extended and Kershaw subsequently sold the property to the Trustees for five shillings. Up in Grisedale is the Richard Atkinson Memorial Chapel, now a dwelling but built for worship in 1888 to commemorate the work of Richard Atkinson, a Christian gamekeeper living at Grouse Hall, Garsdale. He was only 40 years old when he died in 1884. Mount Zion Chapel at the dalehead was opened in 1876, the year in which passenger trains began to run on the Settle-Carlisle Railway. The congregation was drawn from the farming community and from nonconformists living in the local railway cottages.

The head of Garsdale, six miles from Hawes and ten from Sedbergh, is traversed by the Settle-Carlisle railway. In 1875 the company provided 16 houses at the station and another half dozen near the Moorcock viaduct. A 50-strong community of signalmen, porters and gangers came into being. By 1950 each was paying 7s. 6d. rent a year for a spacious home. A representative of *John Bull* visited Garsdale Junction in that year, when many of its features were still intact, and when 90 express freights and passenger trains, including the Thames-Clyde express, thundered through the station each day. On week-days only half a dozen local trains each way stopped here.

Until recently the 'down' platform waiting room had been used for Anglican services, and a harmoniumist accompanied the hymn-singing. The 'up' platform ladies waiting-room still housed the station's own library, which was presented by a kindly woman in 1906. The county library were sending round the books and, said stationmaster Reginald Berwick, 'they all go for the modern stuff'.

Grisedale, a secluded hollow ringed by soggy fells, is a high Pennine setting for farming, forestry and a few sporting activities such as grouse-shooting. The valley has the map name of Grisdale, from *gris*, a pig. In a document of 1649 the spelling is Grysdale. Grisedale is the home of a dozen or so people. Another half-dozen have homes along the loop road connecting the valley with the Hawes-Sedbergh highway. Local children are conveyed by bus to school in Sedbergh. A grassy hump in the valley is all that remains of the Friends Meeting House which stood by the river. George Fox, founder of Quakerism, visited Grisedale as part of a Dales tour in 1652. Near East Scale is a Quaker cemetery, last used over a century ago.

The population of Grisedale slumped over many years, partly because the cold earth could not sustain a high number and partly as a consequence of some cruel winters. Round Ing, the 'end house' in the dale and a former home of the Pratts, father, mother and six children, was vacated just after the Second World War and is now ruined. The last of the native-born left the valley in 1968. Several of the properties, including a former Methodist chapel, are in occupation. Mouse Sike, the Grisedale farm owned by John Pratt, has extensive new outbuildings. In rainy spells, Grisedale is inclined to be too wet for good farming. A drought suits the farmer.

The dale should be visited on foot. There is no parking space for visitors. Apart from the Cheviot and Swaledale sheep, the scene is animated by ponies and there are large conifer plantations. The dampness of the valley is indicated by the way the conifers thrive. Kingcups, or marsh marigolds, give the dale a golden hue for about ten days in the springtime.

9

SWALEDALE AND ARKENGARTHDALE

SWALEDALE, THE MOST NORTHERLY of the dales, is sinuous, narrow and steep-sided, contrasting with its more spacious neighbours–with Teesdale to the north and Wensleydale to the south. Ella Pontefract (1934) detected an alpine character in the gorge at the back of Kisdon Hill, and grey houses perched on the edge of the fells suggested alpine mountain huts. There is more to Swaledale than meets the eye–valleys within a valley, including Swinnergill and Gunnerside Gill, which walkers enter with a sense of discovery, finding the crumbling remains from the lead-mining days.

Apart from the main road, which tries to maintain a reasonable height above the quick-flooding river, travel in the Swaledale area is akin to mountaineering, with steep gradients and zig-zags. The Buttertubs Pass makes a high-level crossing from Hardraw in Wensleydale, passing the limestone shafts after which the route is named, supposedly through a resemblance to the tubs in which butter used to be delivered to grocers in bulk. The road, for a time a narrow ledge on a plunging fellside, then dips into Swaledale, which is met between the greystone villages of Thwaite and Muker.

To reach Tan Hill, the motorist follows a road which zig-zags up to West Stonesdale and then picks its way between peat hags to the inn which, at 1,732 ft., is celebrated as the highest licensed premises in the land. The road to Arkengarthdale, a tributary valley of the

40 *Summer in upper Swaledale.*

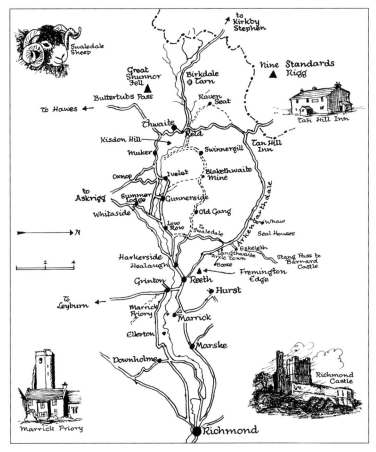

Swaledale and Arkengarthdale.

Swale, begins with an intimidatingly steep climb from Low Row then levels out and wanders for a while through a landscape decked with the ruins of old mine buildings before descending to Arkengarthdale. Swaledale also has moorland road links with Askrigg, Redmire and Leyburn, all in Wensleydale.

Around the head of Swaledale are fells with splendid names–Rogan's Seat, Lovely Seat, Kisdon, a name derived from *kis* and *dun* (little detached hill), and Great Shunner Fell. The undulating moors are, from a sporting point of view, among the best in England, being well-keepered and with the tough old ling burnt off in strips to encourage the growth of new shoots, food for sheep and grouse. There are soft spots, lagged with sphagnum moss, to which a hen grouse takes her brood to feed. The hoarse calls of cock grouse in their territories are familiar sounds to the families occupying the little hill farms.

Upper Swaledale is a colourful area in June, as anyone can see who uses footpaths through the meadowland and negotiates the stiles in the drystone walls, some of which are of the squeeze variety, nicknamed 'Fat Man's Agony'. In Swaledale, that which elsewhere is a tedious summer green is offset by the colour of a variety of flowers. The old-type hay meadows are retained by farmers who have, by and large, kept to the traditional methods, which avoid artificial fertilisers. Mulch from overwintering cattle revives the jaded land. Those farmers do not suffer economically from devotion to the old ways, which enable flowers to set seed and thrive, for they receive grants under the terms of an Environmentally Sensitive Area designation. The number of flower species in the dale is about 600, and contributing to a mosaic of colour, which is dominated by the gold of buttercup, are yellow rattle and the blueish wood cranesbill. Even blighted mining areas and spoilheaps have flowers, in this case the lead-tolerant spring sandwort, which in springtime is a mass of starry white. The yellow mountain pansy decks old grassland. Hybrid pansies are to be found in various places, including Gunnerside Gill.

The river Swale is swift and powerful. Camden, a visitor towards the end of the 16th century, wrote that it 'rusheth rather than runneth'. Its headstreams are on High Seat and Nine Standards Rigg, which straddle the watershed of England. The Swale's source is where Great Sleddale and Birkdale Becks blend their waters. It soon responds to heavy rainfall, and then takes on a brownish tinge and the current trundles stones along its bed. In post-glacial times, the melting ice produced a torrent which reshaped the landscape. Unable to follow its ancient route west of Kisdon Hill because of deposits of boulder clay, the Swale cut a deep course for itself on the other side of the hill. The most impressive inundation in Swaledale in recent times occurred on 26 August 1986. The Swale became ugly but it was Arkle Beck, in adjacent Arkengarthdale, that took the brunt of a particularly heavy downpour, the water rising 12 ft. above normal and, with water from Great Punchard Gill, sweeping away the parapets of the bridge at Whaw and causing serious flooding and much damage to a caravan park and other property at the confluence of Arkle Beck and the Swale near Reeth.

Swaledale has a homely feeling. In the old days almost all the inhabitants were sur-named Alderson, Metcalfe, Harker or Coates, and nicknames proliferated. Alfred J. Brown wrote in 1952: 'Of all the great dales, Swaledale seems to come nearest to one's ideal of a pure, unsullied dale—a true shepherd's dale.' Yet the valley was sullied by industry—by quarrying and by mining for lead and coal. Walkers who follow the Coast to Coast Walk through Swaledale see the valley at its most varied and best and the remoter gills at their most blighted, the crossing from Swinnergill to Old Gang being over what is virtually a desert of mining dross.

Gunnerside Gill, approached from the village of that name, is a good area for exploration, a conspicuous reminder of the mining era being a large compressor. The sides of the valley were scoured by 'hushing', and any ore was collected at the bottom of the slope. In Gunnerside Gill are the ruins of Blakethwaite smelt mill, which originally had two ore hearths, with a roasting furnace. A double flue rises 150 ft. up the hillside to a chimney. This mill worked until 1878. The older mill, Lownathwaite, was last used for smelting in the 1830s.

41 *A conserved chimney and ruined buildings at Old Gang, part of the Swaledale orefield.*

42   *Lead-miners at Nenthead on the northern Pennines.*

A walker from Surrender Bridge, between Low Row and Langthwaite, enters the Old Gang complex, where the annual output between 1800 and 1810 was over 2,000 tons. Old Gang, in a now quiet valley between Swaledale and Arkengarthdale, has a site dominated by a complete chimney, though the smelt mill it served is now sadly ruined. Everywhere in Swaledale is evidence of the activities of 't'Owd Man', as past generations of lead-miners were called. A miner who came across what he thought might be a promising area might be made suddenly aware that 't'Owd Man' had been there before him. Collapsed flues are further evidence of the incredible energy of miners; the flues extending up the sides of gills and across heather moorland to the skyline, where a chimney, if it remains, has the visual effect of an exclamation mark.

Swaledale had the largest concentration of lead mines in the Dales. The villages and hamlets of Swaledale grew with the lead-mining industry. Edmund Cooper recorded that a resident of Reeth who had lived at the turn of the 18th century wrote that, previously, the dale had been occupied by a peculiarly primitive people and that few men from the outside world made their appearances among them. 'But with the coming of these "foreigners" customs began to change and many dialect words which were expressive and comprehensive became obsolete.' Anthony Clarkson, of Keld, writing about 1820, described the Swaledale miners in this lively fashion:

> Wild as the dales in which they dwell
> None can the gruver [mining] lads excel
> In wrestling, leaping, fighting, running,
> Deep drinking, swaring [*sic*], craft and cunning,
> Miracklous tricks and roguish jokes,
> Untoward in their ways and looks.

In truth, the lead-miner had been quickly sapped of his health and energy and was likely to spend the last months of his life in bed, coughing and shivering with the gruver's complaint, a form of silicosis. In some individuals, mining and farming were combined, the miner also having a smallholding which was run in his absence by his wife. Notice the many smallholdings along the south-facing slopes of the dale all the way from Thwaite to

Reeth. The family was virtually self-sufficient, for a cow or two provided milk, some of it being converted into butter and cheese. A pig, fed on household scraps, was slaughtered to provide a reserve of tasty food. Hens scratching in the farmyard yielded eggs for the kitchen and were eventually themselves eaten. With a good-sized garden or a potato garth, a Swaledale or Arkengarthdale miner lived relatively well.

The most striking evidence of mining is on the north side of the valley, where mineral veins which formed some 300 million years ago occupy a concentration of east-west faults. Fieldhouse and Jennings (1978) mention two compensating advantages which lead-miners might set against their relatively low and highly variable wages. These were a short working day (which may have been due in part to the traditional combination of mining and farming) and the feeling of independence which came from contract work. The diary of an upper Swaledale miner-farmer included the following entries for September 1840:

September	8th	Bargain day at Lane End and Keld Side mines.
"	15th	Put mugs into fog [the second flush of grass after haytime].
"	21st	John Alderson and myself started dressing at Keldside.
"	22nd	Selled yearling stag to George Metcalfe.
"	30th	Finished working at Keldside–2 bings 7 cwts.

By 1851, the number of men and boys employed in mining totalled 1,129, quite apart from surface workers, the washers, dressers and smelters. In about 1880, however, the industry, beset by problems related to production from thin deposits at depth, and the importation of cheaper foreign lead, notably from Spain, went into a decline which continued until, by 1900, hardly any mining activity remained.

The novelist Thomas Armstrong studied the period of the early 19th century in Swaledale and used it as the background in his epic novel *Adam Brunskill*, which was painstakingly researched and written in longhand in an attractive Georgian house on the banks of the Swale at Low Row. When he and his wife bought it in 1946 the front garden was clogged with weeds and an old hen house leaned drunkenly over the river bank. When he had his book about Adam Brunskill in hand, he would write in the morning and spend an hour or two in engineering work in the big garden during the afternoon.

His story of Swaledale lead-mining days begins with the return of Adam to his native dale from Spain, where, as a member of a community of lead miners who migrated from Yorkshire, he was anxious to rehabilitate the reputation of his dead father. He believes his father's mysterious flight from the Dales was owing to the malice of his wife's relations, the Nattrass family. He champions the cause of a shaky lead-mining company against the unscrupulous rivalry of a company controlled by those enemies.

A Yorkshire ballad claims for Swaledale that it is 'twenty long mile', but from its beginnings in a peaty landscape, the dale unfolds grandly for 30 miles down to the market town of Richmond. The bleating of sheep has been a dominant sound for centuries. Edmund Cooper, a local historian, recorded that from the sheep walks of Swaledale and other parts of Yorkshire in the 13th century, Rievaulx Abbey produced for export 60 sacks of wool per annum, a sack representing 364 lb. William

43 *Thomas Armstrong, author of* Adam Brunskill, *an epic story set in Swaledale when lead-mining was taking place.*

Marshall, in his account of the rural economy of Yorkshire (1794), was impressed by the stamina of the moorland breed of sheep, which

> has always been different from that of the vale, and has not varied perhaps during a succession of centuries ... They live upon the open heather the year round ... Their wool is somewhat larger and much coarser than the Norfolk sheep. The covering of their buttocks is little more than hair ... but this is considered as a mark of hardiness.

The type of sheep which carries the Swaledale name, and which has colonised most of the northern fell country in recent decades, was fixed by farmers living on and around Tan Hill, at the head of the valley. In the Swaledale, quick and bright eyes stare out from a head which is dark complexioned on the upper part, grey or mealy lower down. Strong horns curl round low on either side. A sturdy body is clothed tightly and thickly with wool. No written records of the Swaledale breed have been found before 1920, when a Breeders' Association was formed. In February of that year, interested farmers met at Barnard Castle. The main marketing centres for Swaledale sheep today are at Hawes and Kirkby Stephen.

Tan Hill Inn, formerly a building connected with the local colliery, and standing in grand isolation, surveying the empty acres of Stainmore Forest, is the setting for a springtime show of Swaledale sheep from local breeders. The oldest patrons remember when Susan Peacock was the characterful landlady, from 1902 until her death in 1937. Though somewhat brusque in her manner, she made travellers welcome and under-played the bleakness of her surroundings and the severity of winter weather. In addition to the supplies she received in autumn–enough to carry her and her visitors through the worst type of winter–she had poultry, a pig or two and a goat which was not fussy about what it ate, and received from visitors everything from sandwiches to liquorice allsorts. When this well-loved daleswoman died, 40 cars followed the hearse from Tan Hill to the burial place in the yard at Keld Chapel.

Tan is a Celtic word which alludes, appropriately, to fire. Tan Hill was a useful source of coal which, though hard and brittle, served the needs of dalesfolk well before improved transport led to the use of deep-mined coal from South Yorkshire. Tan Hill coal formed a seam in the upper parts of the Yoredale Series and was being mined up to 30 fathoms deep. In 1384, coal from the Takkan Tan Mine was being delivered to Richmond Castle. The smelt mills of the orefield took large quantities of coal and there was a brown variety much sought after by blacksmiths, for it did not cake in the forge. Coal from Tan Hill, transported by packhorse, was used in the hearths of Jervaulx Abbey and Bolton Castle and, in the 17th century, at Appleby Castle, for the benefit of Lady Anne Clifford. Mining, then as now, was hazardous. In 1641 Robert Grummett fell to the bottom of a mine shaft on 'Tanhill'. He 'dyed' from his injuries and was buried at Muker. In 1670, when rights were owned by Lord Wharton, he leased them to three men providing he was supplied with up to 150 loads a year without charge at his home, Wharton Hall, near Kirkby Stephen. Colliers who worked on the Hill in 1833 lived after a fashion at cottages adjacent to what is now the *Tan Hill Inn*, and coal in panniers was transported from the Hill by donkeys owned by 'Awd Helkanah'.

44 *Mr. Harker, Muker, 1900.*

The main period of mining was in the late 18th and early 19th centuries, when large quantities were needed for the field kilns at which lime was burnt to be spread on the land, and was the fuel for the new reverberatory furnaces at the smelt mills. The last time Tan Hill coal was in popular demand was during a national miners strike in the 1930s.

Keld, the first (or last) settlement in the valley of the Swale, at 1,050 ft., has a disproportionate number of public buildings, including two chapels–Congregational (latterly United Reform) of 1840 and Methodist of 1841. Here, too, was established a school and a literary institute, as befitted a well-developed mining community. The *Cat Hole* inn was privatised as a dwelling in 1954. The village is relatively quiet and the Swale is noisy as it plunges down a series of limestone steps. The name Keld is derived from the Norse *kelda*, meaning a spring of water.

Angram, the next village down the dale from Keld, is the highest at 1,185 ft. William Alderson, who grew up here, slept with his bedroom window open and awoke one winter morning to find everything covered with snow. He used to say, 'It's aw reet as long as thoo doesn't git snawed up i' bed.' Angram has a splendid view of Kisdon Hill which, thatched with heather, has its own special little community of red grouse. Lord Peel, who took over the running of the 32,000-acre Gunnerside estate in 1970 and held it until quite recent times, was a principal advocate of a research project into red grouse, at a time when there was concern about numbers. The red grouse, a British version of the willow grouse which is spread across northern lands, feeds predominantly on heather. One of the greatest aids to the modern biologist is the small radio transmitter fitted round the neck of individual birds, enabling a check to be kept on their movements and habitat preferences to be determined with the minimum of disturbance to the birds.

In 1946 Lord Peel's father bought an estate that had formerly been owned by Lord Rochdale, who in the 1920s developed a shooting lodge from a nucleus of old Dales buildings. Gunnerside Lodge was for many years a hotch-potch but now, under new ownership, has been developed on a grander scale. In Lord Peel's time in Swaledale, two miles of new road were laid across virgin peat and a further five miles upgraded, giving ready access to a vast area of moorland. Of the total acreage of the estate, about 22,000 acres consisted of commonland, on which Lord Peel owned the freehold as lord of the manor, and the shooting rights. The land was subject to the grazing rights of various farms, rights stipulated under the Commons Registration Act. The rest was in-bye land: either upland pasture or hay meadow.

The settlements of upper Swaledale are little more than hamlets. Their names have a Norse ring. Keld has been mentioned. Others are Thwaite (from *thveit* or clearing), Muker (cultivated area) and Gunnerside (the summer grazing land of one Gunnar). At Thwaite lived a gamekeeper called Kearton, two of whose sons, Richard and Cherry, became pioneers of wildlife photography. On the lintel of the family's cottage doorway are now carved the figures of animals and birds, together with the initials RK (1862-1928) and CK (1871-1940). Richard in particular did pioneering work in popularising natural history and recording it by camera. As a boy, he fell from a tree while bird-nesting and the leg he broke was imperfectly set by a drunken physician at Kirkby Stephen. Richard grew up crippled yet managed to remain active.

A chance meeting with a London visitor to the grouse moors determined his future life. When it looked as though sport was ruined by thick mist, Richard imitated the call of a hen grouse and brought some fine cock birds to within range of the guns. The Londoner, who was associated with the publishing firm of Cassell, gave him a job with the firm. His brother Cherry joined him. They became interested in photographing bird's nests, which led to wildlife photography in remote parts of the land. Richard devised a variety of ingenious hides from which pictures of the birds themselves might be taken at close quarters. Then, taking advantage of the new half-tone process of block-making, introduced from America, they compiled books that were illustrated with photographs. Cherry later made a name for himself through his photography of African wildlife. Richard, in his autobiographical *At Home with Wild Nature* (1922), wrote of his love for Swaledale, mentioning 'its fresh, cool breezes, grey limestone crags, and chattering becks tumbling over mossy boulders'.

When, in 1580, a church was built at Muker and land consecrated for burial, it was no longer necessary to convey the bodies of the dead for 12 miles, in some cases, along the grimly-named Corpse Way for burial at the parish church of Grinton. The journey could not usually be undertaken in a day. The bearers, who worked in relays, carried a wicker basket, which was lighter and less rigid than a coffin. The sad little party would cross the 'island hill' of Kisdon, ford the river Swale, ascend the northern bank and take the high road to Gunnerside, climbing still higher before descending to Reeth, and thence to the parish church at Grinton.

At Low Row are traces of what life was like on the old common pastures. Much of the roadside land between here and Gunnerside is open grazing, which explains the presence of traffic signs featuring a cow. In summer, cattle seen on the main road are there by ancient right. The pasture is stocked from May until October and is administered by a committee which meets annually to discuss such matters as the date on which the 'break' (turning-out day for cattle) occurs. The maximum number of cattle allowed on the common is 128. Years ago, some cattle were milked on the common, the milker sitting on a three-legged stool and transporting the milk back to the farmhouse kitchen by back can.

The basic grazing unit is a stint or gait, which in this instance represents the pasturage of a cow. In winter, three sheep per gait are permitted. Low Row Common extends from the road to a stone wall at the edge of the moor. Moorland sheep have been known to dodge round it and descend to lusher grazings. Such sheep are 'partial' to garden plants! Within living memory, up to 20 farm horses have been grazed near the houses and farms under ancient right, one horse being equal to two gaits. Geese are 'stockable', but this does not apply to hens, which cannot be restrained or controlled. The land is rested for about six weeks in spring. Huts were once permitted on the common, the charge for a hut being a shilling per annum.

45   *The edge of Low Row Common, Swaledale.*

The junction of Swaledale and Arkengarthdale is at Reeth, which occupies a commanding position on the slopes of Mount Calva, and was awarded a market charter in 1695. It was important as a market at a time when local industries included lead-mining and hand-knitting. A boost came in the 18th century with the turnpiking of the road to Tan Hill. The population reached 1,300 but is now about 350, many more people being evident in summer when roadsides on and around the huge sloping green are packed with the cars of day-trippers. The Swaledale Folk Museum is full of local interest. The village also has a pottery where the products are inspired by features and creatures of Dales life.

Arkengarthdale, a northern offshoot of the valley of the Swale, begins near Reeth and peters out some 11 miles later on the way to Tan Hill. The main road is unfenced at both ends and sheep are at liberty to cross. A road beginning near the *CB Inn* traverses the Stang Pass to Barnard Castle. Another, heading south, connects with Swaledale at Low Row. Arkengarthdale is drained by Arkle Beck, a name derived from a doughty Norseman, Arkil, who enclosed a tract of land. There is one village, Langthwaite, which achieved modern fame in a curious way. Its bridge appeared in an introductory sequence to BBC television films based on the writings of Alf Wight, alias James Herriot.

The church in Arkengarthdale is unusual, being one of the 'Waterloo' churches constructed in 1817 with money provided by parliament when there was concern, following the French Revolution, about an increase in freethinking, this being considered a threat to the British establishment. The *CB Inn* is named after Charles Bathurst, the grandson of Dr. John Bathurst, physician to Cromwell and a somewhat high-handed individual, who purchased the Manor of Arkengarthdale from the Crown in 1656, but showed the favourable side of his character when he founded a Free School in 1657 and arranged for the master to receive £16 a year.

Dr. John might have exploited the labour of the fathers but he was liberal over the education of their sons. The Bathursts, father, son and grandson, the last two named Charles, were considerable mine owners. They built a hexagonal powder house in 1807 where the main smelt mills were situated. The smelt mills have gone but the powder house remains. The Bathurst connection with Arkengarthdale ended in 1912, which was also when the mines closed. When the family was still a power in the land, a visitor to the dale was Charles Fothergill, who noted, in 1805, that the main amusements among the miners were fives, cricket, wrestling and leaping. Belts were wrestled for and gloves were given to the best leapers. He heard that the men of Arkengarthdale were famous for their skill at football, a sport popular in the lead-mining communities but one which had been dropped 'in consequence of accidents happening not unfrequently, particularly broken legs in consequence of the players wearing such terrible thick shoes armed with iron'. In later times, miners used a Mechanics' Institute at C.B. Terrace and smallholders had their Cow Club.

Fothergill described the miners as being generally tall and muscular,

> tho' not particularly stout nor of very healthy appearance in the face. They wear a kind of short shirt or jerkin over their cloaths made of coarse linen or canvass ... On their feet they wear very formidable clogs, so large, loose and ponderous that they give their wearers a peculiarly lingy and awkward gait; they must be worn large and loose because the soles, being made of thick wood and shod with iron cannot spring or be in any degree elastic: there is more iron put round the soles of these clogs than is used in the shoes or plates of race horses; indeed it is nailed on and formed in a similar manner.

Some of the women walked to the Old Gang, knitting socks as they went and earning a shilling for a 12-hour day at the mine. Among them was Old Ruth, who had an invalid husband. She smoked a clay pipe and carried food in a white-spotted red handkerchief. Instead of eating it in the warmth of the blacksmith's shop at Old Gang, she went outdoors. One day a woman followed Ruth and saw her open her handkerchief, which was full of stones, she had given her dinner to her ailing husband but was too proud to admit there was nothing for her to eat. Such women did the domestic chores when they returned home and had children 'amanghands'.

Arkengarthdale is given character by the varied appearance of its six hamlets. The place attracting most interest is Booze, reached by road from Langthwaite. The other hamlets are Arkle Town, High Green, Eskeleth, Seal Houses and Whaw, beyond which the road–a former turnpike–makes its lonely way to Tan Hill. The scatter of buildings at Booze has a name said to mean 'a house on a curve'. Alfred J. Brown wrote of Booze in 1952 that 'despite its encouraging name, it is about the most teetotal hamlet I have ever explored hopefully from end to bitter end'. It was not always 'dry'. In 1840, it had an inn, and also a chapel, necessary in a community of 42 houses, most of the residents being lead-miners. At Arkle Town was an inn called *The Jolly Dogs*. The dale used to have five inns and four beerhouses. Sir Walter Scott stayed at *Lily Jock*. Attached to the inn were rooms used as a miners' club. On special occasions, such as a Club Walk, the miners wore off-white fustian trousers, coats with tails, known locally as claw-hammer jackets, and cravats in which *Lily Jock* pins were stuck.

Chert, a hard, flint-like stone varying in colour from a deep slate-blue to almost pure white, was recovered from Fremington Edge in the early part of this century. The chert was hacked out by hand in small blocks and loaded into wagons operating along narrow gauge rails leading from the entrance to the mine. It was ground into a fine powder and used in the manufacture of chinaware.

St Andrew's Church, Grinton, which at one time presided over one of the largest parishes in the country, was founded in Norman times by the monks of Bridlington. It is an impressive building, like a small cathedral, the style being Perpendicular, though there is much work dating from Norman and medieval times. The castellated building at the moor-edge, high above the village, was a shooting lodge which, in the 1940s, became a youth hostel. During 1996, the main consolidation programme at Grinton Smelt Mill was completed.

Back in the main dale, Marrick had a nunnery which at the time of the Dissolution in 1539 had a prioress and 16 nuns. Subsequently, the priory church was used for public worship. A few substantial pieces remain of the old priory.

Richmond, the market town for much of Swaledale, was not mentioned in Domesday Book, growing up beside a castle in an area of great strategic importance; Stanwick, a little to the north, had been a Brigantean stronghold, and Roman troops had been based at *Cataractonium* (Catterick). Alan Rufus (Alan the Red), whose cousin was Count of Brittany, chose, in 1071, to build his castle on an eminence beside the Swale, the name Richmond being Norman and meaning 'strong hill'.

The big cobbled market place of Richmond is rarely quiet. Over the years it has seen dalesfolk and others assembling to sell farm produce–butter, eggs and livestock. The fairs at which men were hired for work on the farms took place here. There is still a Saturday market, with stalls, continuing a tradition that spans nine centuries. The traditional bell-ringing continues at Holy Trinity, once a church, now the Green Howards' museum. The prentice bell is rung at 8 a.m. and the curfew at 8 p.m. each day. On Shrove Tuesday, the sound of the pancake bell is heard and housewives prepare to fry the pancakes. The Georgian Theatre is one of the two oldest in the land. It was built by actor-manager Samuel Butler as part of his Northern circuit and was opened in 1787. Among the actors who appeared in productions here were Kean and Kemble. The theatre fell into disuse in the 1840s and after a chequered career was re-opened as a theatre in May 1963. Thus does Richmond take care of its most interesting features.

10

WENSLEYDALE

JOHN WESLEY, HAVING CROSSED from Swaledale into Wensleydale in 1790, described his new surroundings as 'the largest by far of all the Dales and the most beautiful'. Charles Kingsley, parson, novelist and enthusiast for the north country, shared Wesley's impressions of Wensleydale. Here was a 'beautiful oasis in the mountains' and 'the richest spot in all England'. Wesley, a bustling servant of the Lord, shuddered at the bleak hills, acknowledged beauty where he found it and rejoiced in his converts to Methodism. Kingsley, whose chief Dales pleasure was tempting the lordly trout to the hook, did have a local connection as canon of the collegiate church of Middleham. He was, indeed, the last canon for the collegiate foundation was suppressed by Act of Parliament in 1845. Some people have revelled in Wensleydale's botanical wealth–some 700 species. Dr. Arnold Lees wrote that this dale

ranks second only to Teesdale in the richness and variety of its plantlife ... by reason of the successive alternations of shales, flagrock, limestone and grits which its slopes present, from the Yore bed at 500 feet altitude to the fell ridges at over 2,000 feet.

The valley is named after the village of Wensley which, though of modest size, was its only market town during the 13th century. The river Ure, anciently Yore, has its nursery reaches in a wild, remote area. In contrast, the main dale is broad, verdant and open-ended, providing with the extension offered by the deep trough of Garsdale a spendid east-west route through the Pennines. Jervaulx, as applied to a local abbey, is derived from Yoredale, a name commonly used until the start of the 18th century. The name Yoredale was chosen by the Yorkshire geologist John Phillips (1836) for a group of strata which is locally prominent and which he examined and described. The Yoredale Way, a long distance footpath, begins in York and passes through Wensleydale to end at Kirkby Stephen, a distance of 100 miles.

46 *John Wesley, a visitor to the Yorkshire Dales, where Methodism became well established.*

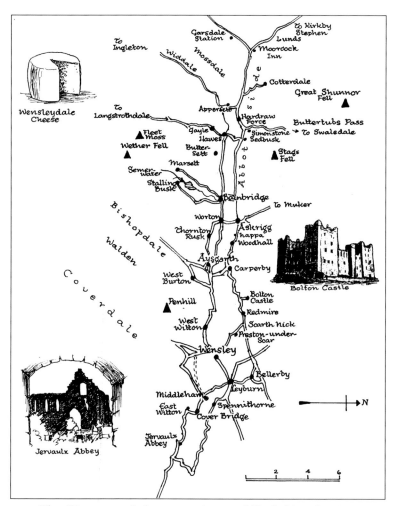

Wensleydale

The Ure, one of the great rivers of Yorkshire, begins among the rush-bobs at Ure Head, on Lunds Fell, and is inconspicuous to travellers for most of its course, the valley being so broad there are two roads with the river taking a quiet course in between. To see the Ure at its most spirited, a visitor uses a link road at Aysgarth, where the river descends 26 ft. on broad limestone steps. In the higher dale, near *The Moorcock Inn*, the bed of the river is on the 1,000 ft. contour. From here for 26 miles, to Kilgram Bridge, the Ure flows through a benevolent countryside.

In 1805, Charles Fothergill and a friend named Dinsdale set out from Simonstone to visit the source of the Ure, 'which I have long wished to see. I moreover wished to know how far the maps are correct: we furnished ourselves with a wallet containing some cold provisions and a small bottle of rum, beside our drawing utensils.' They walked to where 'the romantic stream of Cotterdale' had its confluence with the major river.

> Our road for the greater part lay over wild uncultivated moors feeding a few Scots and black-faced sheep, amongst high and bleak hills with the river Ure now in a little compass winding and foaming in the bottom with her banks naked and bare and unadorned even by a single tree ... Having walked about 6 miles, Wild Boar Fell and Bow [Baugh] Fell made their magnificent appearance.

The main dale is flanked by scarped hills, including Addleborough (1,542 ft.) and Penhill Beacon (1,685 ft.), a notable viewpoint, marginally lower than the highest point on Penhill Crags (1,726 ft.). The name Addleborough is derived from the Old Norse, *Authulf's burh*, and perhaps the skeleton found beneath a cairn was that of the ancient chief. Wensleydale is generally a quiet dale, though in periods of torrential rain Hardraw Force, a magnificent waterfall, roars out like a prophet in the wilderness. At Hardraw, a beck from Great Shunner Fell (2,349 ft.) plunges over the limestone lip of Hardraw Scar and descends unimpeded for 90 ft. into a plunge pool. A novel approach to the great waterfall is through an inn, the *Green Dragon*, a path following the gorge which the fall has eroded back for about 1,000 ft. The Wordsworths, William and Dorothy, were at Hardraw in the winter of 1799, the year in which they had settled at Grasmere, in their native Lake District. As they stood behind the waterfall, they marvelled at the pendant icicles, which were 'lofty and magnificent'. The artist Turner sketched the fall and worked his impressions up into a splendid canvas. In recent times, the gorge, with its impressive acoustics, has been the setting for band contests and for a time choirs mustered at the head of the fall for competitive events.

Wensleydale draws to itself a number of little dales. Some, like Mossdale and Fossdale, are diminutive. Others, like Cotterdale, have a tucked-away character. Cotterdale, a Nordic name, said to mean 'the valley with huts', is a half-forgotten little valley, once populated by three families, the Halls, Kirks and Kings, hence a frequently quoted couplet: 'Three halls, two kirks and a king; Same road out as goes in.' It is now the setting for a sprawling conifer forest, though there are plans to offset the effect of grim regimentation by planting some other species for variety. What was grandly known as 'The High Way', at the mouth of the valley, was a pre-turnpike track, following a band of limestone in otherwise soggy terrain on its steep way by Cotter End, thence to Hell Gill and Mallerstang. The turnpike kept to the lower ground.

Gayle and Hawes are close neighbours but differ in background and appearance. Gayle, the older place, was the Norse *geil* or ravine, a reference to Duerley Beck, which has a ford as well as a bridge and lively waterfalls. The three-storey mill at Gayle, a unique survival of early industrialisation, occupies a site by Gayle Beck. Constructed in 1784 as a 'cotton factory', it is thought to be the earliest mill of its type to survive unaltered. The internal timber construction of North American pitch pine for the roof and floors would presumably have been hand-hewn before being shipped across the Atlantic. Raw material for the textile machinery was transported by packhorse from ports on the west coast.

The mill had ceased to be used for processing cotton by the early 19th century. It was adapted for processing flax and then wool, supplying yarn to the local hand-knitting industry. Towards the end of the century, Gayle Mill became a saw-mill. The waterwheel was replaced by a water turbine, built and supplied by Williamson Bros. of Kendal in 1878. It is believed to be the oldest *in situ* turbine in the world. The machinery installed was capable of converting tree trunks to finished products. Early in the 20th century, the turbine also generated electricity for public lighting in the village. A second turbine, built by Gilkes in 1920, produced electric light for the mill itself.

To Alfred J. Brown, a hill walker with a fanciful turn of phrase, Hawes was 'a grey, rugged market town with a cobbled main street, narrowing near the bottom, and with its houses and inns hobnobbing together'. It was marked on Saxton's map of 1577 as Horse-house, from the Norse *hals*, meaning a narrow pass, possibly that up Widdale. Situated in an area which in medieval times was forest, Hawes was soon the main trading centre of the upper dale though it did not become a market town until 1700. It evolved steadily through the 18th and 19th centuries, benefiting from the re-routing through Hawes in 1795 of the Lancaster-Richmond turnpike.

47   *Market day at Hawes in Wensleydale.*

Charles Fothergill, staying with relatives in Wensleydale in 1805, visited Hawes Fair, which was held on the day prior to the more celebrated Brough Hill Fair, notable for its cattle and ponies, which were known hereabouts as Galloways. Fothergill observed that the little Galloways, bred amongst the hills, had never been broken in.

> They are driven from the moors, on which they have roamed like shaggy bears from the day of their birth, to the fair in large companies ... This race of horses is chiefly confined to the mountains and even there they are gradually becoming less and less numerous.

Livestock was sold in the main street until 1887, when the auction mart was built. Hawes acquired a market hall in 1902 and hosts one of the principal autumn sales of Swaledale tups.

At the point of convergence of several important roads, Hawes is sufficiently far away from other towns to have retained a strong local character. The next populous places, Kirkby Stephen, Sedbergh, Leyburn and Ingleton, are about 16 miles away. A railway link with the outer world was secured in the 1870s, when the Midland branch from Garsdale, on the Settle-Carlisle, joined up with the North Eastern system. From Hawes, by rail, were despatched farm products, milk and cheese, and vast quantities of stone from local quarries. The branch line was closed in 1954 but the Wensleydale Railway Association was established in 1990 to investigate the possible reinstatement of a passenger rail link between Garsdale and Northallerton on the East Coast Main Line. At present, the only remaining track on the 40-mile route is the 22 miles linking the East Coast line with a railhead at Redmire. Meanwhile, the old station goods shed is now part of an extended Upper Dales Folk Museum, based on a collection of Dales bygones donated by Marie Hartley and Joan Ingilby.

A local celebrity, Kit Calvert, was born at Burtersett, began his working life as a farm lad down at Colby Hall, near Askrigg, and became widely known in 1935 as the saviour of the Wensleydale cheese industry. When it seemed that the local creamery would be closed, Kit and others took on the factory production of cheese which Edward Chapman had begun in 1897 in a substantial beckside building. He bought milk from local farmers, who in those days were keeping the dual-purpose Shorthorn cattle, and manufactured cheese on a larger scale than was possible domestically.

Cheese-making thrived under Kit. According to him, the farmhouse variety of 'Wensleydale' had its demise in the Second World War, at the start of which there were still over 100 Dales farmers' wives who made this type of cheese. High-moisture cheese did not fit in with the Ministry of Food's rationing scheme, for weight might be lost through evaporation. Therefore, much of the farmhouse Wensleydale was reprocessed for distribution among the armed services. Farmers' wives, who had been proud of their products, were disheartened when they heard that their cheese was simply re-mulched. By 1945 only six farmhouse cheese-makers were left. None of them was in Wensleydale, five being in Teesdale and one in Swaledale.

Cheese-making remains a major feature of the industrial life of Hawes. Another threat of closure occurred in May 1992, when a firm called Dales Crest, having decided that cheese production would be moved from Hawes to a larger creamery in Lancashire, shut the Wensleydale Dairy, having sacked its 59 workers. A management buy-out was agreed and cheese-making resumed under the direction of Alice Amsden, David Hartley, Michael Webster and Richard Clarke. Dairy Crest had stripped the creamery and £50,000 had to be raised to buy second-hand cheese-making plant in addition to the £300,000 for the six-acre site. A workforce of 13 resumed production, and in the first year 450 tons of Wensleydale cheese were made. A leaflet issued to visitors describes the appearance, texture and taste of this well-known dairy product: 'When you remove the muslin, you will find inside the rich yellow rind, a delicious creamy-white flaky cheese with a fresh, clean, slightly honeyed aroma.' The texture is said to be firm but not dry and hard. When sliced, the surface is slightly uneven and open, not solid and smooth like a processed cheese. Taste? 'Mild, but with a full creamy flavour which is unique. Eat it with crisp apple, apple pie or with fruit cake.'

The ambition from the start was to use all the milk which Wensleydale farmers could provide. By this time the Shorthorns had been succeeded by the pied Friesian cattle. A visitor centre at the creamery introduces visitors to cheese-making and keeps alive the memory of Kit Calvert, whose portrait by local artist Barbara Drew, showing him with old trilby at the back of his head and clay pipe in mouth, appears on the labels. Kit not only presided over the cheese factory; he owned a remarkable little bookshop in which patrons who wished to buy a book when there was no attendant present left their money on a chapel collecting plate.

48 *Fred Taylor with some dairy utensils collected in the Dales for a private museum at the dairy in West Marton.*

A preacher in the old style, he also translated part of the Bible into Wensleydale dialect. His local version of chapter XV of St Luke's Gospel begins: 'Noo, aw t'Taxgitherers an' knockaboots crooded roond ta hear Him, an' t'Pharasees an' t'Lawyers chuntered an' said, "This feller tek's up wi' good fer nowts, an' itts wi' 'em".' In his translation of St John's Gospel, chapter XXI, Kit dealt in true Dales fashion with the words of Christ and his disciples: 'He ca'ed oot tew 'em, "Lads, hey ye caught owt?" Th' shooted back, "Nowt!" Sooa He sez, "Kest yet net ower t'reet side ev t'booat an' ye'll git a catch." Seea th' threw t'net inta t'watter, an' th'cudn't rive't back fer t'weet o' fish in't.'

Burtersett, a village on higher ground, became a major centre for quarrying from the 1860s, with a peak about 1890 and a steady decline to closure in the 1920s. The products of Burtersett were varied. Suitable material became roofing 'slate'. This and some of the best stone was transported from Hawes railway station from 1878. They were needed by the fast-growing towns of the Lancashire textile belt. Poor quality stone had its use for drystone walling. At Burtersett, the quarrymen were actually miners, removing the best stone from drifts which penetrated the hillside for anything up to half a mile, pillars being left to support the roof. Because no explosives could be used, the men had the laborious task of cutting out the stone with hand-drills. It was 'desperate' work but reasonably healthy. The men gave the sections they created some striking names—Peacock's End, Redgate and Fancy End.

Burtersett stone was brought out of the workings by pony and truck. The worked-out areas were back-filled, leaving comparatively little evidence in the form of heaps of rubble at the surface. The horses which transported the stone were of the Shire type, large and hefty. Mostly they had been bought at the special fairs, such as Askrigg Hill, held in early July as the farmers were preparing for haytime, and Brough Hill, which took place at the end of September. The subterranean world was aglow with the light of tallow candles, bought a hundredweight at a time from Candle Willie (Metcalfe), of Hawes. He rendered down mutton or beef fat in a container over a wire. The 'wicks' for the candles were draped from a wheel-like structure and were gently lowered into the fat. As they were drawn out with equal care, some of the fat adhered to the wicks. The size of a candle was determined by the number of times a wick entered the cauldron. The candles were sold according to the number of dips, twelve dips creating a candle which was no thicker than a finger. The popular cottage size, which could be rammed into a candlestick, had been dipped 16 times. The quarrymen used 20s and the 24s, which were even more durable, found a place in trap lamps.

The village of Bainbridge, named after a river crossing, was an important Roman fort. Many centuries later, in 1227, it became a new settlement associated with the Forest of Wensleydale, which took in the upper dale, the forest keepers living at Bainbridge. By the 14th century it was customary for cattle to be agisted (summered) in the Forest of Wensleydale, and in 1573 such an arrangement enabled Sir Christopher Metcalfe of Nappa Hall to benefit financially from such a scheme, at a cost of £3 9s. The village prospered when, in 1751, the Lancaster-Richmond turnpike road was re-routed through it, travellers seeking overnight hospitality here before braving Cam High Road, the approach to which the Hon. John Byng had described as 'one of the longest, steepest and most stoney in great Britain'. The watercourse, which negotiates a series of natural limestone steps, has the grand title of River Bain, though it flows for only 2½ miles from its source at the lake to the point where it loses its identity in the Ure.

A road from Bainbridge climbs over a hill to a cluster of little dales, notably Raydale or Roedale (from roe deer). For two months of the year, the sun does not shine directly on Raydale House. The main settlements in Raydale are Countersett, which in Norse times was a *saeter* or *sheiling*, and Stalling Busk, 'the bushy place with stallions'. Busk (as it is locally known) throve with the traffic on the Stake Pass from upper Wharfedale, and here were to be found church and school. The old chapel, constructed shrewdly on a drumlin between the village and Semerwater, and dating from 1603, is now a ruin, but dignified and well cared for in its decline. A new church has taken its place and a Methodist chapel at Marsett, just across the dale, is of early 19th-century date.

Much of the fell country is common land. Grazing by livestock is regulated by the old system of stints. The concept of an acre has less relevance in a large area where there might be unproductive bogs or outcropping rock. One of the ancient minute books, relating to Marsett, includes the following ponderous phraseology:

> And I do Hereby Direct that one calf be admitted in respect of one Stint or Right of Pasture; that one yearling heifer or Ox be admitted in respect of two Stints or Rights of Pasture; that one two-years-old Heifer or Ox be admitted in respect of four Stints or Rights of Pasture; that one Cow or Ox three years old or upwards be admitted in respect of Six Stints or Rights of Pasture; and that one Horse be admitted in respect of 12 Stints or Rights of Pasture to the said regulated Pasture called Marsett Green and Rigg ...

The other stinted area is Bardale. At one time Wether Fell was in a similar category, and people from Bainbridge had a right to put geese on Wether Fell even if they did not have a right to graze sheep.

The hamlet of Marsett is said to be on the 'sunny' side and Stalling Busk, high up, at the approaches to Stake Pass, is on 'the money side'. At the Methodist chapel in Marsett the Christmas carol service has been held by candlelight. Busk has two churches, one (as noted) a picturesque, roofless ruin, not far from the lake; there is no road to it—just five footpaths. The new church, built in 1908-9 at a cost of £300, is unusual, with its internal scissor-beam roof supports and a lean-to roof to the baptistry. An extension to the roof protects the single bell. The old school is now a social centre.

Semerwater, a name derived from the Old English *sae*, a lake, and *maer*, a marshy pool, had its origins in the Ice Age when meltwater gathered behind a moraine. The lake was formerly much larger than it is today. A third of Semerwater and adjacent marsh and

49   *Semerwater in Raydale, near Bainbridge.*

wet pasture are situated within a reserve owned by the Yorkshire Wildlife Trust. The floral treasures include bogbean and four species of willow. Semerwater receives water from Crook Beck, which in turn is fed by the becks draining Bardale, Raydale and Cragdale. The outlet was dredged to lower the water level by two feet ten inches. Notorious for its flash-floods, water has been known to overlap the Carlow Stone, a large erratic named from the Celtic *caer*, a rock, which stands near the outflow.

An old tale of a settlement flooded because of its inhospitality to a beggar probably had a basis in lake dwellings of a Neolithic people. Dick Chapman, who spent his later years at Bainbridge, had a bronze spearhead which had been picked up on the northern shore, not far from where he suspected such lake dwellings to have been. The simple structures, if they existed, evolved in Sir William Watson's great poem, 'The Ballad of Semerwater', into an imposing place, being:

> A mickle town and tall,
> King's tower and Queen's bower,
> And the wakeman on the wall.

Today, motor boats with skiers in tow criss-cross the lake in summer. Since 1956, a service has been held at the lake on August Bank Holiday Sunday, when the local vicar preaches from a floating pulpit—a boat on the lake—while on shore the Hawes Silver Band accompanies the hymn singing. In winter, at Semerwater, the voices of whooper swans, refugees from Iceland, are sometimes to be heard.

Askrigg received a market charter from Elizabeth I in 1587 but lost its importance rather more than a century later when Hawes was granted a charter and took over much of the trading. The market cross, near St Oswald's Church, is a reminder of past glories, as indeed is the church itself, with its substantial tower and a fine peal of bells which is heard each Sunday. St Oswald's is largely of the 15th century, with 16th-century additions. When the Old Hall, dating from 1678, burnt down in 1935, Askrigg lost a venerable building, though much of the rest of the village is old enough not to be obtrusive. From a distance, the buildings blend with the landforms.

Askrigg was the first village in the Dales to be lit by electricity, the pioneer being William Handley Burton, a local millwright, joiner, general builder and maker of hay-rakes, who in about 1900 met some Lancashire electrical engineers and heard how, in Italy, the mountain torrents were used to drive electric generators. Returning to Askrigg, Burton studied Mill Gill Force, a mile west of the village, as a potential source of power. In 1910, at Mill Gill House, William Burton and Ernest, his son, pulled the switch by which their home became the first in the dale to have electric lighting. The *Darlington and Stockton Times* for 15 October 1910 reported:

> Mr. Burton, of Askrigg, has purchased a portion of the old Arkle Mill and has repaired the mill-dam. Soon the old building will be demolished preparatory to the building of an electric power station so, in the future, Reeth will be illuminated by electric light.

The building remained standing but its inside was gutted to find space for the turbine and generating plant.

In 1814, when George Walker compiled his *The Costume of Yorkshire*, he could confidently include a plate showing 'The Wensleydale Knitters at Askrigg', and he wrote that

> their wants ... are few; but to supply these, almost constant labour is required. In any business where the assistance of the hands is not necessary, they universally resort to knitting. Young and old, male and female, are all adept in this art. Shepherds attending their flocks, men driving cattle, women going to market, are all thus industriously and doubly employed.

When building Nappa Hall in about 1460, Thomas Metcalfe had provision made for two towers—a west tower was the main unit, a hall was central, and the eastern part was in the form of a lower tower which housed the service rooms. The Metcalfes, who have a strong association with Nappa Hall, form a clan in the sense that everyone bearing that name and its several variants have a common ancestor in one William de Dent, not de Wensleydale, the 'calf' in the name being a hill, Calf Top, overlooking Dentdale. In 1194, when that eminence was divided into three, William, who was head warden of the Royal Forest, bagged the central piece and was known as William de Medecalf.

Sir Christopher Metcalfe, Sheriff of York in 1556, impressed the county by forming a bodyguard of 300 of 'his own name and kindred, all mounted on white horses and clad in uniform'. It is questionable whether the horses were white. The type favoured by the family was the grey. As with the modern muster of the Metcalfe Society, some of the bodyguard, though having some Metcalfe blood flowing through their veins, might have borne other surnames. Nappa, incidentally, means 'turnip patch'.

In June 1617, a squabble between Sir Thomas Metcalfe of Nappa and William Robinson of Worton flared up over the lease of land to such an extent a force of about forty men bearing guns, swords, pikes and other warlike instruments was used when Sir Thomas laid siege to Raydale House. This little army was reported to have stopped at the *Rose and Crown* in Bainbridge on their way to Raydale. The affair lasted three days and one of the attackers was killed. Three days after the siege of Raydale House began, a relief force of sergeant and soldiers arrived from York. Ten years more elapsed before the right of tenancy of Raydale was settled, in favour of the Robinsons. Sir Thomas, along with Lady Metcalfe and followers, was heavily fined and he was also imprisoned.

The parish church at Aysgarth is big, set in an extensive graveyard, a consequence of the time when it was the largest parish in England, presiding over 80,000 acres of the upper dale. The churchyard covers five acres. Today's church, which is conspicuously Victorian, replaced a building of the 13th century. In the chancel is a rood screen dating from the early 16th century, which was conveyed from Jervaulx Abbey to Aysgarth at the Dissolution. The Ure is spanned here, just below the upper of three sets of waterfalls, by a bridge which springs from one rock ledge to another and was widened in 1788. In the tourist boom, the bridge was a prime vantage point and cars were known to stop here so the occupants might get out to admire the view; the bridge is now distinguished by having double yellow lines! The large number of visitors are accommodated by a car park between the river and the old rail track. An information centre has recently been refurbished. One footpath takes a woodland way to the bridge, and another path enters Freeholders' Wood, with viewing areas for the middle and lower falls.

Yore Mills, which dates from 1784, is used as a carriage museum. As industrial premises, the mills have a fascinating history, originally built for worsted yarns but later turning to cotton. A fire of 1850 gutted the building but it was soon rebuilt and produced, among many other products, red shirts for Garibaldi's army. The premises became a corn mill, and so it remained, using water turbines installed by Gilkes of Kendal in the 1930s, until 1968, by which time it had become a depot for the distribution of animal foodstuffs.

Aysgarth Falls have impressed tourists for centuries. The three groups of falls at Aysgarth have the neat appearance caused by the erosion of beds of limestone. Geologically, they are in steady retreat upstream. Some 8,000 years ago, the local glacier, in slow retreat, left a mix of clay and stones (boulder clay) which created an impervious barrier behind which a lake was formed. When water flowed over the barrier there began a process of erosion which reached the Yoredale series of rocks and cut through them to where the Great Scar Limestone, which now forms the river bed, lay. The stepped appearance came

50   *The Low Falls at Aysgarth in Wensleydale.*

into being through the erosion of an underlying layer of shale, which undercut the limestone and broke it off. Bishop Pococke (1751) compared Aysgarth Falls favourably with the
cataracts of the Nile. John Ruskin, the Victorian philosopher and art critic, thought of them
as being 'out and out the finest thing in water I've seen in these islands ... the rocks going
out in perfectly flat tables'. This area was 'wilder than the Highlands'.

Freeholders' Wood, some thirteen hectares purchased by the Dales Park Authority in
1982, is named after the rights held by Carperby villagers. This is a survival of a coppiced
wood which has not outgrown itself. The wood, which is predominantly of hazel, also
includes ash, wych elm, rowan, birch, holly and wild cherry. It continues to be coppiced
in the old way, whereby broad-leaved trees are cut down to the stools (stumps) and throw
out poles (new shoots) which in due course can be harvested every few years. The poles
had a number of uses, from firewood to fencing. In spring, wood anemones and bluebells
carpet the woodland floor.

Bishopdale, some six miles in length, the largest of the tributary valleys of Wensley-
dale, extends from near Aysgarth to where Kidstones Pass gives a high-level approach to
Wharfedale. It is a fertile dale, the fine soil being formed of silt from a large glacial lake.
The Nevilles of Middleham had Bishopdale Chase from the middle of the 15th century.
Some of the most attractive farmhouses of the 17th century are to be seen at Thoralby and
Newbiggin. West Burton, one of a trio of unspoilt villages, has a huge triangular green from
the side of which access is gained to the secluded valley known as Walden, where two
roads connect the farmsteads, the longest road ending near a farmstead called Kentucky.
Beyond this point, in an area where coal and lead were mined, a moorland track leads to
Wharfedale, making the final descent into Starbotton.

Back in Wensleydale, the valley is dominated visually by the sandstone castle of the Scrope family (pronounced 'Scroop'). They were here as early as the 13th century, a William le Scrope paying an annual rental of nine shillings in 1285. The Scropes went up in the world when William's son became Sir Henry and was at different times Chief Justice of England and Chief Baron of the Exchequer. Bolton Castle, which has corner towers each nearly 100 ft. high, stands in isolated majesty on an exposed hillside. It was built for Richard Scrope, who became the first Lord Scrope in 1371. He was granted a licence in 1379 to crenellate his manor with a wall of stone and lime. His plan was not for a castle (there is no moat) but, in effect, apartments within a secure area. The master mason, John Lewyn, who was well known as a rebuilder of castles, was employed to carry out the work, using stone quarried on Ellerlands Edge, not far away, and timbers reputed to have been brought from the Penrith district of Cumberland on ox-wagons, via Lunds, Askrigg and Carperby. Bolton Castle, completed in 1399, cost Richard the impressive sum of £12,000.

The most notable occurrence at Bolton was the stay here of the doomed Mary, Queen of Scots and her 40-strong retinue. Her term in Wensleydale lasted from 13 July 1568, until 26 January 1569, while she was in the custody of the ninth Baron Scrope and Sir Thomas Knollys. Mary had been at Carlisle Castle for 19 years. Sir Francis Knollys, who was deputed by Queen Elizabeth to check the suitability of Bolton Castle, found it to be 'very strong, very fair and very stately after the old manner of building. It is the highest walled house that I have seen.' Mary and her followers had comfortable quarters and, in the case of Mary, a view across landscaped ground, deer parks and the main dale to Pen Hill. There was a special treat for her each week when venison was on the menu. She was also allowed to hunt. Mary was moved on, and in 1587, still proclaiming her Catholic faith, was taken to the scaffold and executed. The church of St Oswald, first recorded at the end of the 14th century, relatively small, aisle-less, and contemporary with the castle, is literally over-shadowed by the larger building.

The village plan, its long green overlooked by a neat arrangement of house plots (or tofts), is a delight to visitors. The plots lying south of the village green date from the period just after the Civil War, when Castle Bolton was laid out afresh. There is a memorial in the church to Fred Lawson, who arrived in the village for a month's holiday in 1910 and died here in 1968. The inscription reads: 'A man for all seasons, Fred Lawson, artist and good companion, 1888-1968'.

Bolton was at one time the home of lead-miners employed in nearby Apedale. Redmire, a name which is probably derived from a reed-fringed mere (long since drained), was, like Bolton, frequented by miners, and Thomas Maude, a poet who wrote about the village in 1780, began one verse with the words: 'Of Redmire's mining town how shall we sing?' Happily, the mines were tucked out of sight, over the rim of the moor, and Redmire retained its delightful unpretentious appearance, its houses set round a green. G.L. Harriman (1982) recalled Redmire Feast as

> a picturesque remnant of the old Feast held on the green ... It was, in the old days, the holiday of the year. People who had left the village came back and every house was full ... Donkey racing and quoiting were two of the main features. Another game still played is wallops, in which skittles were put on the ground and a stick thrown at them to knock as many down as possible in one 'go' ... The young men of the village dressed up and went from house to house begging cheesecakes.

Leyburn's importance is seen by a glance at a road map. The dale road here has several branches of 'A' classification–to Richmond, to Bedale and to Ripon. The largest of the Wensleydale settlements, the town has a broad market square ringed by houses, shops and inns. Its market charter was granted by Charles I and the market was moved from Tuesday to Friday in 1696. St Matthew's Church dates from 1836, and in 1858 the appearance of the town was enhanced by the Town Hall, now shops. Frances I'anson, the 'sweet lass of Richmond Hill', was born in Leyburn, not Richmond, though anyone going from Leyburn to Richmond via Bellerby is said to be going 'up Richmond Hill'. Leyburn Shawl, a limestone terrace 800 ft. above sea level, offers wide-ranging views of Wensleydale. The name is said, somewhat fancifully, to come from an incident when Mary, Queen of Scots, having escaped from Bolton Castle, dropped her shawl here. Shawl is more likely to be a corruption of the Norse *skali*, referring to huts used in summer by those who tended stock. The Leyburn Shawl Tea Festivals of last century were extremely popular, and in 1845 no fewer than 1,000 people had tea in a marquee while an estimated 2,000 strolled around or danced.

Middleham, two miles from workaday Leyburn, is a town which has kept the village 'feel'. It is notable for the substantial remains of a castle. Indeed, what was dubbed the 'Windsor of the North' has had two castles, the oldest of motte and bailey form, the style in early Norman times, known today as 'William's Hill'. The builder of the later castle, Ribald, was the brother of the Count Alan who was responsible for the initial work on Richmond Castle.

Middleham Castle, dating from 1170, has a Norman keep, said to be the largest in the north country. This settlement came into the possession of the Nevilles of Raby, in Teesdale, and its heyday was from 1461, when the youthful Duke of Gloucester (who would become Richard III) arrived here to be trained for a noble life by the Earl of Warwick. Richard married Anne, the Earl's daughter, in 1472, and in the following year their only son, Edward, was born at Middleham. Richard is well remembered in this little Wensleydale town, benevolent deeds including a collegiate foundation at St Alkelda's Church in 1478 and, in the following year, the ratification of the market charter which had been granted by Ralph Neville, Earl of Westmorland, a century earlier. The Swine Cross in the upper market place at Middleham commemorates this deed.

Middleham was Richard's home until 1483, when he became King of England. The 500th anniversary of his coronation was celebrated at Middleham in 1983, and at that time Middleham associated itself in friendship with the French village of Agincourt. Royal duties kept Richard in the south but he made one more visit to the north, in 1484, on the death of his son. Shortly afterwards, his wife died. Richard survived until only 1485, when he was slain at Bosworth. The castle was acquired by Henry VII but was allowed to fall into a state of disrepair, enjoying a brief time of importance in the Civil War when it accommodated prisoners.

Middleham church, dedicated to St Mary and St Alkelda, dates from around 1280 and, as noted, was made collegiate by Richard, Duke of Gloucester. Only two churches, Middleham and Giggleswick, have St Alkelda as their patron. Some people believe the name Alkelda, incorporating *keld*, refers to the spirit of a well taking the form, in popular thought, of a Saxon princess strangled by two heathen women while on her way to Middleham in about A.D. 800.

The town of Middleham is notable for many fine Georgian houses and inns, some of the gracious houses being associated with stables where racehorses are trained. Each morning, the clatter of hooves against the road marks the passage of strings of racehorses to the gallops on the 363-acre Low Moor, where up to the end of last century the celebrated Middleham livestock fair took place. In summer, the horses have a slightly longer journey to gallops on the High Moor, part of Pen Hill, a name which means 'hill-hill'. Pen Hill was part of the lordship of Middleham and the whole area, including the Forest of Wensleydale, belonged to the king. Charles I sold part of the lordship of Middleham to the citizens of

London in 1625. The land was subsequently split up and most of it bought by local people. Even then, horses were being exercised on the High Moor. Race meetings were first held at Middleham from 1739 and this was the first place in the land where what is now regarded as the modern way of training racehorses was employed. The track across the Low Moor, where are to be found the all-weather gallops, was once used by the illustrious Nevilles and their friends when on hunting excursions from Middleham Castle to Bishopdale Chase. The High Moor, used during the summer, is at that time empurpled by the blossom of large tracts of heather.

A dozen trainers continue to use the Yorkshire town from where, in 1849, Tom Fobert's horse, Flying Dutchman, won both the Derby and the St Leger. This achievement was exceeded in the 19th century by Tom Dawson and Johnny Osborne, the last-named riding a dozen Classic winners from 1846 until 1892. The Peacock family has brought renown to Middleham, Matt winning the Derby with Dante in 1945. Neville Crump produced three Grand National winners from Middleham and, in 1994, Mister Baileys, a racehorse belonging to Mark Johnston, won the 2000 Guineas in a record time.

51 *Middleham in Wensleydale.*

Coverdale is a world unto itself–too large to be thought of simply as an adjunct to Wensleydale, and in part a royal hunting forest of the lords of Middleham. Caldbergh is the reputed birthplace of Miles Coverdale, scholar and priest, who in 1535 was the first to translate the Bible into English. He was responsible, in 1539, for the publication of the Great Bible, a copy of which Henry VIII had decreed should be provided to every church in his realm. The road through Coverdale was no backwater, being at a much later period part of the well-used coach route between London and Richmond. The moors of Cover Head and South Walden were highly productive of grouse and within living memory, when there was a large well-managed estate, the average bag was 600 brace. The village of Horsehouse is so named because it stood at the crossing point of two packhorse routes– the major way, connecting Lancaster, Skipton and Middleham, another route from Walden, passing Fleensop colliery and lead mines. At Horsehouse packhorses were baited (fed).

The river Cover, some twelve miles in length and with a name derived from 'stream in a deep ravine', is fed by many moorland springs in the shadow of the two Whernsides, Great and Little, and joins the Ure at Ulshaw near Middleham. Carlton, with *The Forester's Arms*, comes fully to life on the second Wednesday in June every other year. It is then that the Foresters' Walk takes place. The Foresters, clad in green jackets, with peaked caps and green silk sashes, carry staves topped with carved emblems depicting forest animals, including deer and foxes. They are celebrating the founding of a court of The Ancient Order of Foresters on the banks of the Cover in 1837. Their procession starts in Carlton and, led by the Muker Silver Band, is concluded with celebrations at Melmerby. Before the days of social security, friendly societies such as this were formed in many villages.

52   Jervaulx Abbey was established in Wensleydale in 1156.

In the lower part of the valley, on private land, are what remains of the Premonstratensian Abbey of Coverham, dating from 1212. The Premonstratensian Order of White Canons moved to this sheltered part of Coverdale from Swainby, in the Vale of Mowbray, and were thus nearer Middleham Castle, from which they derived patronage. The abbey soon owned most of Coverdale, that part of Wharfedale around Kettlewell, and certain lands near Sedbergh. The most conspicuous remains are parts of the gatehouse and a double arch, part of the division between nave and south aisle which is of mid-14th century date. An awesome stillness is felt in Holy Trinity, once the parish church and now redundant, possibly because of its isolated position. The remains are well preserved. The inscriptions on local tombstones will give you much on which to ponder.

Jervaulx Abbey was established in 1156 by Cistercians, who had previously lived at Fors near Askrigg. They bred horses both here and in North Ribblesdale; they farmed and made ewe's milk cheese, the precursor of the Wensleydale which was subsequently made throughout the dale from the milk of the Shorthorn cow; and they had mining interests. Jervaulx suffered dissolution in 1536. The last abbot, Adam Sedbergh, was executed in 1537, having unwillingly taken part in the armed rebellion known as the Pilgrimage of Grace. Today, the remains of the abbey, in the grounds of what is now a hotel, may be visited, motorists using a car park across the road from the hotel entrance.

Kilgram Bridge–Leland's 'great old bridge of stone'–is said to mark the end of Wensleydale. A ponderous structure with six arches, this is one of the oldest bridges in Yorkshire, dating back to at least the 1540s.

11

WHARFEDALE

THE WHARFE, WHICH DRAINS one twentieth of Yorkshire, begins at Beckermonds, a hamlet with a Norse name which means 'meeting of the becks', the source streams arriving from Greenfield and Oughtershaw. The river has a catchment area extending to 1,008 square km and takes its name from *guerf*, meaning swift. The average flow is 17.4 cubic metres a second, except at floodtime, when the figure rises to 430 and the level of the water rises perceptibly. It is also topped up from the Skirfare, a river which flows down Littondale, the major tributary valley. Normally, the Wharfe seethes where it is pent in by rocks at Ghaistrills Strid, above Grassington, and at the Strid proper, on the Bolton Abbey estate.

Anglers venerate the brown trout of the Wharfe and about 70 per cent of the angling is done with wet flies. The trout run to about 1½ lb., their growth being related to the food supplies and size of the population. Joe Smith, who worked for the Burnsall Angling Club, had seen a Wharfe trout which weighed over 14 lb. Kilnsey Estates founded a fish farm, rearing rainbow trout within sight of the famous Crag which, with a height of 140 ft. and a overhang extending some 30 ft., is a dominant feature of the upper dale.

Walkers on the Dales Way, which was devised by Colin Speakman in 1970, best appreciate Wharfedale and the distinctive U-shape of its glacial trough. The sides are scored by V-shaped gills, where rushing water has cut deeply into the landscape and produced gravel patches on which villages such as Buckden, Starbotton and Kettlewell were built. The Dales Way of 73 miles follows the valley on its way from Ilkley to Bowness-on-Windermere. The section of Wharfedale within the Yorkshire Dales National Park, which ends near Bolton Bridge, is 23 miles long.

The headwaters of the becks which combine to form the River Wharfe are in an area which also sees the beginnings of Cam Beck, one of the principal tributaries of the Ribble. The Greenfield valley, through which lay a famous old packhorse route, is now largely swaddled with conifers, the new plantings extending to the north of Penyghent. Yet at the farmstead of Greenfield in the 1770s, when much open land was enclosed by drystone walls, the acidic soil was sweetened by an application of lime from field kilns. Oughtershaw, at 1,200 ft., is a scattering of buildings beside the Fleet Moss road which, attaining 1,934 ft., is the highest stretch of road in Yorkshire. A two-mile-long spur leads from Fleet Moss to Cam Houses.

At Beckermonds lived the Fosters and Beresfords, who occupied much of their spare time in music and dancing, their feet and those of their neighbours and friends tapping to the strains of 'Buttered Peas' and 'Huntsman's Chorus'. The river Wharfe flows over well-worn limestone bedrock down Langstrothdale, which on a fine summer day can resemble Blackpool as hundreds of people, many with deck-chairs, picnic on the unfenced land beside

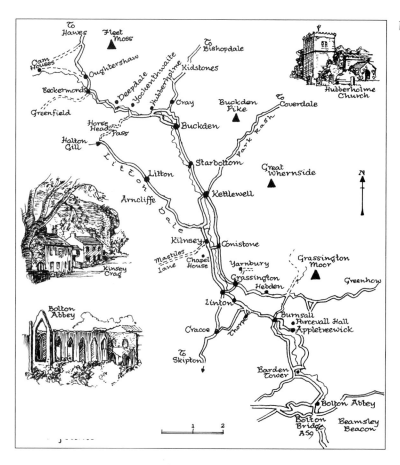

Wharfedale

the river. Within a few yards of the river, near Yockenthwaite (Eogan's Clearing), is a circle of 20 stones which, it is claimed, were put in place during the Bronze Age, some 4,000 years ago. Another theory is that it is the remains of a tomb. Judging by its untypical low-lying position, it may be nothing more than a picturesque sham. The most conspicuous feature at Yockenthwaite is the bridge, a single stupendous arch of stone.

To the Normans this area was Langstrothdale Chase, a *foris*, or land set apart for hunting. Many such tracts in England were royal forests. Those in the dales were not originally designated as such, the term chase here denoting a forest which was private. In Langstrothdale, the chief hunters were the Percies and, by descent, the Cliffords of Skipton. The hamlets of Beckermonds and Yockenthwaite, though having older histories, were eventually lodges in the forest, the chief officers of which lived at Buckden. Marie Hartley and Joan Ingilby, in *Dales Memories* (1986), note that as late as 1608/9 a lease by a Clifford to Richard Slinger relating to a farm at Kirkgill (Hubberholme) in Langstrothdale stated that fishing, hunting and hawking were reserved, and that the deer were to 'goe feed as aforetime hath been used upon the premises, and that the foresters were to be free to range and ride over them'.

The Church of St Michael and All Angels at Hubberholme, once a forest chapel, has a history dating back to the 12th century, the arches and piers of the north aisle being original but the rest, including the tower, taking their present form in the 16th century. Occasionally the church has paid for its fine position near the river by an inundation, which on at least one occasion is said to have led to fish swimming in the old pews, new ones having been provided in recent times; they bear the carved mouse of Robert Thompson, craftsman of Kilburn. The most distinctive feature in Hubberholme church is a rood loft, painted red, black and gold. It is a feature of the medieval church which was supposed to have been removed at the Reformation. This loft bears the Percy badge, William de Percy having given Hubberholme to Coverham Abbey in 1241.

At the Dissolution in 1539 it became a chapel-of-ease to Arncliffe, and was served by the curate at Halton Gill, who had to travel over the often wild and occasionally snow-bound Horse Head Pass, which crests at 1,985 ft. Miles Wilson, one of the curates, wrote in 1743 of the great danger and difficulty in winter of passing over 'very high mountain and large drifts of snow'. One of the stained glass windows at Hubberholme has a picture of Thomas Lindley, another indomitable curate, riding a white horse on Horse Head Pass in snowtime. Also in the church is a memorial to the celebrated writer, J.B. Priestley, whose ashes were deposited in the churchyard after spending the week before the funeral service under the stairs at a local farmhouse, a circumstance which would have appealed to Priestley's comic sense. At *The George* inn, once the property of the benefice, the custom of Land Letting has been held for 200 years, originally on the first Monday of the New Year and then a few days later. The land in question is a pasture of 16 acres, the rent from which has traditionally been given to the poor of the parish. It is a candle auction, at which the vicar and his wardens officiate; a candle is lit and the letting must take place before it burns out.

53 & 54 *Hubberholme Church, which stands close to the river Wharfe in Langstrothdale.*

Buckden, 760 ft., has a name which proclaims its old forest associations. Buckden lost its original importance along with Langstrothdale Chase, but *The Buck* inn is a reminder of the glory days. The term 'buck' applies to either roe or fallow deer, and within living memory a stock of fallow was emparked on land belonging to the Stansfield family. Buckden's impressive backdrop is Buckden Pike, 2,302 ft. A section of the Roman road which connected Bainbridge and Ilkley is found on Buckden Rake, the old route to Cray.

Starbotton, between Buckden and Kettlewell, has had an uneasy relationship with the beck flowing down the gill at the mouth of which the hamlet stands. Several times, a rampaging beck has engulfed it, the most notable instance being in 1686, when bridges were demolished and dwellings destroyed. Starbotton has no church but there was a burial ground for Quakers. The hall belonging to John Symondson was at the disposal of Lady Anne Clifford when, in July 1667, she broke her journey from Skipton through the Dales to her Westmorland properties. The *Fox and Hounds* has a strategic position beside the dale road. Less conspicuous but worthily representing the best of Dales architecture are properties dating back to the 17th and 18th centuries. At this time, lead mines flourished on the fell and there was a beckside smelt mill, the remains of which may be seen above the village.

Kettlewell (Chetel's spring), a village dominated by Great Whernside, was on the Roman road from Ilkley to Bainbridge and, much later, was an important halt on a coach road between Skipton and Richmond, the road continuing with a 1-in-4 zig-zag up Park Rash, and through the 15th-century Scale Park, where deer had been restrained at the behest of Ralph, Earl of Westmorland, to Coverdale. The old road was rough, and horses could therefore keep their feet. In 1953 Park Rash was given a coating of tarmacadam for the benefit of motor traffic.

Kettlewell once prospered through lead-mining, and at Providence mine, at the head of Dowber Gill, a peak of production of 325 tons of lead ore was attained in 1867. The village is now devoted largely to tourism. The summer sun brings a reflective gleam from scores of cars parked near the river bridge, while two historic inns keep an eye on each other near the bridge which spans Cam Beck: *The Bluebell* dates from 1680 and *The Race-horses* had a facelift in 1740.

Littondale, which, like Wharfedale, bears the distinctive U-shape of glacial erosion, begins where the Foxup and Cosh Becks combine to become the river Skirfare, haunt of dipper and grey wagtail in a seven-mile course to Amerdale Dub, where it blends its waters with the Wharfe. The Skirfare spends much of its life underground in limestone passages. Cosh, a mile and a half beyond the hamlet of Foxup, where the road ends, was a farmstead which later became a centre for school parties on Dales study courses. Littondale is named after Litton, a hamlet rich in ancient buildings which is now presided over, in the absence of a church, by *The Queen's Arms*, known far and wide for the appeal of its local delicacies, including rabbit pie. Arncliffe, the largest settlement, which stands on a gravel delta above the floodplain of the river, has a name said to be derived from *erne*, or white-tailed eagle; *The Falcon* inn, overlooking the green, takes its name from another predatory bird. A former host at *The Falcon*, Marmaduke Miller, celebrated his native dale through distinctive watercolour paintings.

A riverside church, St Oswald's, is, like so many Dales churches, pretentiously Victorian, though the foundations are Norman and the 15th-century tower harks back to glory days. The first rector held office about 1180. Local lads who followed their Clifford lord to Flodden Field in 1513 included Knolle, who was 'able, horsed and harnished [*sic*]', and Tennant, who had only a 'bille'. During a break from fishing in Malham Tarn, Charles Kingsley had afternoon tea with Miss Hammond at Bridge House and, in *The Water-Babies*, described the valley as Vendale, 'a quiet, silent, rich, happy place ... three hundred feet of

55   Langstrothdale in 1900.

limestone terraces, one below the other, as straight as if they had been ruled with a ruler and then cut out with a chisel'.

This has been a well-farmed valley ever since the land was deforested. In medieval days, sheep belonging to Fountains Abbey grazed here, and after the Dissolution the wealth of Littondale was mainly in its livestock, both sheep and cattle, which was exceptional; Littondale is untainted by mining. The best views of the valley are from the hill routes, such as where the road from Stainforth begins to dip to Halton Gill, or from Horse Head Pass, the old track which leads from Halton Gill to Langstrothdale. Apart from the simple, clear lines of the glacial trough are broad flat stretches indicative of a glacial lake and, all along the valley, connected by miles of drystone walls, an assembly of field barns, some of the typical Craven type, being large with conspicuous porches, dating from a time when corn was grown. The double doors and threshing-floor are reminders of days when wheat and chaff were separated using the flail.

Kilnsey Crag dominates upper Wharfedale at the point where Littondale joins the main valley. The Crag was formed when a glacier left a vertical face. Subsequently, it is thought, a smaller glacier cut into it still further, leaving an overhang. The Crag forms a splendid backdrop to a floodplain on which, each summer, Kilnsey Show is held. In August 1997, which was centenary year, the attendance at the show was 14,000 people. Kilnsey Crag is a resort of climbers. It was first climbed using 'hardware' in 1957. The greatest achievement was the first free climb, by Mark Leach from Lancashire, on 16 September 1989.

Fountains Abbey established a grange at Kilnsey in the later part of the 12th century, using 200 acres given to it by Alice de Romille and her husband. This was in addition to lands on Malham Moor. Kilnsey, 22 miles west of the abbey, was connected to it by tracks, some of them crossing the moors. Kilnsey supervised the Abbey's large Malham estate and was a good stopping place on the route, known in part as Mastiles Lane, which led to their properties in the Lake District. The Kilnsey grange would have been of timber construction, with wattle and plaster walls and a thatched roof, incorporating a hall, chapel and rooms for guests. Every aspect of its life was accounted for meticulously, and checked by a visiting cellarer who also received any rents. It would be a remarkable day if the Prior or Abbot of Fountains deigned to call at Kilnsey. Eventually a sub-grange of Kilnsey dealt directly with monastic concerns in Malham and on the Moor, most of it being austere moorland with a few scattered habitations. The Forest of Gnoup or Knipe, which took in the highest summits of Fountains and Darnbrook Fells, was the resort of red deer.

Conistone ('farmstead of cows') was mentioned in Domesday but had its greatest period, judging by the present buildings, during the 17th century. Conistone Dib, a narrow gorge cut out by post-glacial floodwater, leads upwards to an area of stupendous limestone scenery, especially pavements. There is also a knoll with a distinctive shape which is known as Conistone Pie. Grass Wood, between Conistone and Grassington, remains well wooded, extending up a rocky hillside from the Wharfe, the tree species changing with the differing conditions. Lower Grass Wood, adjacent to the river, is owned by the Woodland Trust and contains ash, oak, buckthorn and bird cherry. Primrose is succeeded by cowslip and, in May, by a carpet of bluebells. Grass Wood proper, which lies on the top side of the road, is owned and managed by the Yorkshire Wildlife Trust. Here the plant species include lily of the valley and Solomon's Seal, with violets, harebells and field scabious among the plants which thrive at higher levels.

The cobbled square at Grassington heard the clatter of miners' clogs as the men made their way to and from their small cottage homes. Thomas Airey opened a theatre in modest premises near a 16th-century barn, outside which John Wesley preached on his first visit to the neighbourhood. Airey's son Tom inaugurated a mail coal service not long after the introduction of the Penny Post in 1840. As the coach approached each settlement between Skipton and Upper Wharfedale, a horn was blown to alert the local people of its impending arrival. The grand entry into Grassington followed its crossing of the Wharfe by the three-arched bridge, formerly known as Linton Bridge, which had replaced a wooden structure in 1603. The market charter of Grassington is dated 1282, but Grassington's commercial importance spans the 18th and early 19th centuries, the heyday of lead-mining on the Moor. Small cottages, which just housed a miner and his large family, are now used at weekends or by newly-retired couples from town. In some cases, adjacent cottages have been made into one. Grassington, somewhat shabby in the past, is now smart, elegant indeed, with its square, its narrow streets, its tourist shops, re-styled Town Hall and well-stocked Upper Wharfedale Museum. The place teems with visitors in summer and just before Christmas, when a Dickensian Festival is held. The Yorkshire Dales National Park has a suite of offices and an Information Centre at Colvend. Here, undoubtedly, is the capital of upper Wharfedale, though Linton has the parish church, which is shared by several places round about, and the futuristic Catholic church occupies a pleasant site at Threshfield.

Industrial Grassington throve during the period of mining on the Moor and when the machinery of textile mills was harnessed to the power of the river Wharfe. The Yorkshire Dales Railway, from Skipton to Threshfield, was opened in 1901, serving the interests of both commuters and tourists. A row of red-tiled houses just over Grassington Bridge from the railway station became known as Boiled Egg Row, because in the time needed to boil

56   Grassington, capital of upper Wharfedale, showing the old Town Hall.

an egg the commuter could have walked from the station to his home. Edmund Bogg, writing early this century, in the fulsome manner of the time, observed:

> Standing healthily high on a gently sloping limestone terrace or shelf, Grassington's position full in the sun on the northern slope of the dale is, for Craven-land, unique. The sun's rays light up early and till late gladden the hearts and quicken to fuller life the bodies of its people.

Many people are drawn to the area by industrial archaeology and there is much to interest tourists since the mining area was provided with signs explaining the remains and the processes involved in mining and smelting galena. The last lead was mined over a century ago, but relics of the industry are conspicuous in a tormented landscape. Mining operations were put on a large and efficient scale when Cavendish Estate developed the area, and activities in the mining field were controlled from a manager's office at Yarnbury. Smelting was undertaken on site and the ruins of Cupola Mill are clear to see. This smelt mill, built in 1793 by the Duke of Devonshire, replaced the original peat- and wood-burning smelt mill. Fired by coal from local mines, this new reverberatory furnace ran continuously and required a high input of ore to make it economical. Two flues 600 yards long were constructed from the smelt mill up the hillside to two tall chimneys, one of which stands proud on the moor to a height of 40 ft.

Recovering lead from the mines of Yarnbury and Grassington Moor involved deep mining, with shafts and levels rather than drifts. The orefield on Grassington Moor had some impressively large waterwheels, used for raising the ore or pumping out water from shafts which attained depths of up to 400 ft. When water became a major problem, working at depth was possible only through the opening of the Duke's Level, driven in from Hebden Gill. The work, beginning in 1792 and completed 30 years later, provided an effective drain for water which threatened the future of the mines. The Grassington Moor mines ceased production in the early 1880s, one reason being competition from cheap imported ores, and another the fact that they had been virtually worked out. The output of lead during their almost 120 years of existence has been estimated at 57,000 tons.

Linton, a village with a capacious green, a beck and several bridges, has an outstanding building in Fountaine Hospital (1721), a place endowed by the will of Richard Fountaine for 'six poor men or women'. Sir John Vanbrugh is thought to have had a hand in its design. In the central block is a chapel, and a square tower to the hospital is surmounted by a cupola. Much older, but with an isolated riverside location is Linton church, dedicated to St Michael and All Angels. This church serves the villages of Grassington, Linton, Hebden and Threshfield, each being linked to the church by a durable path. The site may have supported a church since Danish times, and St Michael was often chosen where there had been a pagan site. In the present church is Norman work, namely some arches and a 'tub' font. With its square bell-turret, the church has a venerable appearance. Though it dates back to the 12th century, it was largely rebuilt and extended in the 15th century. A curious feature of parochial life was the fact that until 1866 Linton had two rectors, the consequence of a situation in which there were two lords of the manor, each with the right of advowson. Threshfield Grammar School is another solitary building whose site reflects a handy position for several villages round about. This building of great architectural distinction, and much educational worth, was founded in 1674 by the rector of Linton, the Rev. Matthew Hewitt. A master of the school who was fond of playing the fiddle was transformed by a romantic writer, Halliwell Sutcliffe, into 'Old Pam the Fiddler', who is said to haunt the place.

At Linton Falls, the Wharfe, pouring over rocks along the line of the North Craven Fault, powered Linton and Threshfield Mills on the south bank of the Wharfe, and Grassington Low Mill on the north side. Cotton was being spun at Linton Mill as early as 1840. This mill closed down in 1950 and new houses occupy the site. In the area between Linton and Burnsall are to be seen smooth, rounded hills, like upturned pudding basins, distinct from the gritstone moors in that they are composed of limestone. These are reef knolls. Millions of years ago, in a position near the equator, they were living reefs, glowing with colour, and the haunt of creatures which are now fixed for all time as fossils. The land mass has subsequently drifted northwards. One of the knolls has a modern commercial use as a limestone quarry.

Burnsall is a notable crossing place of the Wharfe. A massive stone bridge with prominent breakwaters replaced one given to the village by Sir William Craven, a memorial to whom is to be found in St Wilfrid's Church, which he 'repaired and beautified' at about the time he arranged to pay for the bridge. Sir William, who has been dubbed 'Dick Whittington of the Dales', was born in this area, went to London to make his fortune and did so, then became Lord Mayor, but he never forget his birthplace. He founded the Grammar School in 1602. It is still used for educational purposes. St Wilfrid's Church, an ancient Christian centre, has some 14th-century masonry but is better known as a repository of fragments of Anglo-Danish crosses of the 9th or 10th centuries and two equally old hogsback tombstones. A carved alabaster panel features the Adoration of the Magi.

Burnsall is in limestone country. Below the village, the dale takes on the dark grandeur of millstone grit, with brown outcrops and skylines tufty with heather. Burnsall's daughter church, St John's at Appletreewick, is a Victorian conversion of two old cottages

(1897-8). Nearby is an astonishing building, Parcevall Hall, transformed in the 1930s from a typical old Dales farmhouse. The story of Parcevall Hall, a grand house with an incomparable view across a quiet dale to the heather-capped Simon's Seat, began in 1927, when William Frederick Victor Mordaunt Milner, a tall, amiable gentleman, bought a farmhouse near Appletreewick from Frank Laycock, a Skipton antiques dealer whom he met in the bar of *The George* inn at Hubberholme. William Milner's builder, Irvine Hargraves, was commissioned after a chat in the bar of the *Red Lion* at Burnsall. William Milner was an architect, in partnership at York with Romilly Craze, who designed the new Shrine at Walsingham.

William, who was fond of cycling in the Dales, longed for a permanent base. He enthusiastically set about restoring and extending the plain old building until, on what had been a bleak Wharfedale hillside, he had a stylish country house with extensive gardens and trees to break the back of the wind. William Milner directed the work himself. He found master craftsmen to re-work stonework, much of it from the old buildings, and created a series of walled terraces to provide gardens worthy of the dwelling. Among the rare plants they contained were varieties which George Forrest and Reginald Farrer had collected when botanising in Western China and Tibet.

The work of construction was labour-intensive, carried out during the 1930s, a time of industrial depression. William Milner thus made a substantial contribution to the local economy in straitened times. With the death of his father in 1931, he became Sir William Milner, 8th Baronet of Nun Appleton. When the work on Parcevall Hall was completed, he was able to divert some of his mental energy towards other projects, notably, from 1949, the gardens at Harlow Car, near Harrogate, established by the Northern Horticultural Society. He served for some years as Honorary Director. When he died in March 1960, his body was interred in the churchyard at Burnsall and not in the specially consecrated ground at Parcevall Hall, which had been his wish. Parcevall Hall and its estate are administered by the Guardians of the Shrine at Walsingham and the house leased to the Diocese of Bradford, where it is used as a conference centre, for retreats, and to provide quiet pleasure for holidaymakers.

Appletreewick, locally referred to as 'Aptrick', was associated with Bolton Priory, which raised sheep and mined lead here. Authority for an annual fair was granted in 1310 by Edward II to the Prior and Convent of Bolton, the charter being renewed by Edward III in 1328. Owen's *Book of Fairs* (1770) gives the 2 October date for cattle and horses. The fair was well supported until the early 1900s. Scottish stock predominated: cattle from the Highlands, sheep from the Lowlands, and a considerable number of ponies which had been bred north of the border. The owner of a house where drink could be purchased during the fair would hang a bush outside. Long stone water-troughs in Cork Street were for watering cattle.

A large field between Appletreewick and the Wharfe, known as Sheeper or Sheep Fair Hill, was the place where stock was grazed immediately prior to the fair, which was on level ground near the river. The fair dwindled with the coming of the railways and rapid transportation of stock from Scotland, but one element continued—the sale of onions. Sir William Craven restored the High Hall at Appletreewick.

Barden Tower, a hunting lodge associated with Skipton Castle, became the main residence of the 10th Lord Clifford after its enlargement in 1485. He died in 1523, whereupon the tower became ruined. Lady Anne Clifford restored it in 1659, though by then it was no longer her property. Whitaker, in his *History of Craven*, includes under Barden Tower an oblique reference to the venison pies being consumed by the Cliffords and their friends. He mentions that one Atkinson was a famous pie baker in 1606, and that in 1634 Widow Bland, a baker of venison pies, was paid £3 4s. 2d. in instalments for her work.

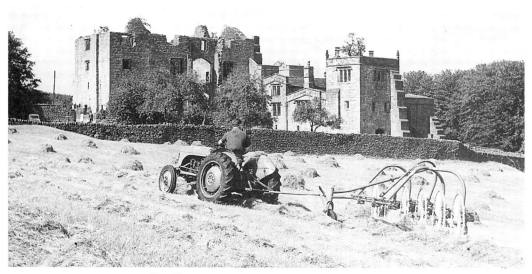

57   'Rowing up' at Barden Tower in the 1970s.

An American visitor, Nathaniel Hawthorne, best summed up the special appeal of Bolton Abbey. He saw the ruined priory 'in the green lap of protecting hills, beside a stream, and with peace and fertility looking down on every side'. In the year 1155, Augustinian canons moved from a somewhat bleak situation at Embsay to a sheltered site at Bolton, in the valley of the Wharfe, a site favoured by the Saxon Earl Edwin before the Norman Conquest. The Augustinians were granted Embsay and the Church of Holy Trinity, Skipton, by Cecily de Rumilly, the charter being a form of insurance for the world to come. It was done 'for the health of our souls and those of our ancestors and successors'. Her daughter, Alice, used almost the same words when she made the transfer to Bolton possible through an exchange of land elsewhere. A legend that her benevolence was a response to her sorrow at the death of her son, William, in the Strid, has long been discounted by historians. William, also known as the Boy of Egremont, put his name to the deed. The canons were originally granted

> the whole manor of Bolton with all its appurtenances, in wood and plain, in water, meadows
> and grazings, by these boundaries; to wit, from Lumgill beneath the game enclosure which is
> called Lobwith, even as it comes down from the moor which is called Lobwithslec along the
> same Lumgill ...

And so on.

Bolton added to its estate through gifts and purchases. Between 1300 and 1317 they acquired land at Appletreewick and here was one of the *bercaries* (sheep farms). The mining of lead became a lucrative additional activity. At Malham, Bolton sheep were on pastures adjacent to those of Fountains Abbey. Dairy products included cheese made from the milk of cows and ewes. Making cheese enabled the monks to lock up the goodness of the summer milk in a form that would sustain them in winter. Goats too were milked. Surplus kids were usually earmarked for the table. Horses were bred and pastured in summer in the limestone country at Malham which was renowned for giving such animals good bone.

Bolton's heyday was from 1286 to 1325, with the exception of a period around 1314 when, following success at Bannockburn, the Scots went on the rampage and the canons became exiles in Lancashire for a while. A relatively small number of Augustinian canons, or Black Friars, being ordained priests, devoted themselves to prayer and meditation, leaving it to some 200 layfolk to do the practical work at the priory and on the outlying farms. Corn was grown here, oats formed the basis for the beer which was their beverage, sheep provided wool for sale, and at Appletreewick was a stock farm, raising the oxen used for ploughing. The canons had quite a varied diet for the time, including bread and cheese, meat, fish from their own ponds and salt herring transported from the east coast. They maintained the tradition of providing hospitality for travellers and alms for local people in need.

Bolton Priory was slow in the making; indeed, the West Tower, begun in 1520, was incomplete at the time of the Dissolution in January 1539 and remained unroofed until as recently as 1985. Little remains of the first group of buildings, which had taken shape by the early part of the 13th century. More grandiose schemes were introduced. The rental taken in 1539 mentions a figure of £62 17s. 8d. for the price of cattle found there and sold to Thomas Proctor. It is apparent that cattle played a more important part in the rental than did sheep. Also detailed are figures relating to wheat and rye being grown in the vicinity of Bolton Priory.

At the Dissolution, Bolton Priory was surrendered by Prior Moone. The nave was retained because it had been used as a parish church by local people for worship. The canons and servants were granted quite generous pensions. The priory was stripped of its valuables and the estate split up. Most of it came into the hands of Henry Clifford, first Earl of Cumberland, who paid £2,490 for it. Those who visit the church hear plainsong relayed as

58 *Bolton Hall in Wharfedale.*

soft background music, and in a moment, or so it seems, they are transported back to medieval days and life at any of 180 Augustinian houses which were established in England.

Bolton Hall, which is neo-Gothic in style, incorporates the 14th-century gatehouse to the priory, which was built at the same time and in the same style as one at Whalley Abbey, in the Ribble Valley. At Bolton, the combined inner and outer gateway form a most unusual dining room for members of the Cavendish family and their guests. The Bolton Abbey estate, one of the largest private estates in the Dales, has for a great many years been open to the public, and after the railway was extended to Bolton Abbey thousands of townsfolk bore down on the area on day trips. A rebuilt Bolton Abbey station is now connected to the preserved railway based on Embsay. Meanwhile, the majority of visitors to Bolton Abbey arrive by car. The Old Rectory, an outstanding building, came into being through a bequest of Robert Boyle, the man who expounded Boyle's Law in physics. English landscape painting owes much to Wharfedale, and more precisely to the area presided over by the semi-ruined priory at Bolton, which has for many years been wrongly but romantically known as Bolton Abbey. The monastic estate passed into hands which cherished it so that today it retains its park-like character. The river Wharfe, after being pent-up in a channel between dark rocks at the Strid, in a wooded area where rain and spray create an atmosphere akin to a rainforest, enters a much calmer landscape, of hills capped with gritstone and tufty with heather.

Thomas Girton, a young Londoner using Harewood, home of the hospitable Lascelles family, as a Wharfedale base, repeatedly visited Bolton Abbey, and in a flurry of activity raised the level of painting from a mere pictorial record to something imbued with the personality of the painter. Girton's experiences and the pictures which resulted from them prompted another young Londoner, Joseph Mallory William Turner, to visit Bolton Abbey in 1797. Turner had the patronage of Walter Fawkes, of Farnley Hall, and returned in 1808 and 1815. Displayed at Chatsworth, the Derbyshire home of the Duke of Devonshire, is a study of the priory under the title 'Bolton Abbey in the Olden Tyme' by Landseer, a favourite artist of Queen Victoria. Landseer arrived in 1833. His painting did not please the duke who commissioned what he doubtless thought would be a study of the ruined priory in its riverside setting. Instead, Landseer presented him with an interior–which could be of any abbey–showing tenants delivering tithes, mainly in the form of dead animals and birds.

Daniel Defoe (an unreliable topographer) had thought of the region beyond Wharfedale as 'a continued waste of black, ill-looking, desolate moors'. The landscape was romanticised by a rector named William Carr who, with the permission of the Duke of Devonshire, opened up the ancient Strid Wood. Those who responded to the cult of 'the Picturesque' might now walk along hard paths to 'stations', or viewing areas, from which to see the works of nature and of man at their grandest. The area was provided with legends by Thomas Dunham Whitaker, in *History of Craven* (1805). William Wordsworth, whose ponderings on the origins of Bolton Priory and the ill-fated Norton family (each versified at length) were once popular, had serious historians of later times throwing up their hands in despair.

The ornate Cavendish Memorial at the roadside commemorates Lord Frederick Cavendish, who was assassinated in Ireland in 1882. In the tithe barn, now used by the estate as a workshop, for storage or for garaging vehicles, the old form of the structure remains: an immense timber framework, with stone walls acting as little more than panelling. They do not carry the weight of the roof as in other barns. A smaller tithe barn was converted into estate cottages last century and has now been restored to display its historic features, being conspicuously barn-like upstairs.

59 *The Cavendish Pavilion and bridge over the Wharfe at Bolton Abbey.*

The Bolton Abbey grouse moors, which occupy about half of the 30,000-acre estate, are world-famous thanks to visiting celebrities, including King George V and Harold Macmillan, when he was prime minister. The moors are considered not just a grouse preserve but the most valuable area for the sheep-grazing associated with traditional hill farms, yet it was on a local moor, Blubberhouses, that, according to the *Victoria County History* of 1907, Lord Walsingham set up a grim sort of record on 23 August 1872, shooting 842 grouse. On 1 August 1888 this 'great' marksman shot for 14 hours and 18 minutes, averaging 108 shots an hour, and his bag was 1,058 birds. Red deer, once locally common, were emparked in a 300-acre tract of rough land called The Nab, where the drystone walls are still much higher than the average. The last red deer, an escapee, was shot as recently as the 1930s.

A 1,200 acre tract of woodland is managed commercially and there are some 600 acres of amenity woodland, most of it by the Wharfe. The river is known for its trout. In 1837 a Mr. Scott, the duke's forester, is said to have landed a trout weighing about eight pounds and having a length of over two feet, which sounds very much like a fisherman's tale. The estate now has its own hatchery and the river is regularly stocked with fish. There is concern for them in dry years, when it is necessary for the water company to take water from the Wharfe, pumping it up the hill to Chelker Reservoir.

As related, thousands of day-trippers to Bolton Abbey once arrived by train. The station was closed and trackless for many years, but a new one was built after tracks were laid from the preserved line at Embsay, the enterprise coming into use in 1997. The Midland Railway had arrived at the ducal estate in Wharfedale in 1888, and drivers on the switchback route between Skipton and Ilkley said they were 'going over t'Alps'. Bolton Abbey, one of the 'alpine' stations, sprang into life on the first Bank Holiday of that year, when 40 extra trains brought trippers from as far off as Liverpool, York and Doncaster. By the turn of the century, there might be 100,000 arrivals each tourist season. Ten coaches

hired by Thomas Cook arrived late because of rail congestion at Skipton. Most of the visitors walked to the village and priory but the more affluent were conveyed in horse-drawn wagonettes belonging to the Steele family, who lived in one of the station houses. In summer, Mrs. Steele catered for the throng. Her boiled ham tea with bread and butter and homemade cakes cost 1s. 10d.

George V, visiting Bolton Hall for the grouse-shooting, always arrived by the royal train and crowds lined the roadsides. Skeps of grouse, their bodies still warm from the moors, were put on an early train to enable them to be served up at dinner in the *Savoy* and other major London hotels on the same day. While at Bolton Abbey, the King attended morning service at the priory church, the lesson being read by the Duke of Devonshire.

During the Second World War, ammunition was stored locally, inviting enemy bombs. One Saturday night a string of bombs pockmarked a large field. Another bomb fell in the cricket field and yet another exploded in the river. On the following day the ammunition in the dump was transferred to what were considered safer quarters. A train bearing George VI on a tour of the north stopped for a while at Bolton Abbey. The train was run into Lob'd (Lob Wood) cutting where the branches of trees met overhead, providing excellent camouflage. A special air raid shelter for the King was constructed 'in the banking'. After the war the shelter was being used by a local man as a garden 'shed'.

Beamsley Beacon, at 1,296 ft. the last flourish of the Yorkshire Dales in the south, has such a fine situation it was indeed used as the site of a beacon, one of a chain which, in pre-telegraph days, transmitted warning of national emergency. Beamsley Hospital, beside the A59, was built in 1593 in a circular form to be almshouses. The benefactor was Margaret, the mother of Lady Anne Clifford, who chose a tract of land which had come into family ownership at the Dissolution of Bolton Priory. Lady Anne herself had a share in the project, completing it by the addition of two blocks of cottages situated at the roadside. And of course, this being Anne Clifford, the family coat of arms was boldly situated on a linking archway.

The stone bridge spanning the Wharfe succeeded a structure of 1318. It was kept in good repair by the canons of Bolton. A new bridge has been constructed for the re-styled A59, now a well-used route over Blubberhouses to Harrogate and York.

12

NIDDERDALE

THE DESIGNATION OF NIDDERDALE as an Area of Outstanding Natural Beauty in 1995 was long overdue. An attractive upper dale, with a distinctive Dales way of life, was excluded from the National Park in 1954, possibly because Bradford Waterworks had modified the landscape with three great reservoirs. Yet much open dale remained and the heather moorland on either side of the dale is outstanding in its extent and grouse-bearing condition, which means it is also good for upland wading birds and for sheep.

The upper two reservoirs, Angram and Scar House, are remote from a public road but may be visited on a water authority road on payment of a small charge. The third reservoir, Gouthwaite, built in 1901 to compensate riparian owners, gives Nidderdale a Lakeland flavour. Some 3 miles long and rather less than 0.5 miles wide, it lacks the bare shorelines of the others and, with large areas of mud frequently exposed at its head, is a major haunt of wild birds–and bird-watchers.

The river has its source at Nidd Head, on the eastern flanks of Great Whernside. Water bubbles out of the hillside at an elevation of almost 2,000 ft. and in one-and-a-half miles it descends 750 ft., losing its identity in a man-made landscape of big reservoirs and hill farms. The upper reservoirs are in an amphitheatre dominated by Great Whernside, 2,310 ft., and Little Whernside, 1,984 ft. It is a desolate area which on the one-inch Ordnance Survey map has bold masses of brown. Above the big dam there is no woodland, no roads, no human habitation. Even tracks are scarce. The fellsides are scored by sheep-trods.

The shining levels of the reservoirs do give Nidderdale some distinction, even an element of novelty, in the Pennine dale-country, and Bradford Corporation built soundly, the big dams having embellishments in the Romantic style of the time. There was a degree of haste, for Bradford was expanding fast and the demand for water was about to outstrip available supplies. In 1891-2, the Corporation acquired the parliamentary powers to intercept the headwaters of the Nidd and its tributaries and to construct works. Bradford became the most 'Dales-conscious' of Yorkshire's industrial towns because 60 per cent of its precious water was derived from the 54 inches falling annually on the heights around Nidderdale.

George F. Renton, a former water engineer at Bradford who had worked on the Scar House project, told me of the earlier Wharfedale works, which had been authorised in 1854 but were not supplying water until 1860 because of delays encountered in the largest of the group, which was Lower Barden. In the 1890s, quiet little Nidderdale became the scene of furious activity that was to continue for 40 years. When the city accountants came to tot up the cost of the Scar House works alone, they found it was £2,200,000.

61   *A view from the dam at Scar House, Nidderdale.*

The dams of Angram (completed in 1919) and Scar House (1936) were the largest in Britain at the time they were created. The Scar House project involved building a dam with a length of 1,800 ft., height of 170 ft. and a thickness at the base of 135 ft. This required 540,000 cubic yards of concrete and masonry, stone being quarried from the fellside on the north side of the valley. James Hoare, in a *Dalesman* article, states that some of the Bradford ratepayers, who were to pay for this 'great and necessary undertaking', thought that Alderman Gadie, the instigator, marched up the Nidd Valley with 1,000 Irish navvies carrying picks and shovels and said, 'Dig here, lads.' That was just a local joke. In fact, 700 men, 13 locomotives, 25 locomotive cranes and three steam navvies were marshalled for the work.

The planners had been working for months on the problem of housing and a workman's village grew up which consisted of 10 hostels and 60 bungalows, a church, school, cinema, concert hall and tennis courts. Families were housed in semi-detached bungalows on three sites, known as East View, The Terrace and The Crescent. The bungalows were rented to the families of the foremen and office staff, a police sergeant, a doctor and a missioner. The main workforce was accommodated in 10 dormitory huts. A fixed sum was deducted from a man's wages and he was issued with a bed card, which was effectively a passport. If a man misbehaved in the hut or village, or at work, his bed card was withdrawn and he was immediately expelled from the village.

Each man had his own cubicle, with adjoining bathrooms and toilets on each corridor. There was a large dining area, also used for games and leisure activities. A separate drying room was used, washing and laundering often being done by the staff for a small charge. The main expense was the 22s. 6d. paid weekly to the landlady. A small church was available for both Anglican and Roman Catholic services and during the period 1922-9 there were 11 marriages, 114 baptisms and 40 confirmations.

A day school accommodated from 70 to 90 children and the brightest of them were awarded scholarships to other schools, where they were boarded out, returning to Scar village for holidays and weekends. The shops included a general store with post office, greengrocer, cobbler and barber. Beer and other forms of 'strong drink' were frowned upon. A wet canteen was open six nights a week and on a Saturday lunchtime, but not on a Sunday. If a man wanted a drink on a Sunday he had the long walk down the valley to Wath or over the hilltop to Horsehouse in Coverdale and back again.

Romantic tales are told of the pre-reservoir Nidderdale. Packhorses travelled from Scotland, via Coverdale and the side of Dead Man's Hill to destinations in the West Riding. The Scottish connection will not be forgotten as long as people recall a tale about Maggie Thompson, who lived at the Lodge, on the north side of Scar House, some two centuries ago. She is said to have murdered three Scottish pedlars for their money and to have transported the bodies by sled to the hill, where she buried them in peat. In 1723, the bodies were discovered by peat-cutters. The murderer was never apprehended.

The service reservoirs are in a stretch of upper Nidderdale which was, until recent years, known only to the local folk and to walkers following the several footpaths of an area which the water authority did its best to protect from contamination. Today, on payment of a fee anyone might drive four miles up the steep-sided valley, the edges of which are tufty with heather, and find adequate car parking and also toilets in the vicinity of the former village, within handy walking distance of the dam. The athletic visitor follows a road to the upper dam.

Down-to-earth Bradford, the wool capital, wanted a copious supply of water that was drinkable and soft enough to meet the requirements of the wool textile industry. A branch line of the North Eastern Railway already extended to Pateley, having been opened in 1862 to serve the lead mines and flax mills but also, it was hoped, to stimulate tourism. Now, with transport to the upper dale a major problem, Bradford built the Nidd Valley Light Railway, a 13-mile system linking Pateley Bridge with Angram which operated from 1907 until 1936. It was intended to carry materials for dam-building but was also made available to fare-paying passengers. For the workers and their families, housed in the bleak upper dale, a train service from Scar village to Pateley Bridge was provided on Tuesdays, Thursdays and Saturdays. Once a month and at holiday times a special trip allowed families to spend from three to four hours in Harrogate. The Nidd Valley Light Railway had stations at Wath, Ramsgill and Lofthouse, the original route up the valley from here including a sharp bend on which buffers locked and derailments were a recurring problem. In 1919, a 600 ft. tunnel was excavated to ease the course of the line. The tunnel has now been sealed off. Two of the steam engines which chuffed their way up the dale from Pateley Bridge had started out life on the pre-electrified London Underground. Coal for the locomotives came from Garforth, near Leeds.

Middlesmoor, the main village in Stonebeck Up, that part of Nidderdale above Stean Beck, stands on a draughty ledge at about 900 ft. Here, where there is a tight cluster of mostly 18th-century buildings around ginnels, courts and small green spaces, the public road ends with a car park for visiting motorists. Walkers enjoy strolling along the green lane which passes through grouse-haunted moorland and descends to the reservoirs, where a figure-of-eight footpath extends across the dams and round their shores. Middlesmoor was once in the possession of Byland Abbey and acquired its chapel in 1484, prior to which the bodies of those who died at the dalehead were borne for 10 miles to Kirkby Malzeard. The present church is of Victorian date. To stand in Middlesmoor churchyard on a clear, sunny day, and to look southwards, over moor and dale to Gouthwaite reservoir, is to enjoy a stupendous view.

Nidderdale was a cul-de-sac from a motoring point of view until a track zig-zagging up the hill from Lofthouse—and heading for Masham and the Vale of York—was given a durable surface. The upper dale lost its secluded nature, though not everyone takes pleasure in the steep, zig-zagging climb out of the valley, especially if they encounter some cows being driven at its steeper stretches. The Nidd flows down its smoothed limestone labyrinth and bursts forth into daylight again at Nidd Heads, below Lofthouse, some two miles below the village of Lofthouse. Lofthouse, originally a grange of Fountains Abbey, who were mining and smelting iron ore in the dale in the 13th century, stands on the bank of a river which for most of the year is out of sight, having gone to ground down Manchester Hole and Goyden Pot, two miles to the north, to reappear at Nidd Heads, a quarter of a mile below the village. Goyden Pot is a limestone cave system in what is otherwise sandstone country.

A by-road near Lofthouse shoots off, initially straight as an arrow-flight, to the hamlet of Stean, a name derived from 'stone', of which there is plenty. En route, the car park at How Stean comes into view. Here the beck has bitten so deeply into a strip of limestone that the gorge was promoted to Victorian tourists as 'Little Switzerland'. The resemblance to alpine scenery is slight, though the gorge impresses, having a maximum depth of 30 ft. Footpaths maintained by the owners, who charge a fee for admission, enable visitors to explore the gorge, a feature of which is Tom Taylor's Cave. In the bed of the beck are rounded potholes, created by the swirling action of stones.

At Stean, an end-of-the-road scattering of buildings 850 ft. above sea level, are gritstone walls, a beck with a bed of creamy limestone and farmsteads composed of stone wrested from nearby quarries. Gritstone crags are a feature of the moorland beyond, which takes in such eminences as the Great and Little Whernsides and Deadman's Hill. Beds of good building stone were disturbed by those who constructed the great aqueduct from Scar House reservoir to the taps of Bradford. At Stean the moor is the main topic. In the old days, Sir Frederick Aykroyd of Birstwith Hall was the landowner, having bought the land when the Yorke estate was sold in 1924. Stean Beck rises 'at the back of Meugher', a peaty hump whose name derives from the Old English *muga*, a stack or heap. Meugher (pronounced Mewpha) is remote and possibly the least-known eminence in the Yorkshire Dales. One reason is that it is on private ground.

The village of Ramsgill, one of the prettiest in dale-country, was in monastic times the property of Byland Abbey. An arch at the east end of the churchyard of St Mary's is all that survives of the grange chapel. A short distance down a by-road leading to the moors is Bouthwaite, with its prominent Methodist chapel in an area where Fountains Abbey had one of its granges; the monastic road ascends the moor to Intake Gate, heading for Kirkby Malzeard. The picture that comes to mind at the mention of a monastic grange is that of a pious monk, in white habit and with sandalled feet, who happens to be a good shepherd in every sense. Yet the key to the success of the Cistercian enterprise at Fountains was the hard work of the lay brothers—men who took their vows but had shorter devotional hours and a longer spell in bed at nights. At the dale-country granges, lay brothers were the farmers while, back at the abbey, the so-called 'choir monks' maintained a strict and prayerful routine.

62 Yorke Arms, *Ramsgill, Upper Nidderdale, is named after a celebrated local family.*

At Ramsgill a former shooting lodge of the Yorke family was transformed into the *Yorke Arms*, rebuilt in 1843 and now creeper-covered, the leaves giving an attractive russet tone in autumn. The Yorke connection with Nidderdale began early in the 16th century when they bought monastic lands from Sir Richard Southwell in 1547 and from Sir Arthur Darcy in 1549. The Yorkes possessed moors, farms and mining interests, mainly at Bewerley and Appletreewick in Wharfedale. Thomas Edward Yorke, who had succeeded to the estate in 1883 and died at Bewerley in 1923, was the archetypal landowner: fond of all field sports, he took a paternal interest in the families on his estate, which he ruled with old-time firmness. He was grouse-

63 *Gouthwaite Hall, Nidderdale, before its demolition. Usable stones went into new buildings in the locality.*

shooting until the age of 82 and laid up his guns after the pheasant season in the following year. On his death, the estate of the Yorkes had to be sold to meet death duties. About 15,000 acres of low ground and moorland changed hands as a single estate. A month later it was split into two through resale.

Gouthwaite, which has a storage capacity of 1.5 billion gallons, looks more like a lake than a reservoir and on calm days it reflects low green hills. It occupies an area where, in post-glacial times, there was a considerable lake. When the valley was dammed, the river spread itself over about 327 acres, forming a lake about two miles long. The reservoir-builders planted many trees in the area of the dam, reducing its visual impact on the landscape. Since then, there has been little disturbance at Gouthwaite. The fishing rights have been exercised and now and again a shooting party arrives, but for most of the time the birds nest, feed or roost in peace. The nesting species include sandpiper, yellow wagtail, lapwing and teal. Among the rarities seen at Gouthwaite have been pied billed grebe, a vagrant golden eagle, rough-legged buzzards, geese and waders. In winter, gulls of several species roost here, and a familiar sight is that of Canada geese, some of which nest on the nearby moorland and bring their young down to the reservoir via the becks.

Below Gouthwaite the countryside is park-like. A reminder of the power of flowing water is to be seen at Foster Beck Mill, where the 35 ft. high breast waterwheel which was installed in 1904 has been kept operational. When its mill days ended, the premises were engaged in spinning. Pateley Bridge has an Anglian name relating to the pate or badger, the suffix *-ley* implying a cleared area in woodland. The little town has an unusual layout. Most settlements run parallel with the river but here the main street extends up a steep hillside, with a further extension that is steeper still, leading to the high moors. Pateley, which received its market charter in 1320, was slow to develop as a market town and enjoyed its busiest period when there was lead-mining, quarrying and reservoir work at the dalehead, supplies being transported by the aforementioned light railway. The last branch-line train, carrying freight, reached Pateley in 1964; passenger traffic had ended in 1951. The story of the town and dale are told in an award-winning museum.

The 13th-century Church of St Mary, now a roofless ruin but dignified even in decay, has a steady stream of visitors, most of whom park their cars near the entrance to the cemetery and walk more or less on the level to where the shell of a historic building—porch, nave, chancel, tower—stands well shielded by trees. A small window frames a view of pastoral Nidderdale. The present parish church, St Cuthbert's, was consecrated in 1827, when it had a gallery and could seat 750 worshippers. The building was refurbished in 1984; the alterations included making a lounge at the west end of the church, which, with kitchen and toilets, means that St Cuthbert's is regarded as a seven-days-a-week church.

Cross the river bridge from Pateley and Bridgehouse Gate, part of Bewerley, is reached, the park being the setting for Nidderdale Show, the last big show of the summer, held in September at the time of the Pateley Rant. Bewerley is another -ley name, this time relating to the beaver. Marmaduke Huby, Abbot of Fountains (1494-1526), caused a chapel and lodging for a priest to be built at the hamlet and this survives as Bewerley Grange Chapel, which has changed hands and uses many times over the years, being used as a school from 1647 until 1831. The chapel was fully restored in 1965.

Thomas Edward Yorke, 't'Awd Squire', the last of the distinguished family to reign locally, lived at Bewerley Hall, a building which, though grand in size and appearance, was not well situated, being down in a hollow. Here was an ice house beside a fish pond which, in the keenest winter weather, provided blocks of ice to be packed into the early form of refrigeration. Grainge's *Nidderdale*, published in 1863, had an advertisement placed by Mr. Warwick, agent to John Yorke, Esq., of Bewerley, inviting tourists to visit the Fish-pond, Ravensgill and Guyscliffe Woods, belonging to Mr. Yorke of Bewerley Hall, open on Tuesdays and Thursday, on payment of sixpence each (schools at reduced rates). The Hall was demolished in 1926 and the park is now owned by the society which organises the Nidderdale Show. Yorke's Folly, on the exposed rim of the moor above Bewerley, is what remains of a structure commissioned by the family to provide employment for needy workers.

64   *The main street at Pateley Bridge.*

Rudyard Kipling had family associations with Pateley Bridge, and one of the stories in *Soldiers Three* has Yorkshireman Learoyd recalling Greenhow Hill and its tewits (lapwings). Greenhow evolved from the early part of the 17th century as a lead-mining community. The road from Pateley to Greenhow via Fan Carl is uncompromising, the road cresting at 1,326 ft. Limestone appears to view near Red Brae. The lychgate of the burial ground has carved upon it the familiar words, 'I will lift up mine eyes to the hills', but here you tend to look down on them. In the late 1970s, when the brakes of a bus heading for Pateley Bridge failed, the vehicle hurtled down to Bridgehousegate at 70 m.p.h.; it brushed against the school wall (where, alas, a woman passenger was killed) and did not stop until it hit a car halfway up the High Street at Pateley, on the opposite side of the dale.

65   *Bewerley Hall, near Pateley Bridge, Nidderdale, the home of the Yorke family (and long since demolished).*

The Greenhow road has a wild setting. Harald Bruff, who wrote about Greenhow folk, frequently referred to the wind, noting that it 'blows fresh and is laden with the fragrance of ling bloom, bent grass and wet moss, the true moor mixture'. Northwards, a tract of moorland extends for some ten miles to Great Whernside. At High Crag, near Stump Cross, in the clearest of conditions a visitor may be rewarded with the sight of the towers of York Minster, 30 miles away. At Stump Cross was the boundary between the Forest of Knaresborough and Craven. Greenhow village straddles a highly mineralised tongue of land, and still has many reminders of the lead-mining which virtually collapsed at the end of the 19th century. St Mary's is, at almost 1,400 ft., reputedly the highest parish church in England; the foundation stone was laid in 1857, volunteers provided most of the labour, and the church was consecrated in the following year. Voluntary effort came into play again in 1985-6 when parishioners re-roofed the building.

The *Miner's Arms* has an apt name, for mining was the principal reason for the growth of this straddling village. The miners found accommodation on the Hill or trudged up the Banks from Nidderdale each working day, one man, according to Fred Longthorne, a fount of information about Greenhow, arriving at 5.30 a.m. and resting for half an hour before joining the shift which began at 6 a.m. Having been permitted to erect cottages on moorland 'intakes', the residents were also able to have crofts. When mining ended, there remained a few stone quarries and opportunities for some men to pick over the old spoil heaps for once-despised minerals such as fluorspar. Farmers were contracted to cart material from the lead-mines, and the last loads contained fluorspar, recovered from the spoil heaps and transported to Pateley Bridge to be forwarded to the steelworks. 'Oade Will', Fred's father, who died in 1933, used to take a horse and cart from Greenhow to Skipton to collect coal. He would set off from home at 5 a.m. and, fearing robbers, usually slipped his money into his clogs. A level named Jackass was driven but in most cases the lead veins were reached by vertical shaft.

Stump Cross Caverns were discovered in 1858, when a small party of miners busy sinking a shaft on the moor found a natural opening at a depth of around 50 ft. Two boys who were working with the men crawled underground, following a winding and tortuous passage, alternately walking and crawling, invariably splashing through water. They arrived in a large chamber, the roof of which was draped with huge calcite formations. Rushing back to the miners, they yelled, 'We've seen a lot of naked men leaning against a wall.' The most easily accessible passages were opened as a show cave. The largest of the calcite formations, known as 'the Sentinel', has linked itself with a stalagmite boss to produce a pillar. Wolverine Cave was named after the discovery of bones from the carnivore which is associated with one of the Pleistocene cold periods over 100,000 years ago.

Brimham Rocks, covering some 50 acres, was willed to the National Trust by R.R. Ackernley. Brimham was referred to anciently as 'Birnbeam', *beam* being an old word for a tree. Roger de Mowbray had given the area to Fountains Abbey and the monks had a grange here, possibly also a chapel. This strange hilltop landscape consists of stumps of sandstone eroded by wind, rain and frost from a thick layer deposited in Carboniferous times, when what was to become Britain lay on the equator and the climate was much warmer than it is today. In the Ice Age, the end of the ridge became frost-shattered, vertical joints developing into deep fissures and lesser lines of weakness, horizontal or inclined, also being eroded. The sandstone along the fissures disintegrated into loose grains and pebbles, which were washed down the hillside. The curious tors and rock-masses are what was left behind.

Brimham House was rebuilt and extended by the Grantleys in 1792, about the time the first tourists were visiting the Rocks. Thomas Pennant (1773) was the first visitor to write about the area as a pleasure ground. In the following decade a Major Rooke read a paper to the Antiquarian Society in which he claimed the Rocks were the work of 'artists skilled in the power of mathematics'. A tourist guide of 1818 made reference to the 'druidical monuments'. A Wesleyan rally held at Brimham in 1885 was attended by 3,000 people, who listened to a brass band and a choir composed of 100 people. There were two sermons and a 'well spread repast'. Early in the 19th century, wagonettes and dog carts carried curiosity-seekers to Brimham, and from 1849 the Nidderdale Omnibus operated regularly from the station at Ripley to Pateley Bridge, further opening up the district to visitors. The opening of the Nidd Valley Railway in 1862 enabled passengers to alight from trains at Dacre Banks.

Nidderdale takes on a rich, fertile aspect at Ripley, a village owned by the Ingilbys for many generations. Ripley is quite unlike any other village in Yorkshire, having been modelled by Sir William Amcotts Ingilby on a village in Alsace-Lorraine, hence the Hotel de Villé. Ingilby remains lie in the Church of All Saints, near the entrance to the castle. On the 1618 tomb of Sir William Ingilby is inscribed: 'No pompe nor pride. Let God be honoured'. Local tradition insists that these words were used by order of Oliver Cromwell. Jane, one of the indomitable Ingilby women, is said to have been wounded at the battle of Marston Moor (1644), after which the victorious Cromwell arrived at Ripley Castle to a less than enthusiastic welcome from Lady Ingilby, Sir William, her husband, being a Royalist. A local story relates how she met the future Protector bearing a brace of loaded pistols and grudgingly allowed him to occupy a sofa overnight. To reassure herself there was no ill intent, she mounted guard over Cromwell and his attendants. When asked why she carried two pistols, she replied that if she missed with one, she could quickly resort to the second.

13

THE DALES TODAY

I N OCTOBER 1947, before the National Park, with its dual role of conserving the land-scape and improving access facilities for the public came into being, the Dales were being exploited to such an extent that a group of local people formed the Craven Branch of the Council for the Preservation (now Protection) of Rural England. At the initial gathering were Arthur Raistrick, historian, Harry J. Scott, founder in 1939 of *The Yorkshire Dalesman*, Marmaduke Miller, artist and mine host of *The Falcon* at Arncliffe, and Sir William Milner, the York architect who transformed an old Wharfedale farmhouse into the stylish Parcevall Hall.

One example of the free development which worried lovers of the Dales was the wooden bungalow at the foot of Malham Cove. Throughout its 50-plus years of existence, the CPRE has relied on persuasion to focus public opinion on matters of concern. The branch came into conflict with the farming community in the 1970s when large silos were the fashion, and after a successful campaign their construction was made subject to planning consent. A stance was taken against caravan sites which were, to quote a branch spokesman, 'spreading like mushrooms out of control up the Dales'. A proposal for a caravan park at Buckden, Wharfedale, would have 'drowned the whole village'.

Curbs were put on the spread of large advertisement hoardings, though this aspect of commercialisation is springing up again, in more subtle ways. An important change in Dales life came in the 1950s with the supply of electricity to villages and farms, but huge pylons do not march up hill and down dale, to provide it. In Langstrothdale, the upper part of the Wharfe valley, it is not easy to pick out the electrical equipment in the landscape.

Much of the Dales landscape is man-made in the sense that humans have tampered with the natural scene. A prime reason for setting up the Dales National Park was preservation of a unique landscape. Many old buildings, such as field barns, bear signs of neglect because of changes in farming practice. Many more would have fallen down but for the grants available from the National Park authority to maintain them. Such is the demand for housing that redundant barns in updale villages are now dwellings. Unlike most field barns, they were handy to basic facilities like electricity and water. At Halton Gill, in Littondale, a church as well as several barns have been brought into the domestic market. Even so over 1,100 new dwellings were permitted in the 1980s within the Yorkshire Dales National Park.

The urbanisation of the dale-country goes on apace, with a vast increase in roadside signs, curbs laid alongside roads and car parks complete with litter-bins. Bureaucracy is rampant. Wardens are now relatively common, yet the Dales population is a mere 18,000. More crucial is the figure for visitor days per annum, which is an awesome 8.3 million. Traffic in the Dales grew by 44 per cent between 1971 and 1991 and if current levels of growth continue, traffic could double by 2025. In the summer of 1997, the Dales suffered

66   *The late Alf Wight, alias James Herriot, the author.*

pollution levels higher than recommended limits for 400 to 600 hours. New roads are not considered to be the answer. Many thoughtful people feel the emphasis should be on a well integrated public transport system. But is not easy to wean Dalesgoers from their cars.

In recent times a rural image of sorts has been created by townsfolk who devise and introduce country programmes. The true voice of the Dales is rarely heard. The dale-country has acquired a romantic aspect through books and television films which stress its farming activity. A vet called Alf Wight, writing as James Herriot about life in the upper dales when he arrived in 1940, came closest to defining the character of Dalesfolk and commended the Dales to readers throughout the English-speaking world. The BBC gave him further celebrity through a series of films based on stories from his books. Hannah Hauxwell, who featured in an official report as a woman living on a high dale farm where her income was less than £200 a year, became a newspaper, then a television celebrity, star of films and books.

Such romanticisation of the Dales has given the impression they have been a quiet farming backwater, which is far from being the case. The industrial aspect is evident in old quarries, the remains of field kilns and, in the lead-mining areas, the shells of smelt mills, peat stores and spoilheaps sprawling in what have reverted to quiet gills without, however, losing their scars. Motorists see little of this former industry but walkers, using fellside paths, gasp whenever they enter areas blighted by mining. Pollution from smelt mill chimneys killed off heather in the immediate area; the watercourses ran grey with sludge.

So much weather-worn limestone has been removed from the glorious 'pavement' areas that a Limestone Pavement Action Group, which includes the Yorkshire Wildlife Trust, has been formed. The group warns that a relatively small area of such pavement remain in England, and of this only three per cent is completely undamaged. The face of a limestone quarry is a prominent scar on the landscape but there is a reassuring sight at old quarries, where the rock has darkened, vegetation has colonised cracks and crannies and once barren quarry floors now sustain trees and a profusion of plants.

Most recently, ancient woodlands, rare mosses, and common but delightful wild flowers in Wensleydale have been under threat from further quarrying. Residents at Preston under Scar, in Wensleydale, were concerned, when learning of plans to extend quarrying, that they might have to suffer from permanent dust in the atmosphere. The quarry owners are beginning to be environmentally friendly. For example, a six-figure trust fund has been set up to pay for ongoing maintenance of Swinden Quarry near Cracoe when quarrying ends in 2020. A harsh commercial environment will then become a nature conservation site, complete with a lake. Another kind of industrialisation in the Dales was textiles, cotton and wool, often located in former corn mills operated by water-power.

The first tourists were folk of leisure and means who ventured into the Dales to see natural wonders such as Weathercote Cave or Gordale Scar. They stayed at local inns and hired local guides. Mass tourism had its beginnings in Victorian days as trains delivered thousands of day-trippers to Ingleton, Bolton Abbey, Grassington or Aysgarth. When, in the 1920s and '30s, the countryside was rediscovered, rambling and cycling were popular and inexpensive occupations. It was the golden age of cycling, for there was little competition from motor vehicles and many of the roads had hardly outgrown their old status of country lanes. They had 'grass up the middle'.

Today, with mass tourism, a large number of specialist firms offer goods and services and the Dales are in danger of becoming a theme park. Within living memory, the tourist season extended from Easter until the end of September and a hush fell on the villages on Sundays. Now there is a seven-day-a-week turbulence which lasts for most of the year. At honeypots, like Bolton Abbey and Aysgarth Falls, there are often hundreds of cars. There might even be difficulty in finding car parking space at Malham in midwinter if a mild spell has encouraged day-tripping. The trippers are usually self-reliant, bringing their own food. Dalesfolk themselves are keen supporters of urban supermarkets for the weekly or monthly shopping and the village shop finds it hard to survive. Over half of England's rural shops selling only food have closed in the last six years. The Rural Development Council is worried that the decline is beginning to affect small market towns as more and more people are lured to 'shopping centres' in town or city.

Hill farming, now in the doldrums, was responsible for the Dales' neat, well-used appearance. The summer sun fell on a riot of colourful plants in the meadows. Great changes began in the Second World War. Mechanisation was represented by the tractor and an assortment of appliances, including the ingenious bailing machine, which took the hard work out of haytime. Such changes greatly reduced the number of people employed in agriculture, impoverishing Dales life. The true hill farms, with little or no valley bottom

67 *Haytime on a Dales farm. The horse-drawn machine is rowing-up the hay.*

68 *'Sweeping up' hay in the northern dales.*

land, such as Penyghent House and Rainscar, beside the Stainforth-Halton Gill road, have 1,000 sheep or more ranging over 3,000 acres, with much depending on the availability of family labour.

The new farming ways–ploughing, draining, re-seeding and the application of artificial fertilisers and slurry–provides wall-to-wall expanses of grass intended for silage-making. An entire dale has the same shade of green throughout. Such improved land offers little food for birds like lapwings and curlews, which had hitherto nested freely and are now becoming scarce. Rolls of silage in black plastic bags lie at the corners of fields rather than being stowed away in the field barns. The driver of one of the tourist buses which regularly come into the Dales refers to them amusingly as 'black pudding factories'.

Changes on the land are legion. Milking no longer takes place on the hill farms; the income is derived from ranching with beef cattle and from the flocks of hardy sheep. Once the Dales farmer was proud of the purity of his stock; now there is a wide variety. In the world of cattle, continental breeds have become prominent. Economics made impossible the continuation of those many smallholdings, where a bright young man might get a start in farming or where a farmer and his wife might rear a large family. In upper Swaledale over 100 smallholdings, each of which once sustained a large family, the husband also working in lead-mining or some other local industry, have been absorbed by larger farms. There is now much concern about the survival of hill farming in its present form, a farmer's annual income being as low as £5,000 to £7,000. A survey conducted by the National Farmers' Union shows that the majority of hill farmers are aged over 50 years and that a minority have a successor within the family to take over their farming business when they retire. The Hill Livestock Compensatory Allowance has been cut, leading to financial stagnation. As the number of hill farms, and those who are capable of operating them, shrinks, so too will the essential knowledge about traditional techniques of stock and land management.

The emphasis today is on diversification, which bemuses the old type of farmer who was brought up rearing cattle and sheep. The Dales, as part of what is being called the Northern Uplands, will benefit financially from a governmental scheme, via the local Tourist Board, which aims to increase a farmer's income from tourism. For a limited period, capital grants are available for the upgrading of existing facilities and the development of new ones. Political leaders tend to think mainly about 'landscape' and to regard 'farming' as a component; the two are interlinked. The work of a farmer in sustaining his land and stock is the key to a varied and well-kept landscape. During the beef troubles of late 1997 the President of the NFU said,

> It is the small and family farms, and hill farms, which are particularly vulnerable. There is no question of just being able to tighten their belts. Their finances are being squeezed to the limits of their financial endurance. They can take no more.

Robert Heseltine, Chairman of the Yorkshire Dales National Park Authority, wrote in *Dales 98*, a community newspaper published by the Authority: 'A devastated agricultural economy leads directly to a degraded landscape.'

With changes in Dales farming practice, hundreds of field barns are under threat because they are no longer needed, and unattended will quickly degenerate into ruin. Now help is at hand from the Dales National Park and also from a grant from the Millenium Trust, which at Darnbrook Farm, one of the Malham Moor holdings of the National Trust, replaced a barn roof and repaired the walls at a cost of about £15,000. The National Trust's holding in the Yorkshire Dales has increased spectacularly in recent years, thanks partly to a grant of almost £600,000 from the National Lottery which in June 1995 enabled 3,000 acres of unspoilt upland landscape to be purchased at a cost of £790,000. The farmland is adjacent to the Malham Tarn estate of the Trust and part of it is included in the Malham/Arncliffe Site of Special Scientific Interest which might become known as the Craven Limestone Complex if plans to designate it for conservation are successful.

The capacity of the uplands to hold water, to release it gradually and to retain the moist areas where moorland birds can feed, have been affected by 'gripping' (mechanical draining). New conifer forests, comprising alien species of trees which grow lustily under grey Dales skies, have since the 1970s clogged many a fellside. Most of the new forests have been planted with the incentive of generous tax allowances. Happily, indigenous species are now coming prominently into modern commercial forestry. Coniferous woodland covers some two per cent of the National Park and has been described by the Park's Trees and Woodland Officer as 'dark, intrusive blobs on the landscape, of little value to wildlife apart from a handful of species'. The National Park is keen to conserve what remains of typical fellside woodland, which is threatened by the browsing of sheep. The Dales landscape is relatively bare, just 3.5 per cent of the National Park area being covered by trees, compared with a national average of 10 per cent.

The proportion of ancient semi-natural broad-leaved woodland of the type which once covered much of the Dales is 0.7 per cent. Co-operation between Park and Forestry authorities, as well as English Nature, has led to the planting of a new native wood in Littondale. Work is under way in conifer plantations in Cotterdale, Upper Wensleydale, to improve their visual impact on the landscape and enhance their wildlife value.

69 *Newhouses, in Langstrothdale, is now owned by the National Trust.*

New problems occur. The air resounds with the thunderous roar of empty lorries returning for more loads of stone from the quarries and the scream of jet engines as military aircraft on exercise follow a dale at less than the height of the flanking hills. Following the introduction of the mobile telephone, and its increasing popularity, the Dales Park Authority has been dealing with a wave of applications for masts, some of them considered to be badly sited. The problem is aggravated by the desire of rival companies to have their own systems.

Conservation has become a dominant topic in the Dales. A stone staircase which has replaced old wooden steps at Gordale Scar, in Malhamdale, is one of a series of improvements being carried out under the £8 million Dales EnviroNet scheme, which is managed by the Yorkshire Dales Millennium Trust. Over 30 tonnes of stone were airlifted to the site by helicopter, the cost of which was met by the National Park Authority.

Meanwhile, firm voices are raised whenever there is a perceived threat to the Dales life and landscape. In matters of conservation, the Yorkshire Dales Society has been effective. One of its founders, Colin Speakman, has written:

> In a deeply uncertain age, where most people live highly mobile lives, in faceless suburbs or traffic-dominated cities which have changed beyond all recognition, the Dales represent for most people something deeply rooted, rural, solid, enduring and understandable.

Escapism? Perhaps. Or, as Speakman says, is it maybe a deeper recognition of all our own roots, in rural or semi-rural communities, a few generations ago. He adds:

> Nobody pretends that we should try and keep old traditions artificially alive—mock peasants dancing in hand-embroidered smocks. The Dales have always been an area of often rapid economic and social change. But the powerful experiences of the past can become a source of emotional and spiritual renewal for present and future generations.

BIBLIOGRAPHY

Armstrong, Thomas, *Adam Brunskill* (1951)

Barringer, J.C., *The Yorkshire Dales* (1982)

Batty, Margaret, *A Bonny Hubbleshoo* (1970)

Batty, Margaret, *Bygone Reeth* (1985)

Beaumont, Heather M., *Sir William Milner* (1985)

Bigland, John, *A Geographical and Historical View of the World* (1810)

Bonser, K.J., *The Drovers* (1970)

Brigg, J.J., *The King's Highway in Craven* (1927)

Brown, A.J., *Moorland Tramping* (1931)

Brown, A.J., *Fair North Riding* (1952)

Calvert, T.C., *Chapters from the New Testament translated into the Wensleydale Tongue* (undated)

Camden, W., *Britannica* (1590)

Craven, S.A., *Christopher Francis Drake Long: a Biography* (Craven Pothole Club, 1975)

Dalesman, monthly magazine founded in April 1939

Dawson, Christopher, *Memories of a Victorian Childhood* (printed privately, 1949)

Drayton, Michael, *Polyolbion* (1598)

Duerden, Norman, *Portrait of the Dales* (1978)

Fieldhouse, R. and Jennings, B., *A History of Richmond and Swaledale* (1978)

Glover, R.R., Pitty, A.F., Waltham, A.C., *Caves and Karst of the Yorkshire Dales* (1977)

Grainge, W., *Nidderdale* (1859)

Gunn, Peter, *The Yorkshire Dales: Landscape with Figures* (1984)

Hall, David, *Burtersett Quarries* (1985)

Harriman, G.L., *Castle Bolton and Redmire* (1982)

Hartley, Marie and Ingilby, Joan, *The Yorkshire Dales* (1956)

Hartley, Marie and Ingilby, Joan, *A Dales Heritage* (1982)

Horton Local History Group, *The Story of an Upland Parish* (1984)

Howson, Thomas, *Illustrated Guide to the District of Craven* (1861)

Hurtley, T., *A Concise Account of some Curiosities in the Environs of Malham* (1786)

Hutton, John, *Tour to the Caves, in the Environs of Ingleborough and Settle* (1781)

Mitchell, W.R., *Tales of a Yorkshire Hoffman* (1980)

Mitchell, W.R., *Uses of Horton Flag* (1981)

Mitchell, W.R., *Drystone Walls of the Yorkshire Dales* (1992)

Mitchell, W.R., *Ingleborough: the Big Blue Hill* (1994)

Muir, Richard, *The Dales of Yorkshire* (1991)

New Arcadians Journal No. 13, 'A Landscape Explored: Wharfedale at Bolton Abbey' (1984)

Ogilby, J., *Britannia* (1675)

Palmer, William T., *Wanderings in Ribblesdale* (1951)

Pontefract, Ella and Hartley, Marie, *Swaledale* (1934)

Pontefract, Ella and Hartley, Marie, *Wensleydale* (1936)
Pontefract, Ella and Hartley, Marie, *Wharfedale* (1938)
Raistrick, Arthur, *Malhamdale* (1947)
Raistrick, Arthur, *Green Tracks on the Pennines* (1962)
Raistrick, Arthur, *Old Yorkshire Dales* (1967)
Raistrick, Arthur, *Malham and Malham Moor* (1976 edition)
Raistrick, Arthur, *Monks and Shepherds in the Yorkshire Dales* (1976)
Robson, Peter, *Fountains Abbey—a Cistercian Monastery* (1983)
Romney, Paul (ed.), *The Diary of Charles Fothergill, 1805* (1984)
Sedgwick, Adam, *A Memorial by the Trustees of Cowgill Chapel* (1968)
Sellers, Gladys, *The Yorkshire Dales* (1984)
Shaw, Trevor R., 'John Hutton (1740?-1806)', *Studies of Speleology*, Vol. 2 (1971)
Southey, Robert, *The Doctor* (1847)
Speakman, Colin, *A Yorkshire Dales Anthology* (1981)
Speight, Harry, *The Craven and North-West Yorkshire Highlands* (1892)
Waltham, Tony, *Yorkshire Dales: Limestone Country* (1987)
Watkins, Peter, *Bolton Priory and its Church* (1989)
Whitaker, Thomas Dunham, *History of Craven* (1812)
Whitaker, Thomas Dunham, *History of Richmondshire* (1822)
White, Robert, *Yorkshire Dales: Landscapes through Time* (1997)
Wright, Geoffrey, *The Yorkshire Dales* (1985)
Yorkshire Dales National Park, *Farming in the Yorkshire Dales* (1977)

INDEX

Illustrations are printed in bold type

Abbeys (*see* specific names)
Access to the Countryside Act, 1949, xiii
Ackernley, R.R., 130
Act of Union, 20
Adam Brunskill, 89
Adamthwaite, 76
Addleborough, **I**, 14, 97
Aire Gap, xiii-xiv, 1, 29, 38, 41
Aire, river, xiii-xiv, 41, 43, 46
Airehead Springs, 46
Airey, Thomas Septimus, 34, 114
Airton, 15, 27, 43, 46, 50
Alan Rufus, 94
Aldborough, 29
Alder, 12
Alderson, William, x, 91
Almshouses, Beamsley, 122
Alum Pot, xiv
Amerdale Dub, 112
Amsden, Alice, 99
Anemone, wood, 67
Angles, 14, 15, 43
Anglo-Danish, 15
Angram reservoir, 91, 123-4
Appersett, 15
Appleby, 8, 30-1, 67
Appleby Castle, 90
Appletreewick, 16, 20, 117-8, 126
Arcow Wood, 70
Arkengarthdale, xiii, 6, 8, 16, 18-20, 24, 85-9,
  92-3
Arkengarthdale, Manor of, 93
Arkengarthdale, New Forest, 16
Arkle Beck, 87, 93
Arkle Town, 93-4
Armstrong, Edward, 27
Armstrong, Thomas, 89
Armstrong, William George, 81
Arncliffe, 10, 14, 22, 46, 111
Arten Gill, 81-2
Artists, 25
Ash, 8, 9, 104, 114
Ashwell, William H., 66
Askrigg, **IV**, xv, 22, 86, 98, 102, 105
Askrigg Block, 6
Askrigg Hall, 100
Atkinson, Richard, 84
Austwick, 6, 7, 15, 55, 66, 72
Axe, Cumbrian, 12
Aykroyd, Sir Frederick, 126
Aysgarth, 15, 27-8, 39, 96, 103, 133
Aysgarth Falls, 103-4, **104**, 133

Badger Gate, 32
Bain, river, 29, 100
Bainbridge, 14, 16, 22, 29, 100, l02-3, 112

Balcome, Graham, 61
Baneberry, 68
Baptists, 26
Barbondale, 6
Bardale, 101
Barden, Forest of, 16
Barden Moor, 38
Barden Reservoir, 123
Barden Tower, 19, 117-8
Barley, 12
Barn, 113
Barnard Castle, 90, 93
Barns, field, 40
Barony of Kendal, 61
Barrows, 13
Barytes, 6
Bathurst, Charles, 93
Bathurst, John, 93
Batty, Edward, 61
Batty, Margaret, xv
Baugh Fell, 35, 76-7, 82, 96
Beamsley, 32, 122
Beamsley Beacon, 122
Beamsley Hospital, 122
Beck Head, Clapham, 3
Beckermonds, 109-10
Becket, Thomas à, 67
Bedale, 105
Bedstraw, limestone, 49
Beecroft, Horton-in-Ribblesdale, 22
Beecroft Quarry, 69
Bell Busk, 27, 43, 46
Bellerby, 26
Bell-pits, 8, 32
Benedictine order, 17
Bentham, 22, 56
Bentinck family, 82
Bewerley, 128
Bewerley Grange Chapel, 128
Bewerley Hall, 128-9
Bicknell, P., 24
Bigland, John, 51
Bilberry, 8
Binyon, Laurence, 51-2, 54
Birch, Silver, 104
Birkbeck, John, 12
Birkdale Beck, 87
Birkwith, 63
Birtwhistle, John, 22
Bishopdale, 16, 25, 104
Bishopdale Chase, 104, 107
Black Death, 19
Blackwood's Magazine, 51
Blea Moor Tunnel, 51
Blea Pot, 32
Blubberhouses, 29, 34, 121, 122

Blue Flagstone, 6
Blue moor-grass, 49
Blunt, Dr Alfred, 73
Bogg, Edmund, 115
Bolton Abbey, 16, 20, 25, 28, 34-5, 49, 109,
  118, 121-2, 133
Bolton Abbey Estate, 109, 120
Bolton Bridge, 29, 109
Bolton Castle, Wensleydale, 90, 105
Bolton Hall, 25, 30, 119, 120, 122
Bolton Priory, **IX**, xiii, 8, 26, 43, 45, 117, 119
Booze, 94
Bordley, 13, 30
Boroughbridge, 18, 29
Borrowdale, 18
Bottomley, Richard, 28
Boulder clay, 5
Bouthwaite, 126
Bowland, 1, 6, 16
Bowland Shales, 41
Bowness, 38, 109
Boy of Egremont, 118
Boyle, Robert, 120
Bracken, 8
Brackenbottom, 54
Bradford, 72, 117
Bradford, University of, 12
Bradford Corporation, 123
Bradford Waterworks, 123
Brathay Flagstone, 83
Bray, William, 23, 25
Brennand, Thomas, 66
Brigantes, 14, 29, 56, 94
Brigflatts, 76-7
Brigg, John J., 32
Brimham House, 130
Brimham Rocks, 4, 130
British Rail, 68
Bronze Age, 12-13, 110
Brough, 31
Brough Hill Fair, 98, 100
Brougham Castle, 21
Brown, A. J., xv, 87, 94, 97
Brown, George H., 11
Bruff, Harald, 129
Buck, Dr. C.W., 71
Buck, Ralph, 18
Buckden, 5, 29, 109-10, 112, 131
Buckden Pike, 38, 112
Buckden Rake, 112
Buckhaw Brow, xv, 33
Buckthorn, 114
Burial Cairns, 13
Burnsall, 14, 15, 30, 116
Burnsall Angling Club, 109
Burnsall Church, 116

Burnsall School, 20
Burtersett, 15, 98, 100
Burtersett Quarries, 100
Burton, Ernest, 102
Burton, William Handley, 102
Burton-in-Kendal, 24
Burton-in-Lonsdale, 8, 51
Butler, Samuel, 94
Buttercup, 87
Buttertubs, **XVII**
Buttertubs Pass, 85
Buzzard, 76
Buzzard, Rough-legged, 127
Byland Abbey, 19, 125-6
Byng, Hon. John, 27, 63, 100

Calamine, 45
Caldbergh, 107
Calf, The, 1, 75, 77
Calf Top, 103
Calton, 30, 43
Calvert, Edward, 57
Calvert, Kit, x, 98-100
Cam Beck, xiv, 63, 109
Cam End, 14, 29, 63
Cam Fell, 22
Cam High Road, 14, 100
Cam Houses, xiv, 63-4
Camden, William, 10, 23, 30, 87
Campbell, Thomas, 66
Canal, Leeds-Liverpool, 33, 45
Carboniferous period, 1, 6, 79, 83, 130
Carlisle, 29
Carlow Stone, 6, 102
Carlton, Coverdale, 107
Carperby, 104-5
Carr, Edith, x
Carr, Rev. William, 25, 120
Carrick, John, 66
Carter, Russell, 47
Cartimandua, 14, 56
Casterton Low Fell, 6
Castle Bolton, 15, 26, 105
Cat Hole, 91
Catrigg Force, 70
Catterick, 29
Cattle, Scotch, 64
Cattle, Shorthorn, 99
Cattle, wild white, 49
Cattle-droving, 20, 22, 25
Cautley, 77
Cautley Chapel, 77
Cautley Crag, **XIII**, 1
Cautley Spout, 1, 76
Cavendish Estate, 115
Cavendish Pavilion, 121
Cavendish, Lord Frederick, 120
Caves, 3
Cawden, 41, 49
Cerialis, 14
Chapel-le-Dale, 4-5, 9, 14, 25, 27, 53, 55, 61, 62
Chapman, Dick, 102
Chapman, Edward, 99
Charcoal burning, 18
Chatsworth Estate, 16
Cheese, ewe, 118
Cheese, Wensleydale, 98-9, 108
Chelker Reservoir, 121
Cherry, Matthew, x, 24
Chert, 12, 94
Christianity, 14-15
Christie's Mill, 69
Churchill, John H., 62
Cinquefoil, alpine, 49

Cistercian order, 17, 18, 45
Civil War, 21, 50, 105
Clapdale, 58-9
Clapham, 17, 51, 55, 60-1, 66
Clapham Beck, 3, 59
Clapper Bridge, **41**
Clark, John, 7, 71
Clarkson, Anthony, 88
Clay, laminated, 11
Clifford family, 16, 43, 110, 117
Clifford, Lady Anne, 8, **21**, 30, 112, 117, 122
Clifford, Henry, 119
Climate, 10
Clints, 5
Cloudberry, 8
Clough, river, xiv, 75, 77, 82
Coaches, mail, 33
Coaching, 33-34
Coal, 4, 8, 26, 31-2, 81, 90
Coal Mining, 8, 26, 32
Coal Road, 8, 26, 32, 81
Coalgrove Head Company, 32
Coast to Coast Walk, 38, 87
Coke Oven, 8
Colby Hall, 98
Coleridge, Samuel Taylor, 79
Collins, Major E.R., 12
Colt Park, 9, 68
Combs Quarry, 2, 7
Commons Registration Act, 91
Congregationalists, xvi, 91
Coniston Cold, 33
Conistone, 114
Conistone Dib, 3, 114
Conistone Pike, 114
Conquest, Norman, 16
Conservation, 136
Conyer family, 20
Cooper, Edmund, 88
Coppice wood, 104
Corals, 2
Corbridge, 29
Cordingley, John, 47
Corpse Way, 92
Cosh, 112
Cosh Beck, 112
Costume of Yorkshire, The, 102
Cotter Clints, 30
Cotter End, 30, 97
Cotter Falls, xiv
Cotterdale, 32, 84, 96-7, 136
Cotton grass, 8, 9
Council for the Protection of Rural England, 37, 131
Count Alan of Brittany, 16, 18-9
Countersett, 15, 100
Cover Head, 107
Cover, river, 14, 107
Coverdale, 14, 107-8, 112, 124
Coverdale, Miles, 107
Coverham Abbey, 108, 111
Cow-keeping, Liverpool, 77
Cow parsley, 9
Cowgill, 79, 81
Cowgill Chapel, 81
Cowgill Head, 8
Cowslip, 114
Cracoe, 133
Cranesbill, meadow, 9
Cranesbill, wood, 49, 87
Craven, 14, 16, 21, 26
Craven Fault, 1, 6, 8
Craven Lime Co. Ltd., 71
Craven Limestone Complex, 135
Craven, Margaret, 20

Craven, Sir William, 20, 30, 116, 117
Craven Way, 51
Cray, 5, 112
Craze, Romilly, 117
Crina Bottom, 55
Crump, Neville, 107
Cromwell, Oliver, 50
Crook Beck, 102
Cross Fell, 54
Crosskeys, The, **XIII**
Cross-leaved heath, 8
Crossley, John, 67, 82
Crowberry, 8
Crummockdale, 6
Cullingford, H., 53
Cumberland, Earls of, 20
Curlew, xiii, 36, 134
Cycling, 133
Cyclo-cross, Three Peaks, 53

Dairy Crest, 99
Dalehead, 57
Dales Countryside Museum, 39
Dales Way, The, 38, 109
Dalesrail, 68
Danes, 14, 15, 43
Danny Bridge, 83
D'arcy, Sir Arthur, 126
Dark Ages, 14
Darlington, 82
Darnbrook Farm, 16, 18, 46, 135
Darnbrook Fell, 114
Dawkins, Boyd, 11
Dawson, Christopher, 20, 24, 41
Dawson, Geoffrey, 72-3
Dawson, Josias, 20
Dayes, Edward, 48
Dead Man's Hill, 124, 126
Dee, river, xiv, 1, 5, 14, 75, 77, 79, 81-2
Deepdale, 34
Deepdale Chapel, 82
Deer, Red, 16, 121
Deeside Lodge, 82
Defoe, Daniel, 24, 120
Delaney, John, **69**
Dent, xv, 4, 32, 34, 51, 60, 75-6, 78, 79, 81-3
Dent Fault, 6, 79, 83
Dent marble, 5, 59-60, 80-2
Dent station, **80**
Dentdale, 5, 26, 38, 54, 76, 78
Derbyshire, 20
Devil's Causeway, The, 29
Devonshire, Duke of, 25, 115, 120, 122
Dewhurst family, 27
Dipper, 112
Disappointment Pot, 57
Dissolution of Monasteries, 19-20, 25, 79, 111, 113, 119
Diving, cave, 47
Domesday Survey, 16, 68, 72, 94, 114
Dower, Arthur, 36, 44
Dower, John, xiii, 36-7, 40, 44
Dower, Michael, 37
Dower, Pauline, 37
Dower, Robert Shillito, 36
Dower, Robin, 37
Dower, Susan, 37
Drayton, Michael, 63
Drebley, 16
Drew, Barbara, 99
Droving (see cattle-droving)
Drumlins, 5
Duerley Beck, 97
Dunlin, xiii

Eagle, Golden, 127
Earl Conan of Richmond, 16
Earl Edwin, 118
Easby Abbey, 17, 83
Edale, 41
Edward VIII, 73
Elephant, straight-tusked, 11
Elgar, Edward, **71**
Elizabeth II, Queen, 56
Ellerkin Scar, **IV**
Ellerlands Edge, 105
Ellerton Priory, 17
Elm, 12
Elm, wych, 104
Emmerdale, 28
Enclosures, xv, 10, 22, 29, 38
English Nature, 68
The English Rock Garden, 60
Environment Act (1995), 37
Environmentally Sensitive Areas (E.S.A.s), 39
Erratics, 6
Eshton, 20, 46
Eshton Hall, 50

Falcon, Peregrine, 76
Farming, hill, 28, 133, 135
Farnley Hall, 120
Farrer family, 57, 59, 65
Farrer, Elizabeth, 58
Farrer, James, 3
Farrer, James Anson, 58
Farrer, James William, 58
Farrer, Matthew, 9
Farrer, Oliver, 58
Farrer, Reginald, 51, 58, **59**, 60, 117
Farrer, Reginald, Trail, 60
Farrer, Sidney James, 59, 63
Fault lines, 3, 42, 116
Fawkes, Walter, 120
Fell Beck, xiv, 56
Fell End Chapel, 77
Field systems, 14
Fiennes, Celia, 30
Firbank, 77
First World War, 28, 36, 61, 77
Flagstone industry, 7, 69-70
Fleet Moss, xiv, 109
Flint, 12, 43
Flintergill Outrake, 80
Flower, globe, 68
Fluorspar, 6
Forest Laws, 16
Forestry, 135
Forrest, George, 117
Fossdale, 97
Foster Beck Mill, 127
Fothergill, Charles, 23, 26, 93, 96, 98
Fountaine Hospital, 116
Fountains Abbey, **VIII**, x, 10, **17**, **18**, 19, 29-30, 43, 45, 53, 63, 113-14, 125-6, 130
Fountains Fell, 8, 16, 26, 41, 43, 58, 70
Fountains Fell Colliery, 45, 70
Fountains Hall, 20, 23, 45
Fox, George, 26, 77, 79, 84
Fox Holes, 11, 12
Fox's Pulpit, 77
Foxup, 20
Foxup Beck, 112
Freeholders' Wood, 103-4
Fremington Edge, 94
Friarfold, 6
Friars Head, 20, **21**

Furness Abbey, 17-18, 20, 63

Gale Beck, 63-4, 66
Galloways, 98
Gamecocks, 61
Gaping Gill, xiv, 3, 55-7
Gargrave, ix, 14, 32, 45-6
Garsdale, **XIV,** 8, 15, 26, 34, 75-6, 78, 82-4, 95, 98
Garsdale Church, 83
Garsdale Junction, 84
Garsdale Street Chapel, 77, 84
Garsdale, Mount Zion Chapel, 84
Gayle, 97
Gayle Mill, 27
Gearstones, 22, 64-5
Gearstones Lodge, 66
Gearstones Moor, 66
Geese, 92
George V, 121-2
George VI, 122
Ghaistrills, 109
'Giant's Grave', 12
Giggleswick, 6, 33, 53, 70, 74
Giggleswick Scar, **XVIII**, 72
Giggleswick School Chapel, **50**
Gill, Harry, ix
Girton, Thomas, 120
Gisburn, 70
Gisburne Park, 49
Glaciation, 5
Gleanings in Craven, 49
Globe Flower, 9
Gloucester, Duke of, 106
Gnoup, Forest of, 114
Goose, Canada, 127
Gordale Scar, 3, 25, 42, **48**, 133, 136
Gouthwaite Hall, 127
Gouthwaite Reservoir, 12, 123
Goyden Pot, 12, 125
Gragareth, 53-4, 60
Grass Wood, 114
Grassington, 6, 12, 14, 22, 24, 28, 34, 35, 109, 114, **115**, 116, 133
Grassington Bridge, 114
Grassington Low Mill, 116
Grassington Moor, 6, 20, 23, 32, 115-16
Gray, Thomas, 24-5, 48
Great Burnet, 49
Great Close, Malham Moor, 22
Great Knoutberry, 80
Great Punchard Gill, 87
Great Scar Limestone, 1, 2, 5
Great Shunner Fell, 54, 86
Green Dragon inn, 97
Green Howards, 94
Green Roads', 29
Greenfield, 109
Greenfield Valley, 109
Greenhow Hill, 6, 18-19, 23, 128-30
Greta, by Tees, 25
Greta Gorge, Ingleton, 61
Griffin, Harry, 82
Grigson, Geoffrey, 9
Grinton, 14, 18, 92
Grisedale, 45, 84
Gritstone Club, 53
Grouse, red, xiii, 8, 28, 36, 91, 107, 121-2
Grouse-beating, 28, 61
Grouse Hall, 84
Grykes, 5
Guide to Malham, 28
Gulls, black-headed, 54
Gunnerside, 5, 22, 31, 35, 92
Gunnerside Gill, 24, 85
Gunnerside Lodge, 91

Hadrian's Wall, 29
Halton Gill, 8, 20, 57, 70, 111, 113, 131, 134
Hancock, Heather, 39
Hand-knitting, 78, 92, 102
Hanley, Tommy, 77
Hanlith, 30, 41, 43
Hanlith Hall, 50
Hardraw, 4, 32, 85
Hardraw Force, 97
Hardraw Scar, xiv, 97
Harebell, 114
Hargraves, Irvine, 117
Harker, Mr., **90**
Harker, Bailey J., 34
Harlow Carr, 117
Harpoon, reverse-barbed, 11
Harriman, G.L., 105
Harrison, Col. John, 50
Harrogate, 29, 34, 122
Hartley, David, 99
Hartley, Marie, 98, 110
Hartley, Marie, and Ingilby, Joan, x
Hartlington, 20
Haukswell, Hannah, 132
Hawes, **II**, xv, 8, 28-9, 31-2, 35, 40, 66, 90, **98**, 98-100, 102
Hawes Fair, 98
Hawes Folk Museum, 98
Hawes Silver Band, 102
Hawthorne, Nathaniel, 118
Haytime, **133**, **134**
Hazel, 104
Heather, 8, 9, 28
Hebblethwaite Hall, 76
Hebden, 116
Hebden Gill, 116
Hell Gill, 30, 97
Hellifield, 5, 27, 33, 46
Helwith Bridge, 2, 7, 70
Hemlock, western, 59
'Henges', 13
Henry VII, 60
Henry VIII, 60, 107
Herriot, James, 93
Herriot Country, 28
Heseltine, Robert, 37, 39, 135
Hewitt, Rev. Matthew, 116
Hey, Tom, 56
High Close, 12
High Crag, 129
High Green, 93
High Seat, 87
Highway Act (1555), 32
Hill-fort, 14, 56
Hill Inn, Chapel-le-Dale, 55
Hippopotamus, 11
Hobhouse Committee, 37
Hoffman, Friedrich, 7
Hoffman Kiln, 7, 71-2
Holiday Fellowship, 50
Hollet's Bookshop, Sedbergh, 76
Hollin Tree Fault, 8
Holly, 104
Horner, Michael, 11
Horse Head Pass, 111,113
Horsehouse, 107
Horton-in-Ribblesdale, 7, 12, 22, 53-5, 57, 63, 68
Horton Flags, 7
Horton Local History Group, 69
Houseman, John, 10
How Stean, 126
Howgill, 76
Howgill Fells, xiii, 1, 6, 13, 35, 55-6, 75, 76
Howson, Thomas, 46

Hubberholme, 5, 15, 110, 117
Hubberholme Church, 110, 111
Hubberholme, Land Letting, 111
Hull Pot, 57
Huby, Marmaduke, 128
Humber, 1
Hurst, Ken, 48
Hurtle Pot, 61-62
Hutton, Rev. John, 3, 4, 7, 24-5. 56
Hyena, spotted, 11
Hyne, C. J. Cutcliffe, 55

I'anson, Frances, 106
Ice Age, 5, 12, 61, 130
Ilkley, 29, 36, 38, 109, 112
Industrial Revolution, 27-8
Ingilby, Joan, 98, 110
Ingilby, Sir William Amcotts, 130
Ingleborough, xiv, 3, 4, **5**, 9, 14, 17, 24, 51, 53-7, **55**
Ingleborough Cave, 3, 12, 57
Ingleborough Estate, 3, 65-6
Ingleborough Hall, 59-60
Ingleborough House, 58
Ingleborough Lake, 58, 60
Ingleborough, Little, 55
Ingleton, 7, 8, 17, 25, 29, 35, 55, 62, 65, 80, 98, 133
Ingleton Fell Rescue, 56
Ingleton Fells, 61
Ingleton Glens, 2, 61-2
Ingleton Green Slate, 2, 7
Ingleton, Manor of, 22
Ingleton New Colliery, 8
Ingleton Patent Limeworks, 7, 71
Intake Gate, 126
Irish Sea, 1, 15
Irish-Norse migration, 15, 53
Iron Age, 10, 13-14, 56
Isle of Man, 15
Ivelet Bridge, 31

Jackson, John, 26
Janet's Foss, 42, 49
Jennings, John, 11
Jervaulx Abbey, 16-9, 30, 63, 68, 90, 95, **108**
Jingle Pot, 61
Jobson, Israel, 57

Kearton, Cherry, 91-2
Kearton, Richard, 91-2
Keasden, 66
Keld, 6, 91
Keld Chapel, 90
Kendal, 20, 32, 75-6
Kendalman's Ford, 20
Kershaw, Jonathan, 84
Kettlewell, 5, 12, 108-9, 112
Kidstones Pass, 104
Kilburn, 111
Kilgram Bridge, 30, 96, 108
Kiln, field, 7, 26, 91
Kilnsey, 14, 17, 18, 25, 29, 43, 45, 109, 113-14
Kilnsey Crag, **XI**, 113
Kilnsey grange, 114
Killhope, Weardale, **19**, 23
Kinder Scout, 36
King, Alan, 53
King, Capt. James, 50
Kingsdale, 22, 60-1
Kingsdale Beck, 61
Kingsdale Head, 61
Kingsley, Rev. Charles, 27, 44, 46, 95, 112
Kipling, Rudyard, 128

Kirk Sink, ix, 14
Kirk Yetholm, 41
Kirkby Lonsdale, 32, 76, 82
Kirkby Malham, xiii, 15, 28, 36, 43-4, 46, 49
Kirkby Malham Church, 50
Kirkby Malzeard, 125-6
Kirkby Stephen, 31, 76, 90-1, 95, 98
Kisdon Hill, 86-7, 91-2
Knitting, hand, 20, 92
Knollys, Francis, 105
Knollys, Sir Thomas, 105

Lake District, 1, 24
Lambert, Gen. John, 50
Lancaster, 25, 64
Lancaster Guardian, 71
Landseer, artist, 120
Langcliffe, **2**, 5, 7, 26, 46, 72
Langcliffe Hall, 72
Langstrothdale, xiv, 13, 109, 112, **113**, 131
Langstrothdale Chase, 16, 110, 112
Langthwaite, 24, 88, 93
Lapwing, xiii, 127, 134
Laund, 16
Lawson, Fred, 105
Laycock, Frank, 117
Lea Green, 12
Lead-miners, 20, **88**, 89, 93
Lead-mining, 6, 18-20, **23**, 24, 27, 31, 85-7, 89, 91, 93, 112, 114-6, 118
Leakey, Bob, 57
Lee Gate, xv, 30, 49
Lees, Dr Arnold, 95
Leland, John, 23, 30
Lewyn, John, 105
Leyburn, 35, 86, 98, 105-6
Leyburn Shaw, 106
Leyburn Tea Festivals, 106
Lily of the Valley, 68
Lime-burning, 26, 31, 70
Lime, tree, 12
Limestone, 2, 3, 7, 61
Limestone Pavement Action Group, 132
Lindley, Thomas, 111
Ling Gill, 66
Linton, 14, 114, 116
Linton Bridge, 114
Linton Church, 116
Linton Falls, 116
Linton Mill, 116
Lister, Leonard, 28
Littledale, 67
Litton, 112
Littondale, xiv, 5, 20, 109, 112-3, 131, 135
Lofthouse, 125-6
Long, C.F.D., 62
Long Preston, 74
Longthorne, Fred, 129
Lord, Thomas C., 11
Lord, Tot, ix, 11, 43
Lovely Seat, 86
Low Burrow, Lunesdale, 14
Low Row, 86, 88-9, 92-3
Low Row Common, **92**
Lowgill, 61
Lunds, 96, 105
Lune Gorge, 1
Lune, river, xiv, 75
Lunesdale, 14, 76
Lupton, Roger, 76
Lynchets, 15

Macmillan, Harold, 121
Malham, xiv, 22, 27, 29-30, 38-9, 41-6, 48, 70, 118

Malham Cove, 3, 27, 41-3, 46-7, 49, 131
Malham Moor, x, 8, 13, 15, 18, 22, 41, 43, 45-6, 70, 135
Malham Tarn, **VII**, 12, 16, 26-7, 41-2, 135
Malham Tarn Estate, 44
Malham Tarn House, **33**, **44**
Malhamdale, xiii, xv, 25, 29-30, 37, 39, 42-3, 46, 49-50, 112
Mallerstang, 30, 97
Manchester Anglers, 68
Manchester University, 13, 69
Maple, red, 59
Maple, yellow, 59
Marigold, marsh, 9, 84
Marrick Mines, 23
Marrick Priory, 17, 94
Marsett, 101
Marsett Green, 101
Marston Moor, 130
Martel, Edward Alfred, 57
Mary, Queen of Scots, 105-6
Masham, 125
Mastiles Lane, ix, 18, 29-30
Maude, Thomas, 105
Maudsley family, 71
Mauleverer family, 43
Meadows, hay, 49, 86
Melmerby, 107
Mesolithic period, 12, 43
Metcalfe family, 8, 20, 78
Metcalfe, Candle Willie, 100
Metcalfe, Sir Christopher, 100, 103
Metcalfe, Thomas, 103
Metcalfe, William, 1-3
Metcalfe Society, 103
Methodism, xvi, 26, 84, 91, 95
Meugher, 126
Microliths, 12
Mid Craven fault, 3
Midland Railway Company, 66, 80, 98
Middle House, 22, 43, 46
Middleham, 26, 30, 95, 104, 106, **107**
Middleham Castle, 107-8
Middleham Church, 106
Middleham Moor, 22
Middlesmoor, 125
Milkhouse, 77-8
Mill Gill Force, 102
Miller, Marmaduke, 112. 131
Millstone Grit, 1, 4, 116
Milner, Sir William, 117, 131
Mining, lead (*see* lead mining)
Ministry of Agriculture, 39
Ministry of Defence, 36
Monasteries, 29, 31
Monk Bridge, 43
Monks' Way, 46
Montagu, Frederic, 49
Moone, Prior, 119
Moorcock Inn, **V**, 96
Moorcock Viaduct, 84
Morecambe Bay, 17
Morrison, Walter, 27, 34, **44**, 46, 50
'Mosscrop', 9
Mossdale, 16, 97
'Mosses', 8
Moughton Fell, 2, 69
Mount Calva, 92
Mowbray, Roger de, 130
Muir, Richard, xv, 10
Muker, **XII**, 90-92
Muker Silver Band, 107
Murray, George, 66
Murray, Thomas, 66
Myers, Dr J.O., x

Nappa Hall, 19, 100, 103
National Farmers' Union, 134
National Trust, xiii, xvi, 36, 38, 44, 49, 71, 130, 135
Neolithic period, 12, 102
Neville family, 16, 104, 106
New House Farm, 49
Newbiggin, 104
Newby, 17
Newby Head, 66
Newfield Hall, 50
Newhouse Tarn, 68
Newhouses, Langstrothdale, **135**
Newton, Sir Isaac, 72
Nidd Head, 123
Nidd, river, xiii, 1, 123, 125
Nidderdale, 4, 12, 19, 53, 123, 125-7, 130
Nidderdale Omnibus, 130
Nidderdale Show, 128
Nine Standards Rigg, 87
Norber, 6
Normans, 14, 16, 43, 118
Norse settlement, xv, 15, 43
North Sea, 1
Northallerton, 34, 76, 98
Northumbrians, 14

Oak, 12, 114
Oak, holly, 59
Old Gang, 87-8, 93
'Old Man', 88
Orchid, greater butterfly, 49
Ordnance Survey, 55
Ordovician rocks, 1, 2
Oughtershaw, 109
Ouse, river, 1
Overbarrow, 29

Packhorses, 17, 26, 30-1, 66, 107, 109, 124
Palmer, William T., 54, 58, 74
Pam the Fiddler, 116
Pansy, mountain, 9, 87
Parcevall Hall, 117, 131
Park Fell, 53, 55
Park Rash, 112
Pateley Bridge, 6, 12, 32, 35, 127, **128**, 130
Peacock, Susan, 90
Pearson, Thomas, 24
Peat, 8, **9**
Peel, J.H.B., 57
Peel, Lord, 91
Pendle Hill, 56
Pendragon Castle, 30
Pen Hill, 105-6
Penhill Beacon, 97
Penhill Crags, 97
Pennant, Thomas, 25, 130
Pennine Way, The, xiv, 38, 57, 70
Pennines, 1, 10
Penrith, 29, 31, 105
Penyghent, 4, 14, 16, 24, 51, 53-4, 57, **58**, 63, 70, 109
Penyghent Gill, 12
Penyghent House, 134
Percy family, 16, 43, 110
Percy, William de, 43, 111
Peterborough Ware, 12
Phillips, John, 4, 95
Pickersett Edge, 32
Pig Yard Club, 11
Pike, 26
Pikedaw, 45
Pilgrimage of Grace, 19, 44, 79, 108
Pine, Scots, 59
Pine, Weymouth, 59

Plain of York, 1
Plant, Ian, 47
Plover, golden, xiii
Pococke, Bishop, 104
Poitevin, Roger de, 63
Pony, Dales, **31**
Pony, Fell, 31
Pony, Jaeger, 31
Pottery, 12
Preston under Scar, 133
Priestley, J.B., xi, 54, 111
Primrose, 114
Primrose, mealy, 9
Priors Rake, 45
Procter, W.A., 34
Proctor, Sir Stephen, 20, 23

Quakers, xvi, 26, 31, 69, 77, 84, 112
quarrying, 7, 39, 69, 100, 133

Racehorses, 106-7
Railways: Bolton Abbey, 121; Lancaster-Carlisle, 66; Lancaster & Yorkshire, 34; Leeds-Skipton, 34; Little North Western, 34; Nidd Valley, 125; Settle-Carlisle, 34, 51, 66-9, 72, 80-2, 84; Skipton-Grassington, 34, 114; Wensleydale, 34
Rainscar, 26, 134
Raistrick, Dr. Arthur, ix, xiv, 22, 29-30, 45, 56, 80, 131
Ralph, Earl of Westmorland, 112
Ramsgill, 125, **126**
Ramshaw, Margaret, 81
Ramsons, 9
Raven, 76
Ravenstonedale, 76
Ravenstonedale Chapel, 77
Rawthey, river, xiii-xiv, 75
Rawthey valley, 35, 77
Ray, John, 9, 56
Raydale, 6, 12, 100, **101**
Raydale House, 100, 103
Redmire, 34, 86, 98, 105
Redshank, xiii
Reeth, 14, 16, 87-9, 92-3
Reindeer, 12
Renton, George F., 123
Reservoirs, Nidderdale, 124
Rhinoceros, narrow-nosed, 11
Rhododendron, Farrer, **60**
Ribble, river, xiii-xiv, 1, 20, 63, 70, 74, 109
Ribble Way, 63
Ribblehead, 15, 22, 51, 53-4, 62, 65-6
Ribblehead Viaduct, 66, **67**
Ribblesdale, Lord, 49
Ribblesdale, North, xiii, 20, 55, 58, 63, 69, 108
Ribchester, 29
Richard III, 106
Richmond, 16, 20, 25, 29, 32, 35, 64, 89, 94, 105, 107, 112
Richmond Castle, 31, 90
Richmond Georgian Theatre, 94
Richmond, Honour of, 16
Rievaulx Abbey, 17
Rights of Way, 40
Ripley, 130
Ripley Castle, 130
Ripon, 105
Rise Hill, 82
Road traffic, 34
Robinson, John, 32
Robinson, William, 103
Rochdale, Lord, 91
Rogan's Seat, 86
Roger de Poitou, 16

Rokeby, Teesdale, 25
Romans, 14, 19, 22, 29, 56, 94, 100, 112
Romantic Age, xvi, 24
Romano-British times, 11
Romille, Alice de, 113
Rood loft, 111
Rooke, Major, 130
Rose, rock, 9
Roughsedge, Hornby, 56
Rowan, 104
Rufus, William, 63
Rumilly, Cecily de, 118
Runley Bridge, 33
Rural Development Council, 133

Salmon, Atlantic, 26, 70
Sandford Committee, 37
Sandpiper, common, 127
Sandwort, spring, 87
Sawley Abbey, 17, 70
Saxifrage, purple, 56
Saxton, map-maker, 57, 97
Sayer, John, 23
Scabious, field, 114
Scale Park, 112
Scar House Reservoir, 123, **124**, 126
Scott, Harry J., xi, 36, 131
Scott, Sir Walter, 25, 94
Scott Report (Nat. Parks), 36
Scrope family, 16
Scrope, Sir Henry, 105
Scrope, Richard, 105
Scrope, William le, 105
Seal Houses, 93
Second World War, xiv, 28, 34, 46, 69, 84, 99, 122, 133
Sedbergh, 1, 6, 13, 35, **75**, 76, 79, 83-4, 98, 108
Sedbergh, Adam, 108
Sedbergh School, 76
Sedge, prickly, 68
Sedgwick, Adam, 4, 6, 32, 79, 81, 83
Sedgwick Trail, The, 83
Sedgwick, Clara, x
Semerwater, **III**, 6, 12, 13, 23, 101-2
Settle, **XV**, 6, 12, 24, 33, 35, 46, 55, 66, 68-70, **73**, 74
Settle R.D.C., 66
Seven Years War, 78
Shakeholes, 5
Sharland, Charles Stanley, 34
Sheep, 45, **65**, 89, 134
Sheep, Dales-bred, 61
Sheep Fair Hill, 117
Sheep House, 45
Sheep salve, 45
Sheep, Swaledale, **40**, 90, 98
Silurian slate, 1-3, 6, 70, 83
Simon Fell, 55
Simonstone, 23, 96
Skell, 17
Skipton, 15, 16, 22, 27, 30, 32, 35, 112
Skirethornes, 69
Skirfare, river, 5, 109
Slates, green, 2
Slinger, Richard, 110
Smelt Mill, 26, 45, 87, 93-4, 115
Smith, Charles Roach, 11
Smith, Joe, 109
Snaizeholme, 16
Snow, 10
Society of Friends, 69
Solomon's Seal, 114
Solomon's Seal, whirled, 68
South Walden, 107
Southerscales, 55

Southey, Robert, 27, 78
Southwell, Sir Richard, 126
Speakman, Colin, xiii, 109
Speight, Harry, 31, 56
Sphagnum Moss, 8
Sportsman's Inn, 82
Stainforth, xiii, 8, 31, 57, 63, 113, 134
Stainforth Bridge, 70-1
Stainforth Foss, 70
Stainforth, Knight, 70
Stainmore, xiii, 6, 31
Stainmore Gap, 1
Stake Pass, 29, 100-1
Stalling Busk, 16, 100-1
Stang Pass, 93
Stanwick, 94
Star of Bethlehem, 68
'Statesmen', 79
Starbotton, 16, 104, 109, 112
Stean, 126
Stean Beck, 125
Stint or gait, 22, 56, 92, 101
Stone Circle, 13
Stone Crosses, 14
Stonebeck Up, 125
Storrs Common, 55
Strid, The, X, xiii, 25, 109
Strid Wood, 120
Studfold Moor, 22
Stump Cross Caverns, 3, 12, 62, 129-30
Sumner, Rev. Joseph, 79
Sundew, 8
Surrender Bridge, 88
Sutcliffe, Halliwell, 116
Swainby, 108
Swale, river, xiii, 1, 14, 87, 92
Swaledale, xiii-xiv, 4-6, 10, 16-20, 22, 24, 31,
   35, 38, 85, 86-9, 91-5, 99
Swaledale Folk Museum, 92
Swan, whooper, 102
'Swarth Moor Jacks', 7
Swift, Col. Geoffrey, 62
Swinbank, B., 27
Swinden Quarry, 39, 133
Swinnergill, 85, 87
Symondson, John, 112

Tan Hill, x, 8, 31, 85, 92-3
Tan Hill Coal, 8, 31, 90
Tan Hill Inn, 85, 90
Tate Gallery, 49
Taylor, Fred, 99
Teal, 127
Teesdale, 85, 99
Tempest family, 70
Textiles, 27
Thistle, melancholy, 49
Thompson, Maggie, 124
Thompson, Mike, 47
Thompson, Robert, 111
Thoralby, 104
Thorns Gill, 31, 66
Thornton Fell, 61
Thornton Force, 2, 61
Thornton-in-Lonsdale, 60
Three Peaks, xiv, 5, 51, 53
Three Peaks Club, 54
Three Peaks Project, 54
Threshfield, 114, 116
Threshfield School, 116
Thwaite, 15, 85, 88, 91
Thwaite Lane, Clapham, 59
Thyme, 9
Tor Dyke, 14

Torfin, 63
Torrington, Lord, 63
Transport, 29, 131-2, 136
Tree cover, 8
Trevelyan, Charles, 36
Trevelyan, George Macaulay, 36
Trevelyan, Pauline, 36
Trout, brown, 26, 44, 109, 120
Trout, rainbow, 109
Trow Gill, 3, 55
Turf Moor Hush, 24
Turner Fell Pit, 8
Turner, J.M.W., 25, 62, 97, 120
Turnpike roads, 24-5, 30, 32
Turnpike, Keighley-Kendal, 33-4
Turnpike, Lancaster-Richmond, 32, 97, 100
Twistleton Scar, 62
Twistleton, Tom, xvi
Tyne Gap, 38

Ulshaw Ure, 107
Umpleby, Walter, 49
Unconformity, 2
Underley Hall, 82
Ure, river, xiii, 1, 14, 30, 95-6, 103

Vanbrugh, Sir John, 116
Venutius, 14, 56
Versey, Professor, 81
Victoria Cave, 11
Victoria, Queen, 56
Vikings, 15, 60

Wagtail, grey, 112
Wagtail, yellow, 127
Wainwright, Alfred, 38
Walden, 104
Walker, Adam, 48
Walker, George, 102
Walls, drystone, xiv-xv, 10, 22-3, 28-9, 36, 39-
   40, 43
Walsingham, 117
Walsingham, Lord, 121
Wandale, 76
Warburton's map, 29
Ward, James, 20, 49
Warwick, Earl of, 106
Washburn Valley, 32
Water-Babies, The, 27, 46
Waterhouses, 16
Watson, Samuel, 70
Watson, Sir William, 102
Weardale, 23
Weather terms, xv-xvi
Weathercote Cave, 4, 25, 61-2, 133
Webster, Michael, 99
Wedber, 49
Weets Cross, VI, 30
Weets Top, 49
Wensley, 15, 26, 95
Wensleydale, xiii-xiv, 4, 6, 8, 10, 14, 15, 20,
   24, 29-32, 35, 39, 54, 63, 76, 85, 95-8, 104-8,
   136
Wensleydale Dairy, 99
Wensleydale, Forest of, 16, 100, 106
Wensleydale Group, 4
Wensleydale Granite, 1
Wensleydale Railway Association, 98
Wesley, John, 24, 114
West Burton, 104
West Stonesdale, 85
West Witton, 15
Westmorland, 21
Wether Fell, 14, 29, 101

Whalley Abbey, 120
Wharfe, hamlet, 9
Wharfe, river, xiii, 1, 15, 30, 109, 112, 114,
   116, 120-1
Wharfedale, xiii, 3-6, 12, 14-6, 18, 20, 24-5, 29,
   34-5, 38-9, 43, 61, 100, 104, 108-9, 111, 113,
   115-6, 117-20, 122
Wharton, Lord, 20, 90
Whaw, 93
Whernside, xiv, 4, 51, 53-5, 60
Whernside, Great, 53, 107, 112, 123, 126,
   129
Whernside, Little, 53, 107, 123, 126
Whernside Manor, 78
Whitaker, Thomas Dunham, 1, 23, 25-6, 57,
   63, 72, 117, 120
White Doe of Rylstone, The, 25
White, Robert, x
White Scar Caverns, 3, 62
Widdale Foot, 26
Wight, Alf, 93, 132
Wild Boar Fell, 6, 96
William I, 16
Williams, F.S., 82
Willow, 12
Wilson, Bernard, 77
Wilson, Sir Matthew, 50
Wilson, Michael, 7, 71
Wilson, Miles, 111
Winder, 1, 75, 77
Winskill Stones, 5
Winterburn, 20
Wold Fell, 63
Wood, Hon. Mrs R., 59
Woodland, 36, 40
Woodland, native, 135
Woodland Trust, 114
Wool, 17, 20
Wordsworth, Dorothy, 9, 49, 97
Wordsworth, William, 1, 25-6, 49, 75, 79, 83,
   97, 120
Worton, 103
Wright, Geoffrey, 31

Yarm, 25, 32
Yarnbury, 13, 20, 115
Yellow rattle, 87
Yeoman farmers, 19, 20
Yew, 2
Yockenthwaite, 13, 110
Yore Mills, Aysgarth, 27, 103
Yore, river, 26, 95
Yoredale, 4, 95
Yoredale Series, 1, 4, 7, 55, 81, 103
Yoredale Way, The, 95
York, 17, 18, 29, 95, 122
York Minster, 55
Yorke Arms, 126
Yorke, John, 128
Yorke, Sir John, 16
Yorke, Thomas Edward, 126, 128
Yorke's Folly, 128
Yorkshire Dales Millennium Trust, 136
Yorkshire Dales National Park, x, xiii-xvi,
   1, 13, 17, 35-7, 40, 46, 51, 54, 75, 109, 114,
   131
Yorkshire Dales National Park Authority, 37,
   39, 66, 68, 70, 104, 135-6
Yorkshire Dales Society, xiii, 136
Yorkshire Ramblers' Club, 57
Yorkshire Wildlife Trust, 9, 102, 114, 132
Young, Arthur, 26

Zinc, ore of, 45